Jie Zhang
Language Policy and Planning for the Modern Olympic Games

Trends in Applied Linguistics

Edited by
Ulrike Jessner

Volume 21

Jie Zhang

Language Policy and Planning for the Modern Olympic Games

Foreword by
Ingrid Piller

DE GRUYTER
MOUTON

ISBN 978-1-5015-2107-2
e-ISBN (PDF) 978-1-61451-495-4
e-ISBN (EPUB) 978-1-5015-0047-3
ISSN 1868-6362

Library of Congress Control Number: 2021931376

Bibliographic information published by the Deutsche Nationalbibliothek
The Deutsche Nationalbibliothek lists this publication in the Deutsche Nationalbibliografie;
detailed bibliographic data are available on the Internet at http://dnb.dnb.de.

© 2022 Walter de Gruyter Inc., Boston/Berlin
This volume is text- and page-identical with the hardback published in 2021.
Typesetting: Integra Software Services Pvt. Ltd.
Printing and binding: CPI books GmbH, Leck

www.degruyter.com

Preface: The paradox of the concomitant rise of China and English

The rise of China has been one of the defining characteristics of the early 21st century. The increase in China's economic, geopolitical, and military clout has been accompanied by a linguistic paradox, though: the language that has most profited from China's substantial investments into education and human resource development has been English. The phenomenal expansion in English language learning amongst China's growing middle classes has been so intense during the past three decades to warrant the label "English fever." As a result, China today has more English speakers than the United Kingdom, and – after USA, India, Nigeria, and Pakistan – China is home to the fifth-largest national population of English speakers on earth.[1]

In this book, Zhang Jie traces the complexities of this paradox: its history, its lived experience, and its future. Taking the 2008 Beijing Olympics as her focal point, the author shows how English became central to this mega-event which constituted a key plank in China's efforts to showcase its national progress to the world.

Based on a wealth of data including policy documents, media reports, English language learning textbooks, signage in Beijing's linguistic landscape, and interviews with policy makers and Olympic volunteers, the book meticulously traces the complex intersections between Chinese national ambition and English language learning. In the process, she also brings Chinese sociolinguistics to an English language audience in an illuminating overview of "language services" research.

To regain its rightful place among the great civilizations and powers had been China's aspiration ever since the humiliations of the 19th and early 20th century. The 2008 Beijing Olympics provided the perfect opportunity to showcase what had been achieved. Therefore, China invested significant resources into its Olympic bid. This included linguistic resources, and Zhang Jie shows how the country went about making that investment: by ramping up English language capacity on all levels of society.

Once the 2008 Olympics had been awarded to Beijing, the ambition was to make it not only perfect but spectacular. In addition to getting the games themselves right, this meant getting the environment right by transforming Beijing into a global city. The meticulous planning and immense resources that went

---

1 List of countries by English-speaking population. (2020). *Wikipedia*. Retrieved from https://en.wikipedia.org/wiki/List_of_countries_by_English-speaking_population

https://doi.org/10.1515/9781614514954-202

into that transformation are staggering. Zhang Jie shows how the language capacities of a population of many millions were carefully assessed and improved. Between 2002 and 2007, the percentage of Beijing residents with foreign language proficiency – mostly in English – rose from 22 percent to 35 per cent. In absolute numbers these are well over five million people whose language capabilities were systematically upgraded.

However, Zhang Jie digs deeper. She not only shows language planning and management for the Beijing Olympics in exquisite detail but also how individuals experienced their transformation into English speakers and global citizens. Most threw themselves dutifully into the effort to improve their English but they were not motivated by a desire for English and the Western cultural values associated with it, as much previous research has found. Rather, they were motivated by a desire for the rewards associated with passing English language tests: university admissions and job prospects.

Not everyone could compete on equal terms, though, and turning performance on English language tests into a gatekeeper for social advancement brought existing inequalities to the fore. Outside of China's metropoles, the material conditions to do well on English language tests – qualified teachers, up-to-date textbooks, or media libraries – simply were not available in many cases.

The single-minded pursuit of English also led to the devaluation of other languages, as Zhang Jie shows with reference to Russian. Russian, which had been learned to high levels, particularly in the northern border provinces, and was of high practical value there in trans-border exchanges, became worthless almost overnight, as university admission was tied to English. As one Olympic volunteer, who had studied Russian throughout her secondary education mournfully complained to the researcher: "There were a great number of Russian people in our county, thus I had never thought of learning English. I didn't realize English is so important elsewhere until I left my hometown. Now, learning Russian has become such a disadvantage!"

That was in 2008. But that is not where this study ends.

Having successfully conducted the Beijing Olympics and continuing its economic and geopolitical rise, language policy and planning have been reevaluated. As China now gets ready to host the 2022 Beijing Winter Olympics, the COVID-19 pandemic has forever changed the meaning of "globalisation" (Piller, Zhang & Li, 2020). This time, China follows a comprehensive language action plan that is quite different to the one for the 2008 Summer Games: there is now a recognition of an oversupply of English language capabilities and the focus is on strengthening language service provision in other languages. Beyond English, China has embraced a truly multilingual vision. There are now programs at Chinese universities in 101 languages – the official languages of all countries that have established diplomatic relations with China. Capacities in most of these languages may still be limited but, as this book amply documents, China has a track record of turning its dream into a reality.

The concomitant rise of China and English may well have come to an end.

Ingrid Piller, Macquarie University

Acknowledgement

The book is based on my doctoral dissertation. When I started this project in 2008, I had limited understanding of language policy and planning in linguistically diverse contexts. I would like to express my deepest gratitude to my supervisor, Professor Ingrid Piller, whose meticulous guidance, constant encouragement, and unfailing support enabled me to complete my dissertation and this book. Her scholarly labours to advance multilingualism and social justice have had a profound influence on me.

Between September 2017 and July 2018, I was fortunate enough to visit Professor Li Yuming at Beijing Language and Culture University (BLCU). During that visit, I gained access to the Beijing Advanced Innovation Centre for Language Resources (ACLR) directed by Professor Li and obtained valuable information about its three language services projects for the 2022 Beijing Winter Olympics. I am deeply indebted to Prof Li, who taught me that being a scholar should not confine us to writing papers and imparting knowledge, but more importantly entails us having a sense of social responsibility along with the awareness and capability to solve practical problems.

In 2013, I signed the book contract with De Gruyter. At that time, I planned to submit my manuscript in 2015. Unfortunately, my life in this period caught me unprepared. Plans could not keep up with the changes. Seven years later, as I finally submitted my book manuscript, I owe my deepest gratitude to the editors of the series *Trends in Applied Linguistics* whose great patience and trust enabled me to complete this book.

My sincere thanks are due to my proofreader Dr. Brett Todd for his insightful feedback and helpful suggestions. In addition, I offer my regards and blessings to all my participants and informants, and to all friends and family who supported me in any respect during the completion of the project.

Above all, I must acknowledge the debt I owe to my father Zhang Xiangsheng and my mother Yuan Lihua for allowing me the luxury to pursue a career and life relatively free of family obligations over the years. Without the powerful backing of my parents' unceasing support, I doubt I would have had the courage to pursue a project of this magnitude. The book is dedicated to you.

Contents

Preface: The paradox of the concomitant rise
of China and English —— V

Acknowledgement —— IX

List of abbreviations and acronyms —— XVII

Chapter 1
The Modern Olympic Games as linguistically complex events —— 1
1	The socio-politics of the Modern Olympic Games —— 1	
2	The Modern Olympic Games as linguistically complex events —— 3	
3	Literature review —— 6	
3.1	Language management of the IOC —— 6	
3.2	LPP studies of the Olympic Games —— 13	
3.3	An expanded view of language policy —— 16	
3.4	Language service as a new explanatory theory —— 18	
3.5	The political economy of language —— 25	
4	Summary —— 27	

Chapter 2
Remaking China in the Olympic spotlight —— 28
1	The historical and realistic significance of the 2008 Beijing Olympic Games —— 28
1.1	Fading glory and lost identity —— 28
1.2	China's identity crisis in the modernisation process —— 30
1.3	China's image crisis in a globalising world —— 32
1.4	Favourable national image as soft power —— 33
2	China's route to the Olympic host country —— 34

Chapter 3
Researching the LPP for the 2008 Beijing Olympics —— 40
1	Language challenges to the 2008 Beijing Olympic Games —— 40
2	Learning from Seoul —— 41
2.1	Public signs —— 42
2.2	Technology-supported language services —— 44
3	Research design —— 49
3.1	Research questions —— 49

3.2	Data collection methods —— 50	
3.3	Data analysis methods —— 56	
3.4	Ethical considerations —— 60	

Chapter 4
Beijing's commitment – international language environment —— 62

1	*The Beijing Olympic Action Plan* —— 62	
2	*The Action Plan of the BSFLP* —— 65	
2.1	Overall objectives —— 65	
2.2	Working procedures —— 66	
2.3	Governmental planning for foreign language popularisation —— 67	
2.4	Governmental planning for language services in window industries —— 68	
2.5	Governmental planning for signage standardisation —— 69	
2.6	Governmental planning for foreign language popularisation in mass media —— 70	
2.7	Governmental planning for technology-supported language services —— 70	
2.8	Governmental planning for regulating foreign language service market —— 71	
2.9	Governmental planning for public foreign language activities —— 72	
2.10	Governmental planning for foreign language volunteers —— 72	
2.11	The implementation and outcome of the *Action Plan* —— 73	
3	The Beijing English Testing System (2006–2013) —— 76	
4	Olympic language services providers —— 77	
4.1	Translation and interpretation service supplier —— 78	
4.2	Language training service suppliers —— 80	
4.3	Multilingual service suppliers —— 87	
5	English language learning and teaching celebrities —— 93	
5.1	Crazy English founder Li Yang: English learning as an act of patriotism —— 94	
5.2	Multilingual policeman Liu Wenli: English learning as empowerment —— 97	
6	Summary —— 101	

Chapter 5
Assessing Beijing's foreign language environment —— 104
1	Assessing foreign language speaking population in Beijing —— 104
1.1	The total number of foreign language speaking population in Beijing —— 104
1.2	Different levels of foreign language speaking population in Beijing —— 106
1.3	Language distribution of foreign language speaking population in Beijing —— 107
2	Assessing Olympic foreign language popularisation —— 110
2.1	Beijing citizens' motivations towards foreign language learning —— 110
2.2	Outcomes of the Beijing speaks foreign language programme —— 112
2.3	Outcomes of Olympic foreign language training —— 114
2.4	Use of foreign language media —— 116
3	Assessing Beijing's foreign language environment —— 118
4	English fever in Olympic city identity construction —— 119
5	Questioning the instrumentalist view of English —— 121
5.1	High expectation vs. low practicability —— 122
5.2	Problems and dilemmas of English language learning —— 125
6	Rethinking the language factor in global city formation —— 132
6.1	The concept and assessment of world/global city —— 132
6.2	English and China's global city aspiration —— 140
7	Summary —— 143

Chapter 6
Imagined communities and identity options in Beijing Olympic English textbooks —— 144
1	Identity options in language textbooks —— 144
2	A Conversational English Reader —— 146
3	Imbalanced gender distribution —— 150
4	Imagined communities —— 154
4.1	Chinese characters as targeted learners —— 154
4.2	Foreign characters as represented visitors —— 158
4.3	Beijing as a harmonious Olympic city —— 162
5	Summary —— 164

Chapter 7
The linguistic landscape of the Olympic city —— 167

1	The language policy environment —— 167	
1.1	Governmental planning for public signs —— 167	
1.2	Olympic English signage standardisation campaign —— 168	
2	Linguistic landscape research —— 170	
3	Standardised official signs —— 173	
3.1	Monolingual signs —— 173	
3.2	Bilingual signs —— 175	
3.3	Multilingual signs —— 181	
4	Language choice, ideology, and identity —— 182	
4.1	Chinese and Beijing as the capital of the harmonious nation —— 182	
4.2	English and Beijing as a global city —— 186	
4.3	English for sale and global elitism —— 188	
4.4	French and Beijing as Olympic city —— 192	
4.5	Other languages and the invisible city —— 194	
5	Summary —— 197	

Chapter 8
China's Olympic language services – legacy, transformation and prospect —— 199

1	The language services legacy of the 2008 Olympic Games —— 199	
1.1	Olympic language services suppliers —— 199	
1.2	The Beijing speaks foreign language programme —— 202	
1.3	Volunteerism —— 202	
2	Transformation in China's foreign language ideology —— 203	
2.1	The *ti-yong* tension in the Beijing Olympic context —— 203	
2.2	Resistance to 'English fever' in the post-Olympic era —— 204	
2.3	National language capacity —— 205	
3	China's language services in the post-Olympic era —— 207	
3.1	China's language services industry at a glance —— 207	
3.2	The standardisation of language services —— 210	
3.3	The technological innovation of language services —— 210	
3.4	Education and training of language professionals —— 212	
4	Looking to the 2022 Beijing Winter Olympic Games —— 213	
4.1	Changing socio-economic environment —— 213	
4.2	*Action plan on language services* —— 216	
4.3	*Action plan on Olympic volunteer services* —— 219	

4.4	Olympic language services suppliers —— **219**	
4.5	Technology-supported multilingual services —— **221**	
4.6	English signage standardisation —— **223**	
5	Summary —— **224**	

Chapter 9
Conclusion —— 226

Bibliography —— 229

Appendix 1: List of interview participants —— 251

Appendix 2: Key to transcription conventions —— 255

Index —— 257

List of abbreviations and acronyms

ACLP	Beijing Advanced Innovation Centre for Language Resources
Aifly	Aifly Education & Technology Co., Ltd.
ASEAN	Association of South East Asian Nations
BBC	British Broadcasting Corporation
BETS	Beijing English Testing System
BFSU	Beijing Foreign Studies University
BOBICO	Beijing 2008 Olympic Games Bid Committee
BOCOG	Beijing Organising Committee for the 2008 Olympic Games
BOCOWG	Beijing Organising Committee for the 2022 Olympic and Paralympic Winter Games
BSFLP	Beijing Speak Foreign Language Programme
CDA	Critical Discourse Analysis
CET-4	College English Test Band Four
CET-6	College English Test Band Six
CPC	Communist Party of China
CPPCC	Chinese People's Political Consultative Conference
EF	English First Co., Ltd.
EFL	English as a Foreign Language
ELLT	English Language Learning and Teaching
ELT	English Language Teaching
ESL	English as a Second Language
EU	European Union
FL	Foreign Language
GDP	Gross Domestic Product
IFs	International Sports Federations
IOC	International Olympic Committee
LCTLs	Less commonly taught languages
LEP	Language Education Policy
LL	Linguistic Landscape
LPP	Language policy and planning
LOTE	Languages other than English
MOE	Ministry of Education of the People's Republic of China
NCEE	National College Entrance Examination (*Gaokao*)
NNESs	Non-native English speakers
NOCs	National Olympic Committees
NSE	Native speaker English
OCOGs	Organising Committees for the Olympic Games
OIF	Organisation Internationale de la Francophonie
PLA	Chinese People's Liberation Army
PRC	People's Republic of China
SL	Second Language
SOCOG	Sydney Organising Committee for the 2000 Olympic Games
TAC	Translators Association of China
TESOL	Teaching English to Speakers of Other Languages

https://doi.org/10.1515/9781614514954-205

UK	United Kingdom
US	United States
VOA	Voice of America
WTO	World Trade Organisation
Advanced Reader	*A Conversational English Reader (Advanced)*
Elementary Reader	*A Conversational English Reader (Elementary)*

Chapter 1
The Modern Olympic Games as linguistically complex events

1 The socio-politics of the Modern Olympic Games

The history of the Olympic Games goes back to Ancient Greece. The Ancient Olympic Games were a series of athletic competitions held between various city states of ancient Greece in honor of the Olympian gods and continued for twelve centuries (776 B.C. – 393 A. D). Olympia became the site of these historic ancient games that sowed the seeds for the world's largest and most influential sporting international event of modern times, the Modern Olympics. On 6 April 1896, the Olympic Games, after an interruption of more than 2,000 years, were revived in Athens by French educationist Baron Pierre de Coubertin with the lofty ideal of promoting international harmony and understanding through sporting competition. The Modern Olympic Games are an international multi-sport event established for summer and winter games and organised every four years. The Ancient Olympic Games celebrated physical excellence and served a primarily religious purpose. In their modern form, while still ostensibly about physical excellence, the Games also play a cultural, economic and often political role (Toohey and Veal, 2007, p. 1). With its swift expansion in all dimensions, the Modern Olympic Games are no longer, if they ever were, just a sports event, but *de facto* a cultural, economic, and political phenomenon.

Within the social sciences, the socio-political significance of the Olympics as a premier sporting event for nation-states has been increasingly acknowledged in recent years (e.g., Blain, Boyle and O'Donnell, 1993; Brown, 2000; Brownell, 2005; Burton, 2003; Dyreson, 2003; Essex and Chalkley, 1998; Houlihan, 1997; Ikhioya, 2001; Jaffe and Nebanzahl, 1993; Smith and Porter, 2004; Toohey and Veal, 2007). The pursuit and sponsorship of mega-sporting events such as the Olympiad has become an increasingly popular strategy of national and municipal governments worldwide. It is widely claimed by Olympic bid cities (in many cases, in tandem with the national governments that back them) that this mega-event can bring about social and material change, such as sport infrastructure improvement, sustainable urban development, global media attention, booms in tourism, and most importantly the promise of long-term image enhancement for strengthening national identity and international recognition.

https://doi.org/10.1515/9781614514954-001

No other events can compete with the Modern Olympic Games in attracting such a large scale of global attention for two weeks. In recent decades, some 10,000 athletes from over 200 countries, accompanied by a similar number of coaches and officials, as many as 15,000 accredited media representatives, and hundreds of thousands of spectators, have gathered every four years for more than two weeks to participate in, report on and watch this sports event which is in turn viewed on television, listened to on radio, read about in the print media and browsed on the Internet by billions of people around the world (Toohey and Veal, 2007, p. 1). In this sense, the Olympic Games are also a global media event. For an Olympic host country, global media exposure is a double-edge sword. The Olympic Games constitute a major opportunity for the host city and country to showcase its culture and project a positive national image through powerful print, broadcasting and electronic media. At the same time, however, the host city and country also open themselves up to intense international media scrutiny.

Hosting the Olympic Games is a mixed blessing commercially, too. On the one hand, the tourism benefits, corporate sponsorship and commercialisation of the Games generate significant income. However, the state-of-the-art buildings and technology needed to attract the Games have rendered hosting both the summer and winter events a rather expensive and grand scale operation (Wamsley and Heine, 1996). Each host city and country, expecting great rewards from the Games, has to pour enormous material and human resources into staging the event. The ever-growing scale of the Modern Olympic Games has actually made it more difficult for the Games to be held in non-Western developing countries. Under the leadership of Juan Antonio Samaranch, former President of the International Olympic Committee (IOC), the Games began to shift toward international sponsors who sought to link their products to the Olympic brand. The sale of the Olympic brand has made the Games move away from the ideals of pure competition and sportsmanship and become indistinguishable from any other commercialised sporting spectacle. In recent decades, the tension between the rhetoric of amateurism and the realities of commercialism has been a central contradiction of the Olympic Games (Blain, Boyle and O'Donnell, 1993, p. 186).

Since the world's nation-states started to come together in 1896 to compete, politics have never stayed out of the Olympic arena. Sport is often constructed as "the great equalizer" (Hogan, 2003, p. 100), and as such the Olympic Movement is assumed to foster international goodwill, peace and equality through free and fair competition between the athletes of the world (International Olympic Committee, 2007). Some scholarly and popular discourses also identify sport as a 'universal language' that transcends not only national boundaries but also national identities. However, Dyreson (2003) argues that "sports have almost always been, in their modern form, an arena for the exhibition of tribal and especially national identities rather than an occasion for the celebration of universal human communities" (p. 92). Substantial research on the Olympics has shown that the reality of this mega-sporting event is much more complex and controversial than those rosy promises. The tension between the rhetoric of internationalism and national concerns is another central contradiction of the Olympic Games (Blain, Boyle and O'Donnell, 1993, p. 186). Judging from the management and organisation of the Olympic Games, the Olympic Movement is still Western-dominated and will continue to be so in the foreseeable future (Brownell, 2007). As the capital of an Asian developing and socialist country, Beijing's selection as the host city of the 2008 Olympic Games, therefore, carried profound socio-political significance in Olympic history. Due to the global significance of the Modern Olympic Games, to become an Olympic power has been "the persistent and ultimate dream of China" (Dong, 2005, p. 533).

2 The Modern Olympic Games as linguistically complex events

The Ancient Olympics were not international in the modern sense of the term as they allowed only free men who spoke Greek to participate in the Games. The Modern Olympic Games that have been held since 1896 are multilingual events. Although the Athens 1896 Olympic Games were the biggest international sports event staged at the time, the Games were attended by merely 241 athletes from 14 countries[2] (International Olympic Committee, 2020a). Women and people of colour were not among the athletes. In 2004, one century later, the Summer Olympics returned to Athens, with 10,625 athletes of different races and sexes competing from 201 countries (International Olympic Committee, 2020b). If the first Athens Olympic Games were a set of sports competitions involving just over a dozen countries, all of them except Hungary using Indo-European languages, the second Athens Olympic Games were truly an international mega-event in which communication was conducted across hundreds of countries and languages.

---

[2] The 14 participating countries in the first Modern Olympic Games include Australia, Austria, Bulgaria, Chile, Denmark, France, Germany, Hungary, Italy, Switzerland, Sweden, the United Kingdom, the United States, and the host country Greece.

The Modern Olympic Games, especially those after the Second World War, are complex linguistic events. Due to the grand scale of the Modern Olympic Games and the diversity of cultural and linguistic backgrounds of competing nations, it can be anticipated that communication across languages and cultures would present many difficulties and challenges. Therefore, organisers of such events have to make important language policy and planning decisions to ensure a quality experience for athletes and visitors during the event. However, accommodating the linguistic needs of all participants to the Games is an extremely arduous task. From the translation of all official documents, media reports, tourist information and linguistic signs to interpreting at official ceremonies, competition venues and press conferences, and to providing instant information to foreign athletes, coaches, officials, journalists and visitors in their own language(s), language services are embedded in all aspects of the preparations for the Olympic Games, and play a crucial role in making the sporting events truly global celebrations.

The Modern Olympic Games offer rich resources for the research of Language Policy and Planning (LPP). Firstly, as the Modern Olympic Games involve participants coming from more than 200 countries and regions with over 80 official languages, there are important issues concerning status planning. At the early stage of overall planning, the organiser will make a conscious choice of the language variety(ies) that will become the official and working language(s) of the Games. Specifically, the status planning issues of the Games include the selection of language(s) used for aspects such as official documents, websites and ceremonies, media communication, competition venues, cultural activities, public announcements, signage, accompanying of VIPs, visitor reception, and spectator guidance. Status planning has a close relationship with prestige planning. A language's status is its position with respect to other languages in a specific social environment, and prestige is how this relationship is perceived by those who inhabit that social environment (Ager, 2005). Prestige planning is directed at those goals related to the image of a language. Prestige planning can create a favorable social psychological environment for the implementation of language planning by creating a positive image of a language. Past Olympic Games have witnessed language promotion activities (via official/government, institutional, pressure group, individual) to improve the image and value of languages in the Olympic movement and international domains. In the Olympic spotlight, the Chinese government attempted to use the Games to "teach and promote the Chinese language to the world, and to demonstrate that Chinese is in fact a language used worldwide" (BOCOG, 2002). Promotional programmes have been developed to encourage and assist foreigners in learning the Chinese language, such as contests for debating, singing and storytelling. Starting from 2005, a section on "Learning the Chinese Language" were added to the publicity materials the Olympic organising committee sent overseas (BOCOG, 2002). Moreover, the Modern Olympic Games often promote corpus planning activities in the host city, such as coinage of new terms; spelling reform; compilation of dictionaries; formulation of English translation standards for public signs; creation of a sports terminology corpus and a portal to access it; and development of machine translation software, websites and applications. The recent history of the Olympic movement has seen the attempts of non-Anglophone host countries to develop a set of English translation norms that define "standard" usage of English in the public sphere and rectify "non-normative" English orthography and grammar. Unlike status planning and prestige planning, which are primarily undertaken by the IOC and national governments of host cities, corpus planning generally involves planners with greater linguistic expertise. Finally, acquisition planning (also called language-in-education planning) is used by the organiser to achieve the purposes of status planning, prestige planning and corpus planning through education and training. For an example, in the preparation for the 1988 Olympics, the Seoul Olympic Organising Committee developed a language education plan and employed diverse training methods to improve foreign language proficiency of Games operation personnel. Frequently, acquisition planning is integrated into a larger language planning process in which the statuses of languages are evaluated, corpuses are revised and the changes are finally introduced to society on a national or local level through education systems, ranging from primary schools to universities. This planning process can entail a variety of activities, such as popularisation of a national or international language in schools; language training for athletes, coaches, officials, and Olympic volunteers; cultivation of less commonly taught language (LCTL) professionals; development of bilingual teaching programmes; compilation of language teaching materials; and establishment of language proficiency tests.

To sum up, the Olympic Games are linguistically complex and culturally diverse events which require "a strategic overall plan for the cultural and linguistic dimensions of the Games" (LO Bianco, 1994). Language skills are closely related to the success or failure of the Olympic Games, and the provision of high-quality language services for the Olympic Games needs comprehensive, practicable and sustainable language planning. Comprehensiveness means that language planning for the Olympic Games should cover all targets, domains and types of language services; practicability refers to the fact that the organisers need to formulate Olympic language service plans on the basis of its own sociolinguistic situation, multilingual resources and financial budget; finally, language planning for the Games should be sustainable which requires the organisers to embed language planning for the Games in the host country's long-term strategic plan of political, economic, educational and cultural development, leaving Olympic legacy for sustainable development of the society.

3 Literature review

3.1 Language management of the IOC

The International Olympic Committee is an international non-governmental not-for-profit organisation and the supreme authority governing and organising the Olympic Games. Thus, an understanding of the LPP for the Modern Olympic Games shall start with an analysis of the language management of the IOC. Language management at the supernational level encompasses language management activities inside a supernational organisation and the way the supernational organisation impinges on the language policies of its member states (Spolsky, 2009). In this section, I employ Spolsky's (2004, 2009) language management model in analysing language management of the IOC from two perspectives: internal policies and external influences.

3.1.1 Internal policies

Domain-internal policies of an international organisation mainly concerns language choices for internal legislative and bureaucratic activity (Spolsky, 2009, p. 208), which involve two aspects: official language(s) and working language(s). Spolsky (2004, pp. 219–221) identifies four main conditions that co-occur with language polices: the sociolinguistic situation, identity, changes, and language-related human and civil rights. First of all, the sociolinguistic situation refers to the number and kinds of languages, the number and kinds of speakers of each language, the communicative value of each language both inside and outside the community being studied. The second condition is related with the working of national or ethnic or other identity within the community. Language is not only a tool of communication, but also a symbol of identity. At the supernational level, the symbolic value of languages and the identity and power relations these languages represent is closely related to the image of an international organisation. Thirdly, since the 1990s, human society has undergone drastic changes as a result of globalisation. In the process of globalisation, English has become *the* international language and plays a leading role in many international domains. This force has significantly influenced language policies and practices of international organisations. Finally, the rising recognition that language choice is an important component of human and civil rights has led to a growing value for linguistic pluralism and an acceptance of the need to recognise the rights of individuals and groups to continue to use their own languages. These four conditions directly affect the formulation of the official and working language(s) of the IOC.

Commonly, international policies are expressed in treaties, declarations, or charters which only come into effect when ratified by a certain number of nations and which only bind those nations which ratify them (Spolsky, 2009, p. 206). The *Olympic Charter* is the codification of the fundamental principles of Olympism, rules and bye-laws adopted by the International Olympic Committee (IOC). It governs the organisation, action and operation of the Olympic Movement and sets forth the conditions for the celebration of the Olympic Games (International Olympic Committee, 2020). Clearly, The *Olympic Charter* serves as the (overt) policy basis of IOC's language management. With the development of the Olympic movement, the IOC has made many amendments to the *Charter* in view of the ever-changing internal and external environment on the premise of maintaining the consistency of the basic principles of Olympism. It can be seen from the various editions of the *Olympic Charter* that the language policies of the IOC have changed from monolingualism in the early stage to bilingualism after World War Two and then to multilingualism since the 1990s.

In the early days of the Modern Olympic Movement, French was the only official language of the IOC. Between the 17th century and the 19th century, the prestige of French was greatly enhanced as France became economically and militarily one of the most powerful states in Europe. During this period, French took the place of Latin as *the* language of international diplomacy and was adopted as a diplomatic language for use in international treaties (Rickard, 1989, pp. 117–118). The *Olympic Charter* was first published in 1908, under the title of *ANNUAIRE DU COMITÉ INTERNATIONAL OLYMPIQUE*. On the basis of this document, the principles of Olympism were gradually formed. From 1908 to 1924, the IOC issued seven editions of the *Charter*, all of which were written in French only. Although the IOC started to publish English editions of the *Charter* since 1930, the *Charter* clearly stipulated that French was the sole official language of the IOC. This French monolingual policy continued until the end of World War Two.

After World War Two, the world changed dramatically. The French colonial empire fell apart and French gradually lost its position as *the* language of international diplomacy. Meanwhile, as the largest beneficiary of the two World Wars, the United States extended its political, economic, technological, and cultural influence around the world, which spread the English language further. The global spread of English since the 20th century is closely related to the rise of the US as a superpower, in particular the rising power and prestige of the US economy, technology and culture. Eventually, English developed from a national language and regional lingua franca to a widest means of communication in the world, replacing French as *the* international language. During this period, the Olympic Movement had developed rapidly. The International Sports Federations (IFs) were established one after another, and the number of the National Olympic Committees (NOCs) as well as the number of countries and people participating in the Olympic Games increased continuously. In this context, Article 61 of the 1949 edition of the *Olympic Charter* (International Olympic Committee, 1949, p. 26) listed English as one of the official languages of the IOC for the first time. At the same time, Article 54 of this edition (International Olympic Committee, 1949, p. 23) requires the Organising Committees for the Olympic Games (OCOGs) to produce and distribute a special booklet for each sport containing the programme and general rules in at least three languages (one must be French and another English). Since then, the official language policy of the IOC was changed from French monolingualism to French-English bilingualism. French and English have formed a competitive relationship, and the practical communicative value of English inside and outside the organisation has been continuously improved.

In the 1990s, the bipolar structure of world order formed in the Cold War collapsed. With the development of globalisation and multipolarisation, and a growing awareness of democratic values and human rights, many international organisations including the IOC began to support beliefs about diversity and multilingualism, Lo Bianco (2007, p. 11) explains:

> The modern Olympic Games are [. . .] beginning to stress the democratic ideals of equality, merit, integrity and peaceful co-existence through an awareness of cultural diversity and cross-cultural communication. One demonstration of this [. . .] is the custom of requiring the host country to provide interpreting facilities and language services prior to and during the Games. Language services have become an essential part of the international peace-making role of the Games in that they facilitate an ease of, and accommodation in, cross-cultural communication during all aspects of the Games.

Since the 1990s, the IOC has shifted its the official and working language policies to European language-dominated multilingualism, hoping to strengthen the cooperation with member states and show an inclusive organisational image through offering more equal and diversified language policies. On July 17, 2020, the 136th plenary session of the IOC adopted the latest amendments to the *Charter*. Article 23 of the current edition of the *Charter* (International Olympic Committee, 2020, p. 52) stipulates the language policies of the IOC as below:

23 Languages
1. The official languages of the IOC are French and English.
2. At all Sessions, simultaneous interpretation must be provided into French, English, German, Spanish, Russian and Arabic.

3. In the case of divergence between the French and English texts of the Olympic Charter and any other IOC document, the French text shall prevail unless expressly provided otherwise in writing.

The *Charter* acknowledges the importance of language skills and stipulates that the official languages of the IOC are French and English, with French prevailing in the occasion of any divergence between the texts of the Charter and other IOC documents. Along with French and English, the *Charter* also features Arabic, German, Russian and Spanish as 'working languages' of the Olympic Games. These languages are sometimes supplemented by 'unofficial languages.' Languages spoken by large numbers of National Olympic Committees (NOCs) are often included in the official communication to allow OCOGs to reach a wider audience (Djité, 2009). Olympic Solidarity, for example, has supported translation of the revised *Sport Administration Manual* into Azerbaijani, Bosnian, Georgian, Khmer, Laotian, Latvian, Lithuanian, Portuguese, Russian, Spanish and Urdu (International Olympic Committee, 2019, p. 64). It is worth noting that although English is more widely used in the internal administration of the IOC, communication with and between member states and external exchanges, the IOC still maintain the status of French as the first official language at the legislative level for its symbolic value as the language initiating the Modern Olympic Movement. Like other supernational organisations, the IOC needs to alleviate the tension between the efficiency of a small number (ideally one) of working languages and the symbolic claims of all member states (Spolsky, 2009, p. 208). The *Olympic Charter* (International Olympic Committee, 2020, p. 12) stipulates that the enjoyment of rights and freedoms shall be secured without discrimination of any kind including language. However, in fact, the IOC does not grant equal right to languages of all member states in its internal operations at the legislative and administrative levels. This fact will inevitably lead to the power distance between the official/working languages and the unofficial/non-working languages, and bring issues pertaining to language rights of speakers of less prestigious languages and linguistics minorities.

3.1.2 External influences

An analysis of the language management of the IOC shall also consider its external influence on the language policies of its member states for hosting the Olympic Games. Supranational organisations regularly respect the sovereignty of their member states which constitute them. They do not have much authority to set policy for individual states, but they have the standing to influence their member states to set policy and to inspect the implementation of policy. As the Olympics are allotted to a host city every four years, the organisation of the Olympic Games is entrusted by the IOC to the NOC of the host country. The NOC in turn constitutes an OCOG. For instance, in the case of the 2008 Beijing Olympic Games, the Beijing Organising Committee for the Games of the XXIX Olympiad (BOCOG) was established on December 13, 2001, five months after Beijing won the right to host the 2008 Olympic Games. The OCOG, since the time it is constituted, communicates directly with the IOC, whose guidelines and instructions it follows to organise the Olympic Games. The minimum legal requirement of an OCOG's contract with the IOC is the use of French and English for Olympic purposes.

The efforts of the IOC to influence the language policies of the OCOGs and the host countries are mainly reflected in the maintenance of the status of French as the first official language. Under the background of the global spread of English, French is losing ground to English in language practices of the Olympic Games. After the 1984 Los Angeles Olympic Games, the French-English bilingual policy has not been well observed in the following Games. Since 2004, the Secretary General of the Organisation Internationale de la Francophonie (OIF)[3] has appointed a special supervisor to inspect and report on the use of French in the Olympic Games (French cultural center, 2013). In view of the difficulties in using French by non-Francophone countries, France and the OIF, with the help of its members, provide specific support to the organisers of the Olympic Games so that they can respect the equal status of French and English during the Olympic Games. In 2007, Jean Pierre Raffarin, the former Prime Minister of France and the supervisor of the OIF, signed an agreement on the use and promotion of French in the Olympic Games with Liu Qi, the president of BOCOG, in order to implement the relevant provisions of the *Charter* (Gui and Dai, 2008). The agreement puts forward a series of measures to protect the status of French as the official language, such as, building French websites of BOCOG and the INFO2008 Olympic news platform; producing French versions of BOCOG publications including the introduction of Olympic venues and the guide manual for the audience; recruiting 40 French translators and journalists; providing French training for hundreds of Chinese Olympic volunteers and organising various French cultural activities.

Through the Olympic Games, the IOC has affected the formulation and implementation of foreign language education policies in many host countries. In the run up to the 2000 Summer Olympic Games, the Sydney Organising Committee for the Olympic Games (SOCOG) had provided a French language training

---

3 A French language term coined in 1880 by French geographer Onesime Reclus to designate the community of people and countries using French, is an international organization of French-speaking countries and governments.

programme for SOCOG staff facilitated through Alliance Française de Sydney to ensure that officials and other professionals were proficient in the official language (Djité, 2009). The Organising Committee of the Sochi 2014 Winter Olympics had also conducted official language training in English, French and Russian for Olympic officials and service personnel (Henning, 2014). The success of the 2008 Olympic bid and admission to the World Trade Organisation (WTO) both in 2001 promised China a larger role in the international community. Accompanying China's rise on the world stage in the first decade of the 21st century is growing connections between developing opportunities and the English language (Zhang, 2011). Under the prospect of the Olympic Games and a greater role in global governance, the first decade of the 21st century has seen a major acceleration of provisions and planning on behalf of foreign languages in general and English in particular in China. A series of policies have been introduced to expand English language education throughout the nation and to improve the quality of ELT through reforming curricula, textbooks, teaching methods, and assessment procedures (Zhang, 2011). For instance, in 2001, the Chinese Ministry of Education (2001a) issued a policy statement entitled "The Ministry of Education Guidelines for Vigorously Promoting the Teaching of English in Primary Schools," requiring a lowering of the threshold of compulsory English education from the first year of junior high school to Grade 3 in elementary school. According to G. Hu (2005), the policy initiative was formulated in the hope of addressing the gap between the increasing demand for English boosted by the prospects of China's accession to WTO and the 2008 Olympic Games and the unsatisfactory outcome of ELT reforms at the secondary school level in the 1990s. Between 2002 and 2008, BOCOG and the Chinese government carried out a massive English popularisation campaign, involving over 4,000 athletes, judges, BOCOG staff, 1.5 million Olympic volunteers and several million Beijing residents as learners of English, which will be discussed in detail in Chapters 4 & 5.

The *Olympic Charter* essentially charges the OCOGs with the responsibility of serving Olympic family members (i.e., athletes, officials and media), the primary goal being to facilitate the communication needs of athletes, officials and international visitors (International Olympic Committee, 2020). In the recent past, OCOGs have gone beyond the minimum requirement of two official languages, extending the range to include those of the host country. There has also been a trend to supply services in other 'working languages' in order to provide assistance on a case-by-case basis and to meet the needs of the anticipated mix of the press and visitors. In practice, OCOGs have historically tended to take languages into account at many different levels – such as formal interpreting at official ceremonies; supplying news and information to the world's media; supporting signage and public information; providing medical and security services;

and recruiting volunteers with proven language skills to welcome foreign visitors in their own language (Djité, 2009).

In the recent past, the 1992 Barcelona Games, the Sydney 2000 Games, the Athens 2004 Games and the 2012 London Games have gone beyond the minimum requirement of the Olympic Charter and successfully staged multilingual Games. Barcelona, the second largest city and a famous travel destination in Spain, has two official languages, Spanish and Catalan, which, as members of the Romance language group, are closely related to French. In the tourism sector, many employees in Barcelona can speak English. At the 1992 Barcelona Games, 15 other languages were used in addition to the four official ones of Catalan, Spanish, English and French (Djité, 2009). Australia is not only an English-speaking country, but also enjoys well-developed community-based interpreting services. Such services were set up to meet the needs of immigrants from language backgrounds other than English and to facilitate their access to legal and medical services (Lo Bianco, 1994). The 2000 Sydney Olympics was able to use its multicultural society to provide interpreting services in a variety of languages (Pym, 2003). At the Sydney 2000 Games, the multilingual switchboard operated in over 50 languages and over 1,400 volunteer interpreters worked inside the venues (Pound, 2003). The 2004 Olympiad was held in the Greek capital, Athens. Greece is a European country with a long-established tourist industry where 40% of the population speaks English as a second language, in addition to widespread use of French, Italian and German. London, the host city of the 2012 Olympic Games is the most cosmopolitan city in the world and home to 200 ethnic communities who speak a total of 300 languages (Collis, 2007). London 2012 involved all of these communities in delivering its Games.

It can be seen from the past Olympics that multilingual services based on the national (regional) language competence of each host country (city) have become a new mode of cross-cultural communication in the Olympic Games, which is the *de facto* language policy of the Olympic Movement. In the sociolinguistic ecology of today's world, the dominance of English co-exists with multilingualism. Apart from the United Nations, global supranational organisations "tend to be less predisposed towards a multiplicity of official or working languages" and most, like the IOC, have fewer than three official languages (de Varennes, 2012, p. 154). What's more, most official languages of international organisations are European languages, among which English is the most frequently used official language (Zhang, 2019). Despite the language management of the IOC and the status planning involved in the officialisation of English and French, there are many additional factors at play that impact upon the extent and way(s) in which these and other languages figure within the Games (Vessey, 2018). Therefore, the IOC and the organisers of the Olympic Games need to fully understand the language needs of the Olympic Movement, and actively seek solutions to bridge the gap between the official language policies and multilingual language practices.

3.2 LPP studies of the Olympic Games

The academic literature on the Modern Olympic Games is massive and growing. A search of "Olympic Games" as the keyword in the topic field in Web of Science Core Collection database found 5,292 works on 1 October 2020. Besides sport sciences, most social science disciplines and sub-disciplines (primarily history, sociology, economics, politics and education) have contributed to the study of the Olympic Games (e.g., Baldauf, 2006; Canagarajah, 2005). Above all, the Games have become an intriguing locus for the study of the social construction of national, regional, and civic identity. Existing scholarly publications (Toohey and Veal, 2007, p. 2) have examined a number of significant and contested issues pertaining to the social construction of identity through the experience of hosting the Olympic Games. For example, many Chinese and international scholars (e.g., Blain, Boyle and O'Donnell, 1993; Brown, 2000; Brownell, 2005; Burton, 2003; Dyreson, 2003; Essex and Chalkley, 1998; Houlihan, 1997; Ikhioya, 2001; Jaffe and Nebanzahl, 1993; Smith and Porter, 2004; Toohey and Veal, 2007) have shown the strategic use of the 2008 Games for increasing the prestige of the Chinese government while concurrently arousing national consciousness and identification within the Chinese population. However, despite the increasing academic attention on the Olympic Games, there is a scarcity of literature in Olympic studies exploring the role of language policy and planning in the Games and its relation to identity construction.

Only a few studies situate the discussion of language policy and planning and identity construction in the context of the Olympic Games. One category of studies explores language planning and policymaking for the Olympic Games by synthesizing official reports and independent research. In preparation for the Sydney 2000 Olympic Games, Lo Bianco (1994) urges the Australian government to adopt a language and cultural plan to complement the infrastructure, sports and telecommunication planning. He explains that such a plan involves eight aspects, including: 1) creation of a language services division within the official Games organising structure; 2) establishment of exact terminological equivalences for a range of languages for all the sports represented at the Games as well as for typical sports medicine terms and for dispute resolution terminology; 3) market research of the actual experiences of visitors from language backgrounds other than English to the Atalanta Games, as well as of the teams and samples of individual athletes; 4) exploration and encouragement of market innovation and institution of a system of approval for technology-supported language services; 5) negotiation of the imagery or iconography to be present at the Games and examination of overseas expectations about this; 6) linking English as a foreign language and tourism activities to the Great Family Reunion ideas for 2001 and to the Games; 7) provision of translating and interpreting services to police, hospitals and emergency services in the planning for the numbers of visitors and the likely languages required; 8) systemic association, alongside the professional services, of volunteers representing the diversity of the religious, cultural and linguistic make-up of the host country. In his later publication, Lo Bianco (2007) provides extensive detail about the language planning and policymaking for the Sydney Games. In particular, the book focuses on the role of the Language Service Programme, which was responsible for a range of translation and interpretation services at pre-Games and Games events. In a similar vein, Djite (2009) notes that international sporting events, such as the Olympic Games, are linguistically complex events that require large-scale language planning and policy, and language skills and services (such as translation and interpreting) are crucial to the success of any such event. With a particular focus on the Sydney Games, he examines how language issues were addressed as part of the planning of the Olympic Games and discusses the range of activities involved in facilitating international collaboration in the preparation for and conduct of the Games. Collis (2007) analyses the language services opportunities at the 2012 London Olympic and Paralympic Games, underscoring the importance of multilingual support in London in sectors such as public services, transportation, tourism, education, business and communities. Huc-Hepher, Kelly and Phipps (2008) provide extensive detail not only on the planning for London 2012 but also on the successes and failures of previous Games. The authors emphasise the relevance of "internationalisation" and the pivotal role of cultural and ethnolinguistic diversity in London, which the authors argue served as an asset for Games organisers. Zhang Jie (2011) situates language policies, language practices and language ideologies within China's broader social, economic and political changes and, in particular, the preparation and hosting of the 2008 Beijing Olympic Games. Specifically, the study interprets China's desire for English in relation to the identity construction of the Olympic host city and its citizens. Although not focused specifically on the Olympic Games, De Varennes (2012) explores language policymaking and planning in supranational organisations such as the IOC. This book chapter discusses the relevance of multilingualism and the dominance of English in international contexts, particularly with reference to the gap between the language(s) used by supranational organisations and those understood by the individuals. Vessey (2018) examines the gap between official language policies and actual language practices by reviewing historical perspectives, specific recent cases and core issues involved in the language planning and policy of the Olympic Games. Drawing on the concept of 'superdiversity,' the chapter asserts that the Games can be considered 'superdiverse' events that bring together "significant new conjunctions and interactions of variables" such as country of origin, ethnicity, language, religion, gender (Vertovec, 2007: 1025) and create 'ephemeral' speech communities of shared indexicalities that emerge in practice (Blommaert & Backus, 2013: 12). In past Games, the official and working languages function alongside a range of bottom-up linguistic practices used by athletes and audience members who communicate in person and via media technologies in a range of contexts across the globe.

Another category of studies investigates language ideologies in the context of the Olympic Games. For instance, Pan (2011) provides an overview of attitudes and ideologies concerning the English language in the context of the Beijing Games. The author suggests that the attitudes and ideologies are the result of social, cultural and political factors at play in China. Vessey (2013) discusses a language ideological debate over the status of French in the Vancouver Olympics that took place in two Canadian national newspapers. Reports on the insufficient use of French during the opening ceremonies sparked protest from politicians, official commentators, citizens and online newsreaders alike. She finds that this debate involves not only ideologies of language, but also ideologies of identity and belonging.

In addition, a few studies focus on the translation and interpretation services for the Olympic Games. For instance, Pym (1996) discusses the role played by translation and language policy at the 1992 Barcelona Olympic Games. Stuker, et al. (2006) look at speech-to-speech translation services for the 2008 Beijing Olympic Games. Henning (2014) examines the role of language services in the 2014 Sochi Winter Olympics.

In contrast to existing literature that has been primarily concerned with socio-historical or political and economic aspects of the Games, this book takes a language policy and planning perspective to identity construction in the preparation and hosting of the Olympic Games. Of particular interest to this study is the relationship between language policies, language ideologies, language practices and identity construction in the 2008 Beijing Olympic Games.

3.3 An expanded view of language policy

Language policies (LP) are "deliberate choices made by governments or other authorities with regard to the relationship between language and social life" (Djité, 1994, p. 63). These decisions are made especially in relation to "the legitimacy of using and learning certain language(s) (e.g., the right to speak and to learn) in given contexts and societies (status) and their forms (corpus)" (Shohamy, 2006, p. 45). Spolsky (2004) argues that a useful first step is to distinguish between the three components of the language policy of a speech community: "(1) its language practices – the habitual pattern of selecting among the varieties that make up its linguistic repertoire; (2) its language beliefs or ideology – the beliefs about language and language use; and (3) any specific efforts to modify or influence that practice by any kind of language intervention, planning, or management" (p. 5). In addition to Spolsky (2004), my view on language policy draws upon that of Shohamy. In *Language Policy: Hidden Agendas and New Approaches*, Shohamy (2006) proposes an expanded view of language and language policy. For Shohamy (2006), language is not 'a closed and finite system,' the kind of concept often used by traditional linguists; rather, it is "open, dynamic, energetic, constantly evolving and personal" (p. 5). This implies that language itself is free from any strict or prescribed rules of correctness. Viewing language in an expanded way also implies that it is not limited to words or other linguistic markers but incorporates multi-modal forms of expression and use: visuals, graphics, images, gesture, clothes, architecture, and so forth (Shohamy, 2006, pp. 14–16). In addition, people seem to, on the surface, enjoy a large degree of freedom of expression as they can make decisions about their language use in everyday life. However, more often than not, people's use of language is regulated, both overtly and covertly. Language is not empty of ideology; rather, it is a symbolic tool for the manipulation of the state's political, social, economic and educational agendas by the imposition of specific linguistic behaviours, and at the same time a tool of control that creates and perpetuates group membership, identities, hierarchies and a variety of other forms of imposition (Shohamy, 2006, p. 1).

Based on this broad view of language, Shohamy makes a distinction between overt LPs and covert LPs. She (2006, p. xvi) argues that an in-depth understanding of the LPs of a political and social entity should not be observed only through explicitly declared, formalised and codified policy documents such as laws, curricula and tests, but rather through a variety of covert and implicit mechanisms used mostly (but not exclusively) by those in authority to affect, create and perpetuate language practices, "de facto LP," which are not conventionally viewed as policy devices.

According to Shohamy (2006), LP plays a key role in manipulating language behaviours and ensuring that ideologies turn into practice. There are a variety of overt and covert mechanisms of LP that fall between language ideology and practice. Figure 1 provides a graphic representation of these mechanisms, or policy devices, within the framework of ideology and practice. In order to understand real LPs and their "hidden agendas," Shohamy argues that it is not enough to study overt and declared policies but rather that there is a need to study covert and de facto policies. Adopting Shohamy's expanded view of LP, this book explores language policy and planning for the Beijing Olympic Games through a variety of overt and covert LP mechanisms. The specific LP mechanisms discussed in this study include action plans, laws, regulations, language tests, language popularisation programmes, language services suppliers, language training textbooks, linguistic landscape, language learning celebrities, and language learning experiences. Besides overt policy processes, I am equally concerned with implicit policy processes – "the ways in which people accommodate, resist and 'make' policy in everyday social practice" (McCarty, 2015, p. 82). An examination of these overt and covert mechanisms requires the adoption of triangulation as a mixed-method approach.

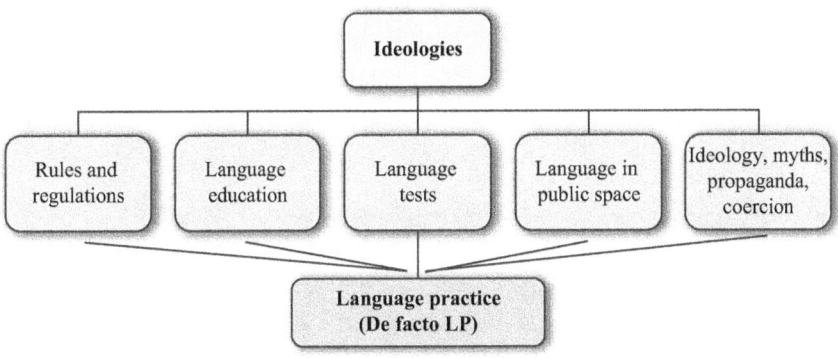

Figure 1: List of mechanisms between ideology and practice (Shohamy, 2006, p. 58).

Language policy is "invariably based on linguistic ideologies, on images of societally desirable forms of language usage and of the ideal linguistic landscape of society" (Blommaert, 2006, p. 244). Language ideology, as succinctly defined by Errington (2001), refers to "the situated, partial, and interested character of conceptions and uses of language" (p. 110). While neutral ideological analysis focuses on "culturally shared" beliefs and practices, critical ideological analysis often emphasises "the political use of language as a particular group's instrument of symbolic domination" (Kroskrity, 2005, p. 501). My view on language ideologies draws upon that of Piller, Gramsci and Bourdieu. From the critical analysis tradition, Piller (2015) emphasizes that language ideologies are constituted by and continuously reconstitute the interests of the dominant classes in society, and are always multiple, fractured, contested, and changing. Gramsci uses the term "hegemony" to describe the way a dominant class makes their ideologies the "norm" (that is, ideas regarded as the most "natural" and "inevitable" and perceived to "benefit" everyone in society) and thereby forms consent among the population at large (Freeden, 2003, p. 20). For Gramsci, ideological hegemony can be exercised by the ruling class not only through exerting state force but also through various cultural means such as education and common sense (Freeden, 2003). Bourdieu's notion (1991) of "symbolic power" and "misrecognition" further elaborates on Gramsci's "hegemony." For Bourdieu, power is transmuted into symbolic form rather than exercised as overt physical force in the routine of daily life. Symbolic power is an invisible power which is "misrecognised" as such and thereby "recognised" as legitimate in the eyes of those subject to the power (Bourdieu, 1991). Following Gramsci and Bourdieu, I argue that ideologies embedded in language policy must not be perceived as "natural," "neutral," or "beneficial" to all members of a society, rather they reflect and serve the interests of the dominant class in that society. As education is a primary mechanism of "ideological hegemony" and "symbolic power," language-in-education policy is considered a powerful tool for the state to exercise its political and cultural governance as it can enforce various political and social ideologies through language education.

3.4 Language service as a new explanatory theory

This section introduces language service as a new approach to analyse and interpret the language planning and management efforts made by the Chinese government and BOCOG for the 2008 and 2022 Olympic Games.

3.4.1 The development of language service studies in China

Increasingly frequent contacts between China and the outside world and transformations in economic and social life in the 21st century have rendered language a key factor in China's modernisation and internationalisation drive. Many Chinese scholars started to reflect on the language issues in the actual conditions of China's social and economic development; thus, studies of language services emerged in accordance with changes in circumstances over time. The concept of 语言服务 yuyan fuwu [*language service*] only began to be employed in China during this period of change, having been developed from traditional translation and interpretation services against the background of the 2008 Beijing Olympics. At present, there is no consensus on its definition in Chinese academia. According to Zhao Shiju (2012), language service is an action and activity of the actor, using language as the contents or methods, to offer help to others or to society broadly. Li Yuming (2016) broadly defines language services as the activities which use language (both spoken and written), linguistic knowledge, language technology and all derivatives of language to meet various language-related needs in social life. Li Xianle (2010) divides language services into two levels: macro level and micro level. Language services at the micro level mainly refer to the paid or unpaid services, with language as the content or tool, which one party provides another party, enabling the receiving party to benefit from it. Language services at the macro level refer to the effective allocation, planning and standardisation of language resources by the state or a government department to ensure that people and organisations in the region under its jurisdiction use the language rationally and effectively.

In the 1986 National Conference on Language and Script Work, Liu Daosheng, Director of the State Language Commission of China, pinpointed that the primary mission of China's language and script work was to strengthen both theoretical and empirical research on language and script, promote social surveys and consultation, and provide services for society (Liu, 1987). Although the term *language service* had not yet been proposed in that conference, there was already recognition of the social service function of language. Under the national strategic agenda, Chinese scholars have taken a constructive approach to language service research from the 1986 national conference. Since the early 21st century, the theoretical framework of language service has been systematically discussed and an independent field of language service studies is beginning to take shape in China. In September 2005, the International Forum on the Construction of the Language Environment of the World Expo was held in Shanghai. A special panel on *language service* was set up in the forum, in which Li Yuming, Qu Shaobing and other Chinese linguists had an in-depth exchange of views on whether *language service* could be used as a term in applied linguistics. In 2007, Qu Shaobing's paper entitled "The outline of language service research" was published. It is the first research paper in which the properties, functions, classification, planning and assessment of language service are discussed in depth. Qu (2007) pointed out that language service research is an inevitable requirement of contemporary social development against the background of internationalisation, marketisation, informatisation and multilingualism. Qu (2007) held that language service as an independent field of study can be classified as a subcategory in applied linguistics and has a close relationship with pragmatics. The scope of language service research includes language education, language planning, sociolinguistics, language information processing and computational linguistics in a broad sense.

The Multilingual Service Centre launched on the eve of the 2008 Beijing Olympics was China's first governmental language service organisation. The centre aimed to provide "barrier-free" language services in 44 languages at Games time. Since then, China's language services industry has entered the fast lane of development. Thousands of language translation and consultation institutions have emerged in China. At the same time, the Translators Association of China (TAC) began to undertake the role of national association for the language service sector. Many government departments, universities, academic organisations and enterprises have participated in the research of language services. A series of academic conferences with language services as the theme were held one after another.

In September 2010, the Translators Association of China and the Beijing Foreign Affairs Office jointly hosted the *2010 International Conference on Language Services Industry* on the theme of 'language services for large-scale international activities.' Guo Xiaoyong (2010) gave the keynote speech, entitled "Chinese Language Services Industry: A Review of the Current Situation, Problems and their Solutions". In that conference, official statistics on the Chinese language services industry were released for the first time. In May 2011, the Department of Language Information Management of the Chinese Ministry of Education and the Centre for Chinese Language Strategy Research at Nanjing University jointly held the *Seminar on Language Economy and Language Services*. In January 2012, Guangzhou University, the Institute of Applied Linguistics of the Chinese Ministry of Education, and the Centre for Chinese Language Strategy Research at Nanjing University co-hosted the *Advanced Forum on Language Service Research*. In December 2012, the *Outline of the Long and Medium-term Reform and Development Plan of Spoken and Written Languages of China (2012–2020)* was issued by the Chinese Ministry of Education and the State Language Commission. The Plan calls for building an information platform on the use of languages and scripts to provide advisory services about language policies, regulations, standards and usages. It also calls for developing 'language services for emergency/assistance response' and building a national multilingual talent pool.

The concept of language service was first put forward in China around 2005. Under the drive of the 2008 Beijing Olympic Games, Shanghai 2010 World Expo and other major international events that needed language services, China's political, industrial and academic circles began to work together closely in relevant research and practices. In 2013 the Chinese government proposed the

"Belt and Road initiative" as a trade and infrastructure network that aimed to connect China with Europe and Africa. This initiative underscored the weakness of China's national language capacity and the urgent need for foreign language professionals in languages other than English (LOTE) in the field of foreign affairs. It is thus clear that the development of language service studies in China has been driven by the government to meet the practical requirements of national social and economic development.

Overall, China's language service research has emerged in the new era of accelerating reform, opening up and economic transformation, in which language competence plays an increasingly important role in the political agenda of the government and in economic development, intercultural communication and the social life of the people. In the past decade, China's language service research has developed very rapidly with the support of the government, but there are also some obvious problems (Zhang and Shen, 2016). First, there is no consensus on the definition of 'language service'. Some broad definitions are very obscure and overlap with existing concepts such as 'language policy', 'language planning' and 'language management'. The different interpretations of the concept of language service have led to different research directions and approaches to this subject by Chinese scholars, which is not conducive to the disciplinary development of the field. Second, the existing research on language services in China is mostly theoretical analysis or policy discussion. There is a paucity of empirical research, especially studies on language needs and language services in specific industries. Moreover, most of the existing empirical research on language services adopts quantitative analysis methods, such as questionnaire survey, which can be useful for describing the general tendency of language service provisions at the macro level but is ineffective in interpreting how language policies and ideologies influence people's language choices and language practices at the micro level. Therefore, it is suggested that language service research should draw on qualitative research methods, such as interview, observation and ethnography, in order to understand the relationship between official language policy and individual language practice.

3.4.2 The system of language services

The system of language services can be studied with a focus on providers, recipients, or content:

1) Language services provider

Government, society and individuals can all be providers of language services. The government is the largest provider of language services. Firstly, the government is the policy maker with respect to language services. In China, language norms and language service standards were formerly formulated by government agencies. Now, due to the change of administrative functions of governments, industrial organisations are in most cases in charge of formulating language norms and language service standards. Nevertheless, standards formulation in the language services industry is still subject to governmental guidance and supervision. Secondly, governments supply funds for public language services, including scientific research, construction of the academic discipline, training of language professionals, and language services for some special groups. Finally, governments have the most abundant resources relating to language services, such as language service human resources, construction of language service markets, and various data resources related to language services. For these reasons, responsibility for the development of the language services industry lies with governments.

In addition to government agencies, a range of social actors, including individuals, can become providers of language services. Institutions such as schools, scientific research institutes, and industrial associations can be the providers of language services, whereas high-tech language services and innovative language services are mostly provided by business enterprises. Language experts contribute the most in terms of the language services provided by individuals. Language experts are distributed across many industries and disciplines, such as linguists, language technology experts, language artists, language teachers, translators, broadcasters, commentators, operators, programme hosts, performers, lexicographers, calligraphers, language pathologists and therapists, psychological consultants, negotiation experts, mediators, font designers, proofreaders, text recorders, copywriters, product spokesmen, tour guides, shopping guides, ceremony hosts, network anchors, customer service personnel, and so on. All of these people have language expertise and are mainly or partially engaged in language services. Most of the language services provided by governments and general society depend on language experts.

2) Recipients of language services

Receiving paid language services can be considered as 'language consumption,' therefore recipients of paid language services are 'language consumers' (Li, 2016). Paid language services make language service a commodity, a product that can be sold for economic value. When the development of paid language services reaches a certain scale, the language services industry and language service market are formed. Governments are the most important recipient of language services. When they formulate language policies such as national language standards and industrial standards for language services, they need to consult experts and purchase language services. At the same time, governments also have the responsibility of providing the public products of language services to society, such as language education in the compulsory education stage, promotion of a national/official language, protection of minority languages and dialects, and so forth. These public products are provided to the relevant language consumers after being purchased by governments.

People from all walks of life and all levels of society can be recipients of language services. For example, people with language-related disabilities, such as the deaf, people with intellectual disabilities, autistic children, or children with delayed language development, have special requirements for language education and training and thus need specialised language services. In order to supply specialised language services, language experts themselves must first receive language education for specific purposes (which is itself a type of language service) provided by enterprises and institutions specialising in the appropriate language services.

Acceptance of free language services can be considered as the receipt of 'language welfare' (Li, 2016). Free language services are generally provided by government agencies. In many countries, public primary and secondary school students at the compulsory education stage enjoy language welfare provided by state institutions. Li Yuming (2016) calls for more academic attention to the issues associated with language welfare, such as: who should enjoy language welfare, how governments and society provide language welfare, and what system should be used to guarantee people's right to enjoy language welfare.

3) Content of language services

The breadth of discussion regarding the content of language services will depend upon how we define language services. If we think of language services as using language (including text), language knowledge, language technology and all derivatives of language to meet the needs of language life (*Yuyan Shenghuo*)[4] (Li, 2016), then the content of language service is extremely broad.

In addition to language education and training, language translation, language art, advertising, and broadcasting, new forms of language services are flourishing with contemporary advances and developments. For example, language technology services, which are benefitting 800 million Chinese Internet users, are becoming an important support for all trades and professions via

---

[4] Li Yuming (2016) defines 'language life (*Yuyan Shenghuo*)' as various activities of using, learning and studying spoken and written language, language knowledge and language technology.

the Internet. Zhao Shiju (2012) classifies languages services into six types according to the content as follows:
(1) Language knowledge services: such as dictionary compilation, linguistic research oriented to natural language processing, formulation of language norms and standards, digitisation of various language knowledge and materials, corpus construction.
(2) Language-related technology services: such as speech synthesis technology, language and script recognition technology, word bank technology, speech and script identification/detection technology, machine translation technology, data retrieval technology, text conversion technology, text typesetting technology, script carving technology.
(3) Language tool services: such as electronic translator, online translation, intelligent multilingual service system, language and text editing software, audio player, text reader.
(4) Language use-related services: such as shorthand, naming, dubbing, broadcasting, typing, secretarial work, language training, language proficiency test, management of spoken and written language, language consulting, signage production, advertising.
(5) Language rehabilitation services: such as stuttering correction, language training for the deaf and mute, diagnosis and treatment of aphasia.
(6) Language education services: such as teaching of national commonly-used languages and characters, foreign language education, teaching Chinese as a foreign language.

A major characteristic of language services is that they are often intermingled with other activities in accomplishing a task. If a language service contributes the substantial part of a task, it can be regarded as *basic language service*, whereas if the proportion of language service in a piece of work is small, it can be regarded as *auxiliary language service* (Li, 2016). Foreign language training, language proficiency testing, language policy consultation, translation, typesetting and proofreading are instances of basic language services in which language service is the main content. In the retail industry, pre-sale and after-sale customer service communication is very important, and to a certain extent determines customer satisfaction. However, the overall degree of customer satisfaction is ultimately dependent upon the quality of products, therefore language service is auxiliary in the customer service of a retail business. In this book, I take *language service* as a new explanatory theory to analyse LPP for the 2008 Beijing Summer Olympic Games and the 2022 Beijing Winter Olympic Games.

3.5 The political economy of language

In recent years, jobs that involve at least some linguistic and communicative labour have increased dramatically worldwide as part of the expanding service economy (Piller, 2012, p. 88). The academic discourse of language service which was developed in China in the past decade and a half has not been adopted by the international academic community. However, many international scholars have extensively discussed relevant language issues in a globalised new economy and developed concepts and theories such as 'linguistic capital', 'language commodification', 'linguistic labour', 'language work', and 'language workers' since the 1980s. International research that has responded to this new linguistic phenomenon under the shifting political and economic conditions often draws on the work of the sociologist Pierre Bourdieu (1986; 1991) to explore how linguistic and cultural capital can be transformed into economic capital in the globalised new economy. Bourdieu (1986) differentiates between three fundamental types of capital in society, all of which are mutually convertible: economic, cultural and social capital. Cultural capital exists mainly in three forms: in the embodied state as a disposition of the mind and body; in the objectified state as cultural goods, for example pictures, books and instruments; and in the institutionalised state as a form of objectification, such as educational qualifications. 'Linguistic capital' is a form of embodied cultural capital acquired through the legitimation of language practices in the family and school. Moreover, Bourdieu (1991) asserted that language reflects power relations within society. He (1991) made a distinction between two types of linguistic markets: formal and informal, with the former having a stronger connection with the power and authority of the state. In a given linguistic market, linguistic capital is unequally distributed among languages and different expressive styles. Traditionally, national and official languages are highly demanded and valued in formal markets such as government, business and school, whereas local languages tend to be used in informal markets such as within local community (Rassool, 2013). Competence in the national or official language of a country, therefore, represents high-valued linguistic capital within the formal linguistic market of the country, giving those endowed with competence in that language an advantage over others (Nishioka and Durrani, 2019). A lack of linguistic capital in the dominant language(s) can become the basis for exclusion from jobs, education and high-status groups. In the global linguistic market, English has nowadays become a lingua franca for cross-cultural communication and thus has highly valued linguistic capital and symbolic power, which may be converted to economic gains in jobs where English is highly demanded.

Thomas Friedman (2006) distinguishes between three stages of globalisation: Globalisation 1.0 was driven by countries internationalising; Globalisation 2.0 was driven by companies internationalising; and Globalisation 3.0 is driven by individuals internationalising themselves. In response to the shifting features of globalisation, Piller (2012, pp. 76–77) discusses three phases of intercultural business communication: Intercultural Business Communication 1.0 research was focused on comparing the communicative styles of nationals of different countries; Intercultural Business Communication 2.0 research shifted its focus to communication within international corporations; Intercultural Business Communication 3.0, the most recent phase with the individual as the locus of intercultural communication, has seen the emergence of employees who are specifically employed to communicate interculturally. Intercultural Business Communication 3.0 is characterized by the commodification of language and communication skills. In sociolinguistics, linguistic anthropology and language economics, a term closely related to 'linguistic capital' is 'language commodification', which describes how language has become reconfigured for market purposes and treated as an economic resource (Heller, 2010a, 2010b; Heller and Duchêne, 2016). Heller (2010a) asserted that the globalised new economy under the political economic conditions of late capitalism led to an increasing central economic role for language, both as the means through which work is accomplished (the work process) and as a product of labour (the work product). One important result of the many ways in which communication in general, and language and multilingualism in particular, has become central to the globalised new economy is the emergence of 'language work,' and therefore of the 'language worker' (Duchêne, 2009; Heller, 2005; Heller and Boutet, 2006; Tange, 2009). Piller (2012) argues that in an economy where business activities centre on knowledge, information and services, language and communication become a part of people's jobs (p. 88). The term 'language work' describes jobs where a substantial aspect of the work consists of language-related tasks, such as teaching, translating and interpreting or call centre work (Piller, 2012, p. 88). Language treated as a commodity represents a new form of labour in late capitalism (Urciuoli and LaDousa, 2013). Based on studies of work in call centres, service encounters and multilingual workplaces, Urciuoli and LaDousa (2013) argue that in late capitalism language work has replaced the physical labour of earlier times and become today's labour commodity. According to them, 'language as labour' is a commodity, a form of cultural capital which is convertible to economic capital.

Holborow (2018) also comments on the commodification of language. In contrast to some sociolinguistic accounts that tend to see the effects of commodification of language at work as shaping a compliant language worker whose language skills are convertible to economic returns in terms of wage premia, she, through a Marxist lens, argued that labour power, including language skills, is bought as a commodity on the labour market for less than the value that it adds through increased sales (for example, call centre operators). Even though there is some economic value which can be associated with language knowledge and skills, Holborow (2018) argues that the neoliberal claims on language as a human capital commodity is too simplistic: "it artificially isolates language from a range of accompanying skills, it masks questions of social power and of who reaps the profit from language skills in the workplace and perhaps, more worryingly, implies a reductionist view of language" (Holborow, 2018). Moreover, Holborow (2018) explores the active social agent dimension of 'language workers' who resist, in various ways, attempts at commodification of their language.

4 Summary

Given the number and diversity of the participants and TV and Internet users, the 2008 Beijing Olympic Games were probably the most linguistically complex event ever held. Despite the massive scholarly literature on the Olympic Games, the value of the Games as the locus of LPP research has not been fully recognised. In the hope of filling this research gap, this book situates the discussion of language policies, language ideologies and language practices in the context of the Beijing Olympic Games. Adopting an expended view of LP, this book examines not only overt top-down policies (action plans, laws, regulations, language tests) but also covert and de facto policies (language popularisation programmes, language services suppliers, language training textbooks, linguistic landscape, language learning celebrities and language learning experience). This book also attempts to bridge two research paradigms: one is the constructive study of language policies and language services by Chinese scholars; the other is the poststructuralist study of language ideologies and language work by Western scholars. By doing so, the book analyses the challenges and achievements in LPP and language services for the two Olympic Games held and to be held in Beijing, and at the same time reveals how language ideologies motivated decision-making in LPP at the macro level and impacted on the language practices of individual participants at the micro level.

Chapter 2
Remaking China in the Olympic spotlight

1 The historical and realistic significance of the 2008 Beijing Olympic Games

What did the Olympics mean to China? It is an important question to answer before we can understand the language policy and planning for the 2008 Beijing Olympic Games. The XXIX Olympiad came to Beijing at a critical juncture in world history, representing both increasing globalisation and the recent Chinese history of great socio-economic transformation (Xu, 2006). The award to host the Olympiad created an additional impetus for China's modernisation drive and international integration. Both internally and externally, the 2008 Beijing Olympic Games were laden with the historical mission of remaking China, in terms of constructing national identity and pursuing international primacy (Xu, 2006).

1.1 Fading glory and lost identity

China is one of the world's oldest continuous civilisations, with its written history tracing back to the Shang Dynasty (ca. 1700 B.C. – ca. 1046 B.C.). For many centuries, China stood as a leading civilisation, outpacing the rest of the world in sciences and arts. Economically, China had a self-reliant economy and self-sufficient domestic trade. Prior to the 19th century, China possessed one of the most advanced societies and economies in the world. Up until the Qianlong Period of the Qing Dynasty (1711–1799), China's gross domestic product (GDP) still accounted for one third of that of the world (Niu, 2008, p. 40). Social stability and economic prosperity lulled the rulers of the Qing Dynasty (1644–1912) into a Sino-centric world view (Adamson, 2002) and this led to self-imposed isolation from the rest of the world. 天圆地方 *tian yuan di fang* [Round Heaven – Square Earth] is an ancient and long-lasting cultural concept in China and the supreme expression of a Sino-centric worldview. Ancient Chinese people believed that the Heaven projected its circular shadow onto the centre of the Earth (Tang, 2010), therefore 中国 *zhongguo* [China] literally means the Middle Kingdom. The area under the shadow, 天下 *tianxia* [literally, land under the Heaven], was divinely appointed to the Emperor of China. The corners of the square which were not under the celestial emanation were ruled by 夷 *yi* [foreign barbarians].

For thousands of years, this Sino-centric worldview had lain behind Chinese construction of self-identity. Holding a Sino-centric worldview toward the Western "barbarians," the Qing government prohibited local Chinese in the only open port from learning foreign languages (Niu, 2008, p. 34). Like all languages other than Chinese, English was perceived as "a barbarian tongue" in the feudal society of China (Adamson, 2002).

The 18th century witnessed revolutionary changes in Europe, especially Britain, which marked the dawn of a new age and the formation of a new world structure. An agrarian society guaranteed continuous prosperity in ancient feudal China but seriously handicapped the development of social productive forces in the late feudal society of China. The closed-door policy implemented during the Qing Dynasty resulted in China's isolation from the world and even widened the gap between China and European countries in comprehensive national strength. At the same time, however, Europe in general and Britain in particular were being transformed and invigorated by the rise of rationalism, nationalism, colonialism, and ultimately the industrial revolution. The Opium War of 1840 between the United Kingdom and Imperial China marked a turning point in Chinese history. As a result of the War, China was reduced to a semi-colonial and semi-feudal country and the feudal rulers in the late Qing Dynasty were finally awakened to the superiority of the West in science and technology. During the following hundred years, economically backward China suffered from foreign aggression, civil war and various political conflicts until the founding of the People's Republic of China in 1949. Political instability and a backward economy not only damaged the Chinese people's national pride but also undermined their Sino-centric national identity. Since then and for over a century, an inferiority complex has been institutionalised in the Chinese mind (Dong, 2005). The shame and humiliation resulting from foreign invasion after 1840 made the Chinese under Communism obsessed with the desire to put behind them the image of the "sick man of East Asia" (Dong, 2005). Beijing's unsuccessful bid for the 2000 Olympic Games in 1993 further contributed to this national psyche of failure and defeat. Reviving a unified, cohesive, and powerful identity for the Chinese nation and regaining its national greatness became the underlying drive for pursuing the Beijing Olympic Games. It was widely claimed that the successful staging of the Games could bring an end to the century of humiliation by and subordination to Western powers and would be a milestone in the course of the great reinvigoration of the Chinese nation. Attending the Olympics and performing well carried the symbolic meaning of catching up with and even beating the Western powers (Fan, Ping and Huan, 2005).

1.2 China's identity crisis in the modernisation process

China's reform and opening up started over 40 years ago after the 10-year Cultural Revolution (1966–1976), which left the country on the verge of economic breakdown. It was not until the Third Plenary Session of the Eleventh Central Committee of the Chinese Communist Party in 1978 that the Chinese leadership concentrated on economic development. The Communist Party of China (CPC) shifted the focus of all its work from class struggle to the drive for socialist modernisation – that is, the modernisation of agriculture, industry, science and technology, and the military. After starting to open up and reform its economy, China averaged 9.8% annual GDP growth for three decades from 1978 to 2008 (Xinhua, 2008c), and surpassed Japan as the world's second largest national economy in 2010 (Associated Press, 2010).

It is the adoption of capitalist market mechanisms since 1978 that has been leading the once poverty-stricken China into becoming an ever-growing prosperous country. However, the country's traditional cultural beliefs and socialist principles are often irreconcilable in the face of its modernisation drive through decentralisation and marketisation (Wu, 2007). Consequently, economic success has come at the price of national identity. Since the 1980s, tremendous socio-economic transformations brought about by Western-oriented modernisation have resulted in a series of identity crises such as the loss of national identity, and the decline of traditional and socialist values (Zheng, 1999, p. 47).Consequently, China's identity crisis also had an impact on the attitude of the public towards the political legitimacy of the leadership of the CPC. Due to the gap between surging economic reform and lagging political reform, from the 1990s growing public concerns started to emerge about a belief crisis among different social groups, especially among the young generation, who were described by the media as "a contemplative generation," "a wounded generation," "a wasted generation," "a lost generation," and "a fallen generation" (Zheng, 1999, p. 48). It was reported that the public took an indifferent attitude to the society they were part of. In a national survey, it was shown that individuals' loyalty to the socialist state had seriously weakened throughout the 1980s (Zheng, 1999, p. 50). Through "opening wide" to the West, the possibility of the erosion of "Chinese" cultural values by a global culture dominated by American values began to alarm China's leaders and CPC theorists (Knight, 2006). Former CPC General Secretary (1989–2002) and President of PRC (1993–2003), Jiang Zemin, in his speech to commemorate the 80th anniversary of the founding of the CPC, called on the whole party to "advocate the ideology of patriotism, collectivism and socialism among all people" and "combat and resist money worship, hedonism, ultra-egoism and other decadent ideas" (Knight, 2006). The Chinese government came to the realisation that it had to rely more on patriotism for reinforcing its legitimacy, which had been weakened by de-ideologisation and the market-oriented modernisation drive (Xu, 2006). The successful hosting of sporting mega-events and the international success of Chinese athletes were believed to bring the nation pride and hope, which were much needed in the new era of transformation (Fan, Ping and Huan, 2005). In addition, sporting mega-events have been proven to be a major source of national cohesion in many different contexts. National cohesion is a multi-component conception with patriotism, sense of belonging and identity, self-consciousness and subject awareness as its main factors. Because of their manifold links with all these factors, sports are seen as effective in invigorating the national spirit, facilitating the forming of national identity and ultimately enhancing the cohesion of the nation-state. Consequently, the 2008 Olympic Games were assigned a set of Olympic objectives, as in this statement by Jiang Zemin: "the success of the bid will advance China's domestic stability and economic prosperity. The Olympics in China has the objectives of raising national morale and strengthening the unity of Chinese people both in the mainland and overseas" (cited in Fan, Ping and Huan, 2005, p. 514). In another example, He Zhenliang, honorary president of the Chinese Olympic Committee and advisor of the Beijing Organising Committee for the Games of the XXIX Olympiad (BOCOG), declared that China should make the 2008 Olympics a success with national cohesion and self-confidence (Kong, 2006).

It has been China's national ambition to catch up with the Western capitalist world through modernisation, and the Olympics played an important part in stimulating the nation's enthusiasm and drive for modernisation (Fan, Ping and Huan, 2005). Indeed, it can be considered that the 2008 Beijing Olympics achieved the goal of furthering national cohesion and unity. In preparation for the Games, Chinese national cohesion was manifested in the forms of "voluntary service" and "public participation." With a 94.9% support rate and 1.5 million Olympic volunteers, the Chinese people impressed the world with their immense enthusiasm and support for the Games. Never before had Chinese people concerned themselves so much with the Olympic Games. The sentiments inspired by the 2008 Beijing Olympic Games prompted an overwhelming majority of the Chinese population to seize every opportunity to participate in this biggest-ever sporting event and in turn reinforced the cohesiveness of the Chinese people. On the eve of the Games, several surveys (Ogilvy Group and Milward Brown ACSR, 2008; Pew Research Center, 2008) found high excitement for the Beijing Olympic Games, with national pride a key driver of China's euphoria. While the Games were largely held in Beijing, the Olympics were not only about Beijing, but rather, the entire nation.

1.3 China's image crisis in a globalising world

In addition to overcoming China's inferiority complex and enhancing national identity and unity, a third objective of the Olympics was to project a new image of China to the world. China, as a communist state in the Far East, has long had an image as 'the ultimate Other' (Wu, 2007). China's ever-growing economic power has attracted worldwide attention and also excessive concerns in the Western world. The implications of various aspects of China's rise have been heatedly debated in the international community as well as within China (e.g., Agarwala, 2002; Hu, 2007; Huntington, 1996; Kennedy, 1987; Overholt, 1993; Ramo, 2004; Xia and Jiang, 2004; Zhang, 2016). One widely held view is that China's international image greatly lags behind its economic development (Ramo, 2007). Confronted with the complexities of rapid changes in China since the reform and opening-up in 1978, China's image in the international community has failed to keep up with these ceaseless changes. Due to complicated political, historical and cultural reasons, China's image in international society is rather complex, contradictory and mysterious. The 2007 Pew Global Attitudes Survey (Pew Research Center, 2008) showed that attitudes toward China had grown more negative in recent years in most countries. Based on the 2004/05 survey conducted by Y&R's Brand Asset® Valuator Group which involved more than 500,000 respondents in 45 countries, Ramo (2007) pointed out that China was among the most poorly understood countries on earth. General knowledge of China remains quite low: "People know China is different but have little understanding of either the roots or implications of that difference" (Ramo, 2007, p. 26). He further argued that China's image misalignment at home and abroad has become a strategic threat in its efforts to better integrate with the international community.

Due to China's image crisis in the international sphere, the bidding road of Beijing was full of troubles and trials before attaining success. Editorials in Western newspapers during Beijing's Olympic bid in 2001 revealed a high level of hostility: "China Doesn't Deserve the Olympics"; "Unwelcome Bid from Beijing"; "Olympics Tied Up in Chinese Puzzle"; and others (Brownell, 2007, p. 4). The Beijing Olympics were viewed by many people in the developed Western countries as "the harbinger of a new age of Eastern imperialism and the rise of the 'China threat'" (Brownell, 2007). In the lead-up to the Games, Western politicians, human rights groups, and media commentators frequently used the Olympic Games as a platform for their own political agendas. For instance, in March 2007 actress Mia Farrow spearheaded an attack on China's support of the government of Sudan in which she labelled the Beijing Olympics as the "genocide games" (Farrow and Farrow, 2007). Before Beijing's successful bid for the Olympics in 2001, there was increasing awareness in China of its national image crisis and the urgency to build international trust and understanding for further development in the globalising world. The bidding slogan "New Beijing, New Olympics" for the 29th Olympiad unveiled in 2001 best demonstrated China's determination to present a new image in the Olympic spotlight. For China, the Olympic Games offered a legitimate way to present and promote its national identity and seek a greater role on the global stage.

1.4 Favourable national image as soft power

The pursuit and sponsorship of the Olympiad was an important strategy for China to enhance its international image and to seek greater power on the global stage. This strategy is closely related to the soft power that China has long sought. In 2007, *soft power*, a term developed by Harvard professor Joseph Nye (1990), emerged as a hot topic at that year's annual sessions of China's parliament and top political advisory body. Although its usefulness as a descriptive theory has often been challenged, soft power is still being used as a term that distinguishes the subtle effects of culture, values, and ideas on others' behaviour from more direct coercive measures called *hard power* such as military action or economic incentives. For instance, Peng Fuchun, the deputy of the National People's Congress, the highest law-making body in the PRC, expressed this idea as follows: "We should never underestimate the importance of building soft power as the economic miracle is only one side of China's rise in the world arena" (People's Daily, 2007). In light of this, China has been striving to achieve "the other side," namely exerting more international influence through diplomacy and national image building. Fan (2010) stressed national image as the core component of a country's soft power. Thus, the creation and promotion of a favourable national image is an inseparable part of the strategic plan for China's development. There is little dispute that power in the international arena is derived, in part, from a country's ability to project an image that presents its military, economic, political, or cultural importance in a favourable and powerful light. In turn, recognition from the international community of the projected national image is an important assurance for the legitimacy and power of the present government.

If we know the socio-political context in which China's Olympic bids were embedded, it is not difficult to understand why the *Beijing Olympic Action Plan* (BOCOG, 2002), which was released as the general guideline for preparing the Beijing Olympic Games, set one of its main strategic objectives as "creating a new image for Beijing." The 17-day sporting extravaganza represented the culmination of three decades of Chinese efforts to reconnect with the world. The

Project 2008 Poll, a joint initiative of the Ogilvy Group in China and Millward Brown ACSR, probed Chinese residents in locations along the torch relay route in China for their attitudes and opinions regarding the upcoming Olympic Games. The study found the fervour with which China had embraced the Olympics supported the notion that China used the Games as a catalyst in its ambition to show the world a new national image and gain respect while doing so (Ogilvy Group and Millward Brown ACSR, 2008). Soon after, the Pew Research Centre (2008) demonstrated in its Global Attitudes Project that the majority of the Chinese population were confident that the 2008 Summer Olympics in Beijing would change the way their country was viewed. Chinese respondents said their country would be a successful host and that the Olympic Games would uplift China's image and enlarge its international influence. In addition to seeing the Beijing Olympics as good for their country, the Project also found that an overwhelming majority of Chinese across all demographic groups said the event was important to them personally. Beijing citizens were especially likely to say that was the case. The 2008 Beijing Olympic Games, undoubtedly, boosted the confidence of most ordinary Chinese people in themselves and in their nation. The successful bidding and hosting of the Games was regarded by the Chinese government and its people as an important symbol of the great rejuvenation of the Chinese nation.

2 China's route to the Olympic host country

For a century, China's "dream" of hosting the Olympiad has always been intertwined with its dream of building a powerful country. It has been China's national ambition to catch up with the Western capitalist world through modernisation and the Olympics played an important part in stimulating the nation's enthusiasm and drive for modernisation (Fan, Ping and Huan, 2005). China's involvement in the Olympic movement can be traced all the way back to the beginning of the Games, when Pierre de Coubertin, father of the Modern Olympics, wrote to Li Hongzhang, chief minister of the Qing Dynasty, in 1895 urging China to attend the first Games. The preparatory committee of the Athens Olympics also sent China an invitation on August 16 through foreign embassies, but the country was at the time being threatened both by domestic unrest and foreign invasion, and was consequently unable to attend. In 1904, many Chinese newspapers and periodicals covered the third Olympic Games, and beginning in 1907, the Young Men's Christian Association (YMCA) and missionary schools in China started publicising the Olympics. On 24 October of that year, Zhang Boling, an advocate of sports and a well-known educator, delivered a speech to the fifth school athletic meeting organised by the Tianjin YMCA urging China to intensify its preparations and to participate in the Games as soon as possible (Zhou, 2008). In 1908, the Chinese press reported on the fourth Olympics hosted in London and declared that "the Olympic Games are unparalleled in the world." In the same year, a magazine called 天津青年 *tianjin qingnian* [*Tianjin Youth*] carried an article entitled "Athletic Sports" by some students of the Nankai School, in which three questions are raised: "When will China send athletes to the Olympics? When will China win the gold? When will China host the Games? (Zhou, 2008)" The answer to the first question finally came in 1932, when Liu Changchun participated in the Los Angeles Olympics, and the second question was answered when China came away with 15 gold medals at the 1984 Games, also in Los Angeles. The final question was settled exactly a century after being asked, when Beijing played host to the Olympics for the first time in 2008.

Photograph 1: A publicity bulletin in Beijing for the 1993 Olympic bid.

The disintegration of the Soviet Union in 1991 broke the balance of power in the global arena, making China adopt an increasingly "international stance" (Lam, 2002, p. 246; 2005) and thus vigorously conduct multilateral diplomacy for closer international cooperation. This "international stance" pushed China to embrace the Olympic Games as its debut on the international stage. From the early 1990s, the Chinese government had been heavily championing the idea of China's hosting the Olympics. During 1991 and 2001, Beijing made two Olympic bids, one for 2000 and the other for 2008. China's application for the 2000 Olympic Games was decided in April 1991. Upon hearing the news of the government's bid, a wide cross-section of Chinese society appeared to be overwhelmed with joy. The 2000 Olympic Games was especially meaningful because the millennium marked a new epoch in human history and the Games would offer "a very rare opportunity" and be "the focus of world attention" (Li, 2001). For a nation that had been longing to regain its national greatness for over a century, the Olympic Games at the turn of the millennium were believed to be a perfect stage for China to showcase its economic and social progress since the reform and opening-up and to gain international prestige. The anticipation showed clearly in Beijing's slogan to bid for the 2000 Olympic Games: "开放的中国盼奥运 *kaifang de zhongguo pan aoyun* [A more open China awaits the 2000 Olympics]" (see Photograph 1).

On 1 December 1991, a ceremony was held in Beijing to mark the occasion of China's formal application to the IOC for the right to host the 27th Olympic Games in 2000. Three days later, Zhang Baifa, Executive Vice-President of the Beijing Bid Committee, handed Beijing's application to IOC President J. A. Samaranch at the IOC headquarters in Lausanne, Switzerland. In this application, Beijing's international competitors were Berlin, Brasilia, Buenos Aires, Manchester, Sydney, Milan, Toronto, and Istanbul. At the 101st IOC Session held in Monte Carlo, Monaco on 23 September 1993, Beijing lost the election to Sydney by only two votes (see Table 1).

Table 1: Election results at the 101st IOC Session.

Cities	the 1st round	the 2nd round	the 3rd round	the 4th round
Sydney	30	30	37	45
Beijing	32	37	40	43
Manchester	11	13	11	
Berlin	9	9		
Istanbul	7			

Even though the spirit of the Olympic Games goes beyond political systems, ideological differences, cultural traditions and races, the selection of the host country for each Olympic Games has always involved political arm-twisting by competing candidates. Soon after Beijing submitted its application, some western countries used human rights issues as grounds for opposing the choice of Beijing as a possible host for the 2000 Olympic Games. Besides the political factors that severely interfered with the election, environmental pollution, language barriers, and insufficient modern infrastructure were three major concerns of the IOC members about staging the Olympics in China. The 1993 Olympic bid became a mirror for China to address its weaknesses. Having learned a lesson from the unsuccessful bid, Beijing Municipal Government started to vigorously improve public awareness of environmental protection and develop infrastructure construction while continuing to develop the economy. By the time Beijing made its second bid for the Olympic Games in 1999, China as a developing country had maintained an annual economic growth of 10.8% over the previous decade (en.olympic.cn, 2006). Beijing as the capital had also experienced great economic growth, with its gross domestic product surging to 32.78 billion US dollars in 1999, registering a per capita GDP of 2,619 US dollars (Beijing Municipal Bureau of Statistics, 2019). From 1993 to 2001, Beijing's urban green coverage rate increased from 28% to 38% (Yang, 2007). A total of 138.2 billion yuan was invested in the construction of modern facilities in Beijing between 1996–2000, including two beltways and hundreds of sports venues (Fu, 2001). In the meantime, China had begun reaping the rewards of a serious commitment to sport, making great achievements in major world tournaments. At the Atlanta Olympic Games in 1996, China won 16 golds, 22 silvers and 12 bronzes to rank fourth both in gold medal tally and in the total number of medals won (en.olympic,cn, 2006). At the Sydney Olympics in the Millennium Year of 2000, China made a historic breakthrough by collecting 28 golds, 22 silvers and 15 bronzes to emerge the world's third sports power following the United States and Russia (en.olympic.cn, 2006). The record-breaking gold harvest in Sydney constituted the best performance ever by a Chinese Olympic team and it was a strong signal that the nation had made impressive achievements in sports.

In the 1990s, the government's determination to improve national foreign language competence and a widespread desire among the Chinese people to contribute to the successful bidding for the Olympics spurred a nationwide English language fever, especially among Beijing citizens. Unlike in the late 1970s and early 1980s when English was taught strictly as a subject of study rather than a means of communication, the emphasis of the 1990s English language teaching (ELT) syllabuses was more on the communicative purpose of language learning, that is, on oral and written communicative competence, independent learning ability and the use of English. All these achievements helped give an impetus to Beijing's bid for the 2008 Olympic Games.

With the approval of the State Council, the Beijing 2008 Olympic Games Bid Committee (BOBICO) was established on September 6, 1999, with Liu Qi, Mayor of Beijing, as the President and COC President Yuan Weimin as the

Executive President. The motto of Beijing's bid was 新北京、新奥运 *xin beijing, xin aoyun* [New Beijing, Great Olympics], meaning that China's reform and opening up to the outside world had brought about great changes in Beijing, a city with a history of 3,000 years, and Beijing was fully capable of staging a successful Olympic Games. According to the results of a public poll conducted by Gallup Organisation in Beijing in November 2000, 94.9% percent of the residents in Beijing strongly supported the city's bid to host the 2008 Olympics. With regard to whether Beijing would be successful in winning the bid, 62.4% were fairly confident that Beijing would win.

On July 13, 2001, Beijing was elected as the host city at the 112th IOC Session in Moscow, defeating Toronto, Paris, Istanbul, and Osaka by fairly large margins (see Table 2). That night, thousands of people in Beijing and many other Chinese cities poured into the streets in victory processions on a scale rarely seen in Chinese history. Beijing's victory of hosting the 2008 Olympic Games came seven years after it lost the 2000 Olympics to Sydney by two votes. The Chinese Government's enthusiasm and the highest public support rate among the five candidate cities were claimed officially as two of the key elements for the successful bid. The IOC Evaluation Commission concluded that "there is significant public support for the prospect of organising the Olympic Games and a feeling that a successful bid would bring recognition to the nation" (International Olympic Committee, 2001, p. 75). China's state news agency Xinhua commented: "Beijing's winning of the bid to host the 2008 Olympic Games is another milestone in China's rising international status and a historical event in the great renaissance of the Chinese nation (People's Daily, 2001)."

Table 2: Election results at the 112st IOC Session.

Cities	the 1st round	the 2nd round
Beijing	44	56
Toronto	20	22
Paris	15	18

Following the 1964 Tokyo Olympic Games and the 1988 Seoul Olympic Games, it was only the third time that the Olympic Summer Games were held in Asia. The attraction and far-reaching significance of staging the Games in the largest developing country, home to one-fifth of the world's population, is self-evident. Beijing's renewed efforts to bid for the Olympic Games and its final success in the bid not only had significance for sharing the Olympic spirit, celebrating humanity and expanding exchanges between the East and the West, but also helped provide a good opportunity of showcasing the country's economic, cultural, social and political development in a comprehensive way. While showing to the world a new, vigorous image of an open, modernised, civilised and well-developed metropolis in the lead-up to the 2008 Olympics, Beijing was ready to become a truly 'international city' and make every effort to deliver a 'Green Olympics', a 'Hi-Tech Olympics', a 'People's Olympics' and, to top it all, an unprecedented Olympics that would leave, as the IOC Evaluation Commission report believed, "a unique legacy for both China and sport as a whole" (Xinhua, 2008c). China's strong desire to return to the centre of the world stage and reconstruct its identity as an international power gave great impetus to a series of language planning efforts for the Beijing Olympic Games.

Chapter 3
Researching the LPP for the 2008 Beijing Olympics

1 Language challenges to the 2008 Beijing Olympic Games

Beijing 2008 made history in many areas. The Chinese government committed to make all possible efforts to ensure that the Beijing Games would be the largest of all time and "the best-ever Olympic Games in history" (BOCOG, 2002). A total of 10,500 athletes from 205 countries and regions competed in 302 events in 28 sports, which made the Olympiad the biggest ever. The games also involved 21,600 registered media journalists and more than 20,000 non-registered media journalists, 8,000 sponsors and their partners, 1,800 IOC and International Sports Federation officers, 4,000 COC staff, 100,000 venue volunteers, 400,000 city volunteers and 1 million social volunteers. About 2 million domestic tourists and 450,000 overseas tourists were estimated to have visited Beijing during the Olympic Games period, according to the Beijing Municipal Tourism Bureau (Zhang and Zhang, 2008). A total of 280 billion yuan (approximately 42 billion US dollars) was invested in the preparation for the Games in Beijing (Xinhua, 2008f), which is three times as much as the Athens Olympics, four times as much as the Sydney Olympics and twice as much as the Rio Olympics, making it the most expensive Olympic Games ever. During the intensive 16 days of sports competition (8 to 24 August 2008), Beijing became the focus of worldwide attention in the Olympic spotlight. The Olympic Games in Beijing saw the largest media contingent for any event ever – more than 28,000 journalists from around the world relayed the story of the Games to their home audiences (International Olympic Committee, 2009). For the first time, the Olympic Games were produced and broadcast entirely in high-definition television by the host broadcaster and broadcast extensively through live online video. According to the media report by Nielsen (Lu, 2009), the 2008 Beijing Olympic Games attracted the largest global TV audience of any Olympiad – 4.7 billion viewers worldwide, 70% of the world's population, making it the most widely reported games in Olympic history. Further, the 2008 Games were the first ever Olympic Games to have full digital coverage freely available around the world (International Olympic Committee, 2009).

With its unprecedented scale, the 2008 Beijing Olympics became the most complex cross-lingual and cross-cultural event in Olympic history. Many past Olympic Games were held in host countries where the national language is one of the official IOC languages (French and English), or at least a related Indo-European language, but Beijing did not possess either of these linguistic advantages. Facing greater challenges in language services, BOCOG had to make greater efforts in bridging the language gap than its Western counterparts. Firstly, language services for the Beijing Olympics would need to help athletes, coaches, IOC officials, journalists, and tourists from 205 countries and regions who speak more than 80 official languages communicate smoothly. Secondly, language services for the Beijing Olympics would need to facilitate communication in various fields and situations relating to the Games, including competition venues, working meetings, press releases, cultural activities, transportation, security, accommodation, catering, medical care, VIP accompanying, visitor reception, and audience guidance. Lastly, the organisers of the Beijing Olympics would need to be able to provide a variety of forms of language services required by the Games, including translation, interpretation, telephone translation, machine translation, online translation, multilingual service intelligent system, corpus retrieval, multilingual identification, Braille and sign language. During Good Luck Beijing 2007, which was a series of Beijing Olympic test events, BOCOG received negative comments on its language services. Critics pointed out that the quality of English-Chinese interpretation should be improved and language services for the Beijing Olympics should be more multilingual. In the face of these challenges, the Chinese government made its solemn commitment to the world in the *Olympic Action Plan* (BOCOG, 2002): "By 2008, information services will be inexpensive, rich in content, free of language barrier, and personalized and available for anyone, at anytime and anywhere." Twenty years after the Seoul Olympics, Beijing's commitment to hosting the biggest and "best-ever Olympic Games in history" (BOCOG, 2002) meant that language policy and planning would become even more important for achieving the strategic objectives of the Games.

2 Learning from Seoul

In 2002, the Beijing Foreign Language Environment Observation Delegation investigated the foreign language situation in some non-English speaking countries, especially in the South Korean capital Seoul, the host city of the 1988 Olympic Games. The Seoul government's work in standardising foreign language public signs and providing technology-supported language services were used for reference in the preparation for the 2008 Beijing Olympics.

2.1 Public signs

2.1.1 Centralised rectification of road signs and direction signs

According to an official report published by Office of the Leading Group on Foreign Affairs of the Beijing Municipal Party Committee of the CPC, et al. (2008), Seoul government agencies and departments used to be responsible for the production of their own linguistic signs, often with errors. In order to unify and standardise foreign language terminology and rectify errors on street signs and direction signs, the Seoul government formed a Seoul Foreign Language Sign Advisory Group, which consisted of 12 Korean language experts, traffic experts, foreign language experts and native speakers of English, Japanese, Chinese and Spanish. A total of 72,032 linguistic signs were under the administration of the municipal government. In order to correct mistakes on public signs, a foreign language error reporting centre was set up, and 120 telephone numbers and online reporting services (Seoul Focus Website, SEOUL NOW Website) were published for public supervision. After receiving reports of errors, the department in charge was informed first, and measures were taken to rectify them after confirmation. In February 2002, the Seoul government established a unified standard for foreign language public signs and trained relevant staff in accordance with it. In April, a specialised portal for English signs (www.Englishname.net) was officially launched.

Apart from standardising English expressions on road signs, other changes were made: (1) the sizes of road signs were unified; (2) the names on road signs were changed from place names to route names; (3) the background colour of road signs was changed from white to green. At present, most road signs in Seoul are bilingual in Korean and English. Road and traffic signs for main roads are often written in three languages: Korean, Chinese and English. The Seoul Municipal Government subsequently announced plans to add Chinese translations to all road signs and traffic signs.

2.1.2 The website of *English Dictionary for Public Signs*

The Seoul government established the website of *English Dictionary for Public Signs* (www.Englishname.net) for promoting a unified standard of English translation on public signs in Seoul (Office of the Leading Group on Foreign Affairs of the Beijing Municipal Party Committee of the CPC, et al. 2008). The website covered 10 categories, 58 items, and standards and rules of English translation for 20,000 public signs. A search engine was installed on the website, providing online English translation consultation services to the general public. The website of *English Dictionary for Public Signs* greatly facilitated the future work of the signage production department, laid a foundation for the standardisation and unification of signage production, and also provided a unified standard for English terminology used in other public places such as restaurants and hotels. The working procedure for rectifying English signs is shown in Figure 2 as follows:

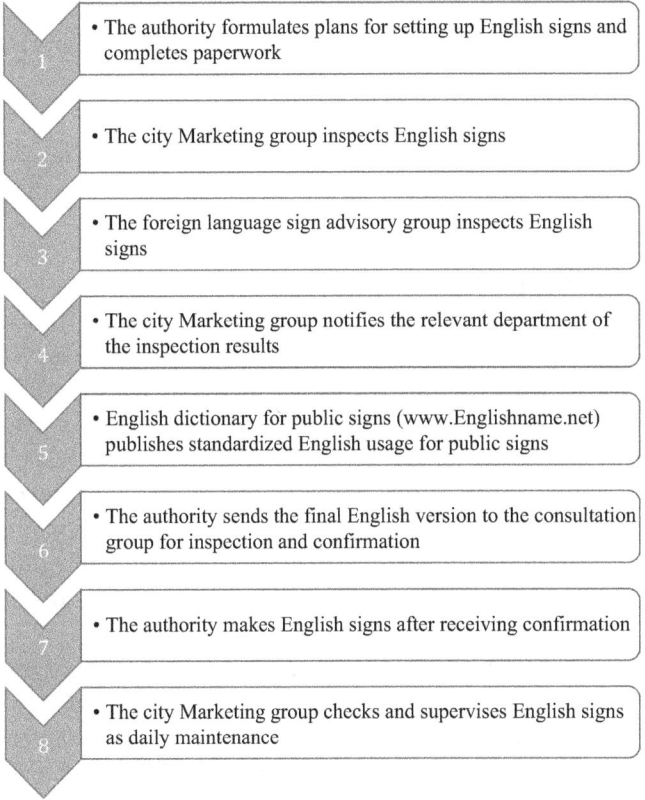

Figure 2: Procedures for rectifying English signs.

2.1.3 Metro signs

According to the official report (Office of the Leading Group on Foreign Affairs of the Beijing Municipal Party Committee of the CPC, et al. 2008), the Seoul Metro signage system mainly includes signs for station names, transfer roadmap, transfer bus route, and for surrounding locations. Metro signs were required to be displayed in three languages: Korean, English and Chinese, while metro announcements were broadcast in Korean and English. During the 2002 Seoul World Cup, Chinese broadcasting was added to the routes leading to the venues and stadiums, and it continued in use after that event.

In 1984, Seoul began to provide English and Chinese training to subway workers. The annual training result was linked to employees' salaries. At present, subway workers are required to have a certain English proficiency and pass a professional English examination for their employment. Officials in charge of Seoul Metro believed that a clear and effective public signage system and foreign language speaking subway workers are important aspects in the construction of Seoul Metro's foreign language environment.

2.2 Technology-supported language services

2.2.1 Seoul hotline

The proportion of foreigners in Seoul's total population of 10.33 million was 0.66% in 2002, of whom 66.1% were Chinese, Americans and Japanese (Office of the Leading Group on Foreign Affairs of the Beijing Municipal Party Committee of the CPC, et al. 2008). Seoul had non-governmental organisations providing tourism information and consultation services for foreigners, but there was no government agency responsible for information and language services for foreigners living in the city. Therefore, the Seoul City Assembly and the Municipal Supervision Conference of Foreigners proposed to set up a Seoul hotline, which aimed to build Seoul into an international city with a comfortable lifestyle and make it a favourite destination for foreign tourists so as to improve its status and image.

Seoul Hotline, sponsored by the Seoul Municipal Government, began operating on April 1, 2002. It provided general services in English, Chinese and Japanese, and had professional translators in these three languages. Information and language services by Seoul hotline could be accessed through telephone (080-731-911), website (www.metro.seoul.kr), fax, and e-mail. Seoul Hotline adopted the following methods in operation: (1) prepared autoreplies for frequently asked questions; (2) consulted relevant departments with questions that could not be resolved on the spot and then tried to reply on the same day; (3) recorded all consultations in the registration book for further management. During the 2002 Seoul World Cup, Seoul Hotline expanded the scope of its services by: (1) adding services in three foreign languages, including French, Turkish and Spanish; (2) recruiting foreign language volunteers and translators; (3) extending working hours from 09:00–18:00 to 07:00–22:00.

2.2.2 BBB (Before Babel Brigade) free translation hotline

BBB Free Translation Hotline was initially proposed by Central Daily News Agency and co-sponsored by various social resources. Samsung Enterprises provided financial support, and Korean News Agency (KBS) was responsible for advertising it. During the 2002 World Cup, BBB Free Translation Hotline provided information and language services in 13 languages, including Chinese, English, Russian, French, Japanese, German, Spanish, Polish, Swedish, Turkish, Italian, Arabic and Portuguese. There were 2500 volunteers, including 350 Chinese volunteers, 850 English volunteers, 500 Japanese volunteers and 8 Swedish volunteers. Multilingual BBB information cards were available to foreigners at airports, tourist information points, hotels and other places (see Photographs 2–6 on pages 46–48). Foreigners who encountered language barriers in Korea or wanted to learn about Korean culture could get help from volunteers by dialling the phone numbers listed on BBB information cards directly.

2.2.3 Foreign language services and simultaneous interpretation in taxis

For the convenience of foreigners travelling in Seoul during the World Cup, the Seoul government built two types of taxis: 'Visitors Guide Taxi' and 'Free Interpretation Taxi'. Visitors Guide Taxis were high-end black cars, which featured a prominent logo of 'Visitors Guide' on their back doors and were often placed at airports and restaurants. The drivers of these taxis were all model drivers who were able to speak basic English and Japanese. Free Interpretation Taxis, which had the logo 'Free Interpretation' on their back doors, were equipped with a free telephone device by the government that could provide simultaneous interpretation services in three languages: Chinese, English and Japanese. Drivers of these taxis could get access to simultaneous interpretation services from the translation centre through the car telephone. As soon as the call was put through, an interpreter would inform a foreign passenger of the destination, time and fare in Chinese, English or Japanese.

2.2.4 Tourist information centres

During the 2002 Seoul World Cup, tourist information centres were installed at major tourist attractions and World Cup football stadiums, providing multilingual services in Korean, English, Japanese, and Chinese. At these tourist information centres, foreign visitors could consult with multilingual service personnel and obtain free multilingual print guidebooks.

South Korea and China are not only geographically close, but both belong to the East Asian culture, with a history of culture exchange for over 2000 years. The language service measures adopted by the South Korean government for the

1988 Seoul Olympic Games provides a useful reference for the Chinese government in preparation for the 2008 Beijing Olympic Games, and also a good sample for the study of LPP for international sports events held in East Asian countries. In this following, I will elaborate on the design of this study.

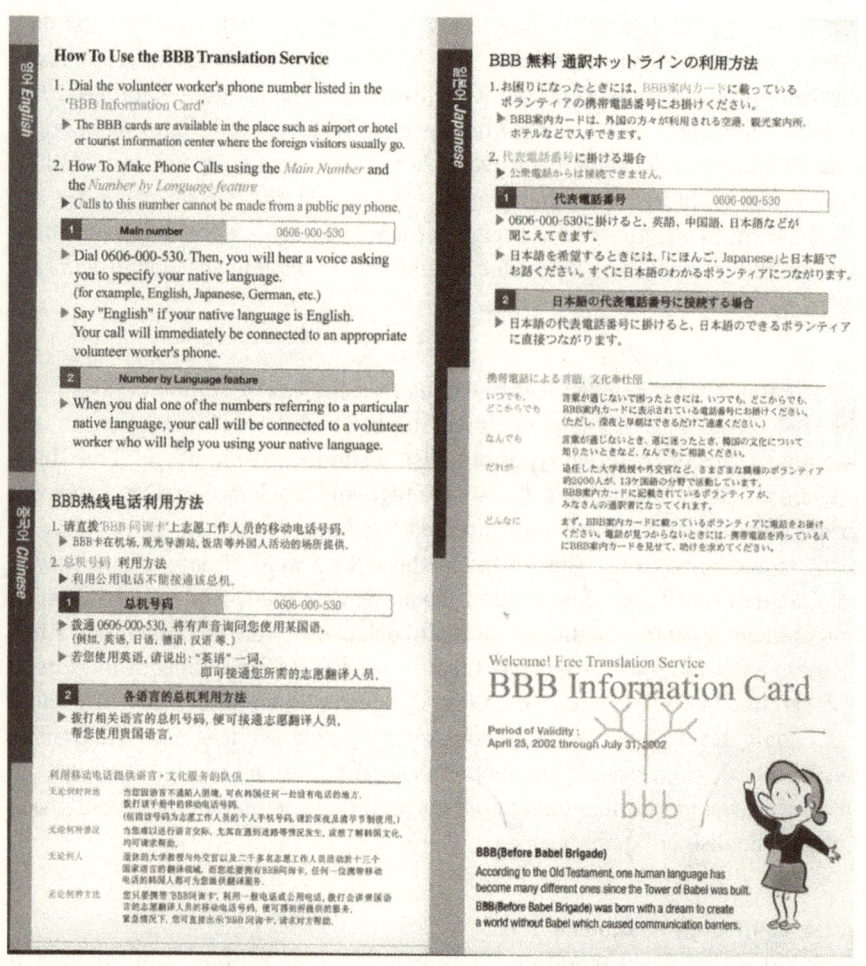

Photograph 2: Multilingual BBB Free Translation Hotline introduction leaflet.

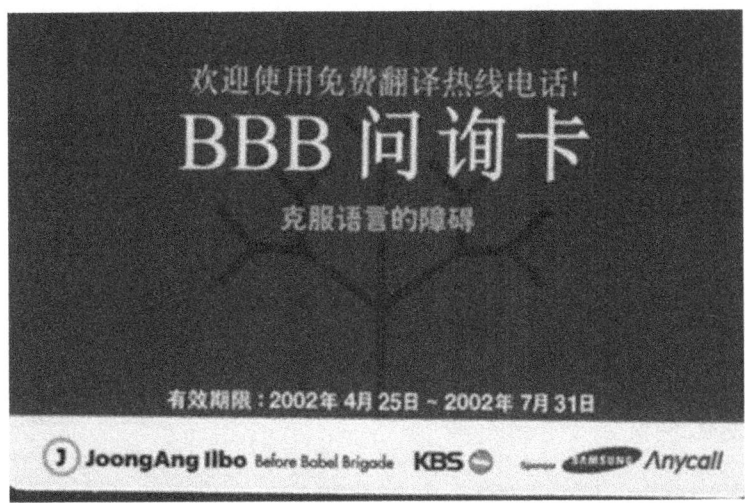

Photograph 3: The front of a Chinese BBB information card.

JoongAng Ilbo 중국어 汉语 该卡为非销售品.

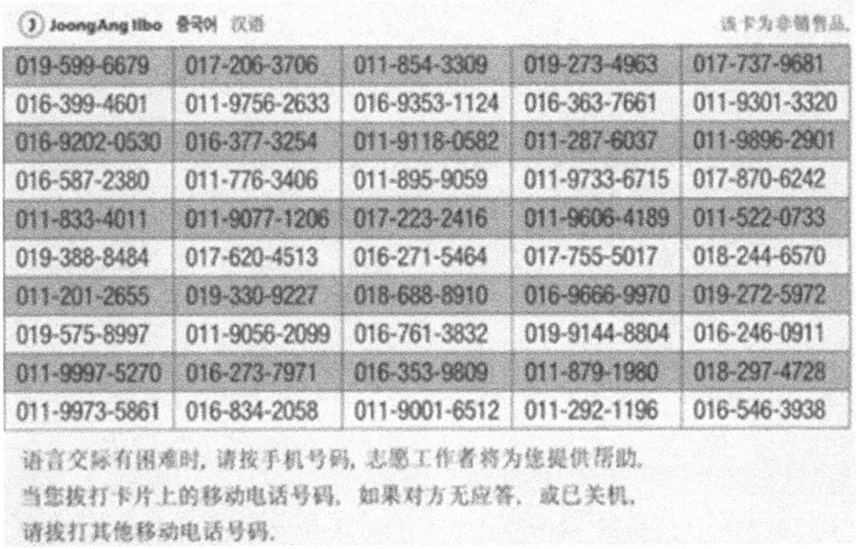

019-599-6679	017-206-3706	011-854-3309	019-273-4963	017-737-9681
016-399-4601	011-9756-2633	016-9353-1124	016-363-7661	011-9301-3320
016-9202-0530	016-377-3254	011-9118-0582	011-287-6037	011-9896-2901
016-587-2380	011-776-3406	011-895-9059	011-9733-6715	017-870-6242
011-833-4011	011-9077-1206	017-223-2416	011-9606-4189	011-522-0733
019-388-8484	017-620-4513	016-271-5464	017-755-5017	018-244-6570
011-201-2655	019-330-9227	018-688-8910	016-9666-9970	019-272-5972
019-575-8997	011-9056-2099	016-761-3832	019-9144-8804	016-246-0911
011-9997-5270	016-273-7971	016-353-9809	011-879-1980	018-297-4728
011-9973-5861	016-834-2058	011-9001-6512	011-292-1196	016-546-3938

语言交际有困难时，请按手机号码，志愿工作者将为您提供帮助.
当您拨打卡片上的移动电话号码，如果对方无应答，或已关机，
请拨打其他移动电话号码.

Photograph 4: The back of a Chinese BBB information card.

Photograph 5: The front of an English BBB information card.

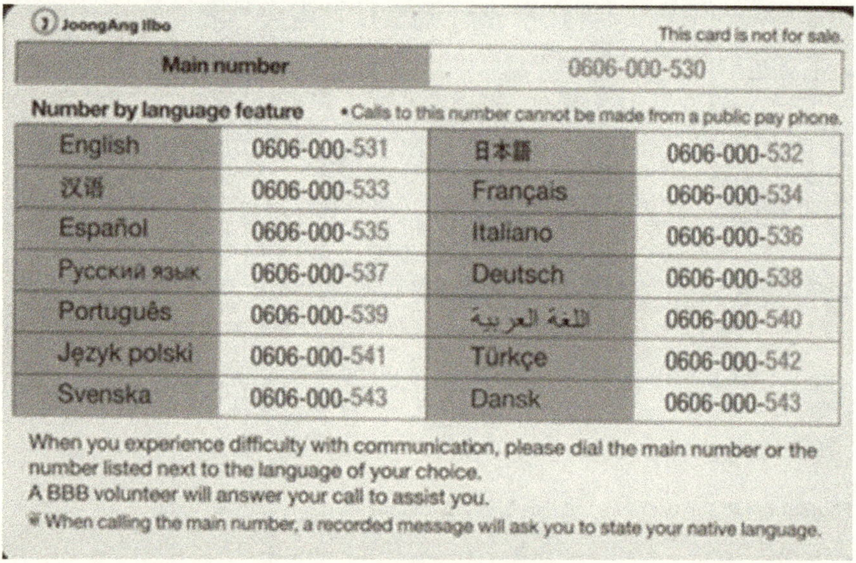

Photograph 6: The back of an English BBB information card.

3 Research design

A research design is the logic that links the initial questions of a study to the data to be collected and the methods of analysis to be adopted. The current study combines multiple data collection and analytical methods in accordance with data types in the investigation.

3.1 Research questions

Under the changing social, economic and political conditions both at home and abroad, the 2008 Beijing Olympics marked a pivotal period of identity construction at national, regional and individual levels. The forces that propelled China towards its biggest-ever sporting event in history also gave impetus to foreign language popularisation campaigns in the first decade of the 21st century. BOCOG and the Beijing government needed to make important language policy and planning decisions to achieve their goal of "barrier-free" language services for the Olympic Games. Seoul's language services for the 1988 Seoul Olympic Games and the 2002 World Cup offered China, another non-English speaking Asian country, valuable experience. However, accommodating the linguistic needs of all participants in the biggest-ever Olympic Games was a much more complex and arduous assignment in language planning. Despite extensive research on the Modern Olympic Games, there is a lack of rigorous research that attempts to make sense of the LPP for the Games. This book situates language policies, language practices and language ideologies within China's broad social, economic and political changes, and in particular, the period from Beijing's bidding for the 2008 Olympic Games to its preparation for the 2022 Winter Olympic Games. Combining macro and micro perspectives, I try to present a holistic picture of the top-down LPP for the two Olympic Games hosted and to be hosted in Beijing, and also give thick description of how language policies and language ideologies impacted on actual language use and speakers' language attitudes in the Beijing Olympic context. The book unfolds according to the following eight questions:
1) Why are the Modern Olympic Games a research topic with unique value in the study of language policy and language planning?
2) What were the historical significance and language challenges of the 2008 Beijing Olympic Games?
3) What official language policies were promulgated and implemented for the 2008 Beijing Olympic Games?
4) What language ideologies and attitudes do these language policies reflect?

5) What language practices were observed in the preparation period and during the Beijing Olympics?
6) What LPP legacy has been left behind after the 2008 Beijing Olympics?
7) What changes have taken place in China's foreign language education ideologies and policies in the post-Olympic era?
8) What language planning efforts have been made for the language services for the 2022 Beijing Winter Olympic Games?

3.2 Data collection methods

This study triangulates data by combining different types of qualitative approaches: semi-structured interviews, participant observations and on-site observations, and the gathering of texts and audio-visual materials. Both micro-domain (interview transcripts and field notes) and macro-domain (policy documents, media texts, signage, teaching materials) data were collected. Due to the evolving nature of qualitative study and the on-going process of the spread of English in China, the collection of policy documents and media texts ran through the entire course of this study. In order to contextualise the discourse analysis of macro-domain data, I conducted a three-month multi-site intensive fieldwork in Beijing (July–October, 2008). After the 2008 Beijing Olympics, I returned to my research sites several times for observation and data collection. Between September 2017 and July 2018, I was a visiting scholar under the supervision of Professor Li Yuming at Beijing Language and Culture University (BLCU). During that visit, I gained access to the Beijing Advanced Innovation Centre for Language Resources[5] (ACLR) directed by Professor Li Yuming and obtained valuable information about its three language services projects for the 2022 Beijing Winter Olympics. All these research activities provided important insights into the research questions under study.

3.2.1 Naturally occurring data
1) Policy documents
English language syllabi and curricula for schools and universities published by the Ministry of Education of the People's Republic of China (MOE) from 1990–2020 were collected for analysis. These policy documents prescribe the

---
5 The Beijing Advanced Innovation Centre for Language Resources (ACLR) was officially established on 25 May 2016. It is a scientific research institution accredited and funded by Beijing Municipal Education Commission and hosted by BLCU.

content of ELT to be covered, recommend teaching methods and assessment measures, and outline the outcomes to be achieved for English in public education. Official policies, guidelines, and regulations on the planning and implementation of foreign language learning and popularisation in preparation for the 2008 Summer Olympics and the 2022 Winter Olympics were gathered from the official websites of the Beijing Organising Committee for the Games of the XXIX Olympiad (www.beijing2008.cn/), Beijing Organising Committee for the 2022 Olympic and Paralympic Winter Games (www.beijing2022.cn), IOC (www.olympic.org/), the Beijing Government (www.ebeijing.gov.cn/), Foreign Affairs Office of the Beijing Municipal Government (www.bjfao.gov.cn/), Organising Committee of The Beijing Speaks Foreign Languages Programme (www.bjenglish.com.cn/), Beijing Education Examinations Authority (www.bjeea.cn/), EF English First Co., Ltd (www.englishfirst.com/index.html), and the Beijing 2008 Olympic Games Language Training Services Suppliers, Aifly Education & Technology Co., Ltd (www.aiflyworld.cn).

2) Media texts
Domestic media reports relating to the LPP and language services of the two Beijing Olympic Games were gathered from several major official newspapers, namely Xinhua (www.xinhuanet.com), China Daily (www.chinadaily.com/), People's Daily (www.people.com) and Global Times (www.huanqiu.com/). These media texts provide a multidimensional perspective on the specific socio-historical context that the Beijing Olympic Games were situated within and the controversy over the *English fever* phenomenon in China.

3) Signage
For an understanding of the linguistic landscape of Beijing as Olympic city, a range of photographs of bilingual/multilingual guiding signs and other linguistic objects was taken and collected at key Olympic venues, tourist sites, commercial areas, and transportation hubs. These naturally occurring observational data include photographs and videos sampled at Beijing Railway Station (01-08-2008), Wangfujing Street (04-08-2008), the Olympic Green (05-08-2008), Tiananmen Square (06-08-2008), Beijing Black Bamboo Park (07-08-2008), the Forbidden City (08-08-2008), Qianmen Street, Beijing West Railway Station (09-08-2008), Beijing Capital International Airport (09-08-2008), Peking University, and Beijing Sport University (20-09-2008). The sampled photographs and videos in this study were recorded by digital camera. These photographs comprise both official/non-commercial (traffic signs, direction signs, information signs, caution and warning signs, tourist map, placards, etc.) and non-official/commercial signs (advertising billboard, notice signs, etc.). The texts on these sampled signs could be monolingual, bilingual or multilingual. A bilingual sign is considered in

this study to be a sign containing at least one language other than Chinese. Thus, a sign could contain just one language and still be categorised as bilingual provided that language is not Chinese. Likewise, a multilingual sign is one containing at least two languages other than Chinese. There are three types of signs that can be distinguished in Beijing's linguistic landscape (LL): monolingual signs (Chinese), bilingual signs (Chinese and English), and multilingual signs (predominately in Chinese, English and French). In Chapter 7, I purposefully select and analyse some photographs depending on whether or not they typify linguistic characteristics of contextual locations.

4) Teaching materials

Three sets of English teaching materials for the specific purposes of serving the Beijing Olympic Games were purchased for the current study: (1) BOCOG publications *A Conversational English Reader* (Elementary & Advanced versions); (2) BSFLP publications (*One World English* 100, 300, 600, 1000); (3) BSFLP and BEST publications (*Olympic English*: Books 1, 2, 3). Shardakova and Pavlenko (2004) stress that language textbooks play a "unique role in the process of potential empowerment or disempowerment of language learners" (p. 28). In Chapter 6, I conduct a multimodal discourse analysis of texts and visual images in *A Conversational English Reader* (Elementary & Advanced). The rationale for selecting the two *Readers* as part of my data is explained in Chapter 6.

3.2.2 Fieldwork

Patton (2002) points out that "the documentation would not have made sense without the interviews, and the focus of the interviews came from the field observation" (p. 307). In order to achieve an in-depth understanding of "a fuller, more meaningful context" (Tedlock, 2000, p. 455) in which the Beijing Olympic events were situated, I combined observation, interviewing and document collection during three months of fieldwork in Beijing (July-October, 2008). The fieldwork serves to contextualise the discourse analysis.

1) Research sites

In order to capture the range of language practices across the city before, during and after the 2008 Beijing Olympics, initially I immersed myself in various places such as Olympic venues, the BOCOG building, the Olympic Youth camp, tourist sites, universities, English schools, central business districts, the airport, train stations, subways, bus dispatching centres, shopping centres, and bookshops. From the initial immersion to more focused research sites, I gradually discovered emerging themes, narrowed down research questions, and gained access to the focused subjects and events. The main research sites where I conducted on-site observations ranged from key Olympic venues (namely, the Olympic Green), tourist sites (Forbidden City, Tiananmen Square), to commercial areas (Qianmen Street, Wangfujing Street), and transportation hubs (Beijing West Railway Station, Beijing Capital International Airport). Most of these research sites are concentrated in the inner city of Beijing. These data collection sites were popular or public locations frequented by tourists and chosen in this study for their respective significance in sports spectating, sightseeing, shopping and commuting experiences that Beijing offered to Olympic visitors. In the above fields I made field notes, took photographs, and recorded audio and/or video of interesting and salient artefacts, activities, and phenomena relevant to the research questions. I attempted to be observant and self-reflective on English learning practices, English-mediated intercultural encounters, and foreign language services and facilities.

2) Recruitment

To identify and recruit participants for this study, non-probability sampling techniques were used: purposive and snowball sampling. Non-probability means sampling without using random selection methods, and therefore non-probability samples are not necessarily representative of the population under study. Burns (2000) points out that the usual form of non-probability sampling is "purposive, purposeful or criterion-based sampling" (p. 178). Purposive sampling is a method where the participants are selected by the researcher subjectively in accordance with his or her criteria for inclusion in the study. The researcher chooses the sample based on who they think would be appropriate for the study. Snowball sampling is a technique for developing a research sample where existing study participants recruit future participants from among their acquaintances who also meet the criteria. The recruiting technique is especially useful when the researchers are trying to reach populations that are inaccessible or hard to find (Trochim, 2006).

The current study started with purposive sampling. I began by contacting several individuals from my existing social network in Beijing. Through my network, I first located information-rich key informants and then clarified to them the characteristics of my targeted participants. As soon as my potential participants were identified, I asked for their initial permission, through my key informants, to accept my interviews. For university students who were sampled through their institutions (e.g., through the teacher of a class or the dean of a faculty), letters of introduction were sent to them in advance to establish initial cooperation and rapport. Having been given initial permission, I made contact with these potential participants through telephone and let them nominate their most suitable interview time and place. After I established a rapport with my existing participants, I used snowball sampling to reach out to more potential participants: I politely requested them to introduce me to their acquaintances who also met my criteria and ask for interview permission.

3) Interviews

There are two main categories of participants in this study: individual participants and institutional participants. The first category of individual participants consists of Olympic volunteers who are college students (aged 18 years old and over) living and studying in Beijing. Olympic volunteers are "accredited personnel, recruited and managed by the Beijing Olympic Organising Committee for the Games of the XXIX Olympiad," who "shoulder critical Games-time responsibilities, work at times and in positions assigned to them by BOCOG during the 2008 Beijing Olympic Games and the Paralympic Games of 2008 without compensation" (Xinhua, 2008a). The Games organiser recruited three categories of Olympic volunteers: Games-time[6] volunteers, urban volunteers, and social volunteers. Games-time volunteers are those who received the most intensive training and were assigned to provide services at Olympic venues (including competition venues, training venues and non-competition venues). Games-time volunteers provided services in designated areas as diverse as guest reception, language translation, transportation, security, medical service, spectator guiding, communication organisation support, venue operation support, media operation support, cultural activity support and other aspects (Nidemike, 2008). Urban volunteers are those responsible for providing information, emergency aid and translation services in urban volunteer service stations set up across Beijing. Social volunteers were extensively recruited and assigned to help with keeping traffic and maintaining social order in the communities and townships of Beijing before and during the Beijing Olympics and Paralympics. At the time of the Games, Beijing university students were one of the major sources for the three categories of Olympic volunteers.

Overall, I interviewed and shadowed 35 participants (Appendix 2: List of interview participants). Of these, 28 were volunteers (26 Games-time volunteers and two urban volunteers) for the 2008 Beijing Olympic Games. The remaining seven institutional participants had been, more or less, involved in Olympic English training before the Beijing Olympics. They included three English teachers, two BOCOG administrative staff, one local government official and one local taxi driver. All the institutional interviewees were highly educated and held a bachelor degree or above.Out of the 35 interviewees, 31 were Han Chinese. The other four are ethnic minority students who were doing their undergraduate study in

---

6 "Games-time" refers to the period from the end of July 2008 to the end of the Olympic Games.

Beijing. Two of these were of Manchu and Hezhe ethnicity and their ethnic languages have died out or faded from everyday usage in their cultures. The other two were of She and Yao backgrounds. They speak Putonghua (Standard Mandarin) and at least one ethnic language, and thus were learning English as a third or even fourth language.

I conducted 27 face-to-face interviews and one telephone interview with these 35 participants between 10 July and 27 September 2008. Of these, 22 were one-on-one interviews and 5 were group interviews (see Appendix 2). For an understanding of participants' experiences and perceptions of English learning and use before and during the Beijing Olympics, I set six main themes as an interview guide. The six themes related to pertinent experiences and perspectives of the participants, namely: foreign learning experiences; foreign language practice at home and in work places; attitudes to English language learning and teaching in China; understanding of the role of English in their respective future lives; opinions on the role of English in relation to Beijing as an Olympic city; personal experiences of using English during the Beijing Olympic events. The framework of the six themes is an informal "grouping of topics and questions that the interviewer can ask in different ways for different participants" (Lindlof and Taylor, 2002, p. 195). Interviews were recorded with an audio-recorder for the purpose of preparing transcripts for data analysis. During group interviewing, conversations among participants and their interactions with other individuals were recorded. All interviews were conducted in Chinese.

4) Participant observation

Due to the sensitivity of most participants' workplaces (they were employed at various Olympics-related venues) and the limited availability of participants (all were heavily involved in their work at the time of the Games), in most cases I was not able to get access to their workplaces and conduct participant observations. On 7 August 2008, I conducted a participant observation with two urban volunteers who were assigned to provide services in their designated urban volunteer service station at the entrance of Beijing Black Bamboo Park for their half-day volunteer service. The aim of my observation was to learn about the two participants' English-mediated intercultural communicative practices in their workplace. Having been given permission, I video-recorded and took field notes on participants' practices in their workplaces and the context they were working in.

3.3 Data analysis methods

3.3.1 A critical discourse analysis perspective

Data analysis means making sense of or interpreting the data. This study aims to interpret the data from a critical discourse analysis (CDA) perspective. CDA is neither a homogeneous nor necessarily united theoretical approach or research method; rather it is "a shared perspective on doing linguistic, semiotic or discourse analysis" (Van Dijk, 1993, p. 253). Four concepts figure indispensably in all CDA research undertakings: discourse, critical, ideology, and power. It is generally agreed that CDA conceives *discourse* as a form of "social practice" (Fairclough and Wodak, 1997) and considers the "context of language use" to be crucial (Wodak, 2001a). Describing discourse as social practice implied "a dialectical relationship between a particular discursive event and the situation(s), institutions(s) and social structure(s) which frame it" (Fairclough and Wodak, 1997, p. 258). In other words, discourse is both socially constitutive and socially conditioned – "it constitutes situations, objects of knowledge, and the social identities of and relationships between people and groups of people" (Fairclough and Wodak, 1997, p. 258). *Ideology* is a topic of considerable importance in CDA. In the social-cognitive theory of van Dijk (1998), ideologies are viewed as "interpretation frameworks" which "organise sets of attitudes" about other elements of modern society. Fairclough, Mulderrig and Wodak (2011) propose to understand ideology not just as "a matter of representing social reality" but also as "a process which articulates together particular representations of reality, and particular constructions of identity" (p. 372). Ideology is produced and reproduced through discourse and serves as an important means of "establishing and maintaining unequal power relations" (Wodak, 2001b. p. 10). A study of ideology requires analysts to go beyond textual analysis and consider "how the texts are interpreted and received and what social effects they have" (Fairclough, Mulderrig and Wodak, 2011, p. 371). In addition, interpretations from a CDA perspective are dynamic and open, and may be affected by new readings and new contextual information. CDA takes a particular interest in the relation between language and power. *Power* is about relations of difference, and particularly about the effects of differences in social structures (Wodak, 2001b, p. 11). For CDA, language "is not powerful on its own, rather it gains power by the use powerful people make of it" (Wodak, 2001b, p. 10). In contrast to non-critical theories and methodologies in discourse analysis, CDA is characterized by "the common interests in demystifying ideologies and power through the systematic investigation of semiotic data, be they written, spoken or visual" (Wodak, 2007, pp. 185–186). Adopting a *critical* goal signals the need for critical discourse analysts not only to describe discursive practices but also to unpack "the ideological underpinnings of discourse that have become so naturalised over time that we begin to treat them as common, acceptable and natural features of discourse" (Talbot, Atkinson and Atkinson, 2003, p. 36) and to make visible inequities in relations of power. The central concerns of researchers working in the critical field include such topics as the dialectal relationship between language and the social; the construction and maintenance of power relations through language; the role played by language in structuring human experience and world-view; and language and social change. CDA researchers, such as Fairclough, are enthusiastically concerned with discourse as an element in the contemporary social changes that are widely referred to as "globalisation." The cultural diversity, contestation and transformation of human discourses, and the development of appropriate and helpful approaches to them, constitute a vast new field in discourse studies. It is believed that awareness of the ideological effects of discourse can lead to changes in discourse practice that will result in greater social equality and justice (Fairclough, 1992).

A critical approach to discourse analysis typically concentrates on data like government documents, news reports, political interviews, schoolbooks and advertising that construct and convey ideology and power relations that have been entrenched and naturalised over time so that they seem to be common beliefs or even common sense in a society. Drawing on a critical approach to discourse analysis, this study explores issues such as ideology, power, identity, class, gender and ethnicity, and examines how they are manifested in texts or speech.

3.3.2 Data analysis procedure

The data for analysis in this study fell into six categories: policy documents, media texts, signage, ELT textbooks, interviews, field notes. The following is my data analysis procedure:

Patton (2002, p. 307) suggests that document analysis can provide "a behind-the-scenes look at the programme that may not be directly observable and about which the interviewer might not ask appropriate questions without the leads provided through documents." At the exploratory stage, the document analysis helped me develop an understanding of the social and cultural roots of ideological underpinnings and identity conflicts related to the spread of English in China. Following Shohamy's expanded view of LP (2006), I set up an analytical framework that addresses language policy and planning issues on the basis of a comparative analysis of language policy documents, language teaching materials, linguistic landscapes, and language learner experiences.

These understandings and the framework informed the directions for subsequent data collection and analysis.

Through my fieldwork, I collected policy documents, media texts, and ELT textbooks took photographs, and conducted interviews and observations. Patton (2002) emphasises that the challenge for qualitative analysts lies in making sense of massive amounts of data, which involves "reducing the volume of raw information, sifting trivia from significance, identifying significant patterns, and constructing a framework for communicating the essence of what the data reveal" (p. 432). The multi-site observation provided me with a general understanding of foreign language popularisation policies and practices and of the pervasive discourses in the field, thereby contributing to defining the focus of my interviews. In the course of interviewing and initial analysis, more focused patterns and themes gradually emerged. At this stage, four major themes are established to explore language policy and planning for the Beijing Olympic Games through a variety of overt and covert LP mechanisms: (1) language policies and practices in the Olympic English popularisation campaign; (2) individual English learning trajectories; (3) imagined communities and identity options in Beijing Olympic English textbooks, and (4) linguistic landscape of the Olympic city.

After the fieldwork, the transcriptions of interviews and field notes were thoroughly scrutinised in an attempt to recheck the analytic insights and interpretations that emerged during data collection and triangulation with macro-domain data. The interview transcripts were first translated into English from Chinese by me and then edited for clarity and grammar by a proofreader (see Appendix 3: Key to transcription conventions). In order to make the translation maximally transparent, I provide all Chinese-language data in the original as well as in translation.

The study employs content analysis for the interpretation of the collected textual and narrative data. Content analysis is one of today's most extensively used analytical methods in the social sciences for categorising emerging themes from textual and narrative data. The choice of the content from textual and narrative data was justified by their relevance to the research questions of the study. For each of the four established themes, I developed a coding scheme inductively from the data. After data coding, I uncovered categories and patterns, made inferences, and presented my interpretations derived from the coded data. I selected some typical quotations from participants that I include in the discussion to reinforce my abstraction of information. At various point, figures and tables are used to facilitate the description.

In order to enhance the credibility of qualitative content analysis, two techniques are used: member checking and triangulation. First, member checks have been done both during the interview process and at the conclusion of the study.

While conducting an interview, I summarised information and then questioned the participant to determine accuracy. After the interview, participants were given opportunities to review the raw data, the analysed data and the reports to ensure that the research adequately and accurately represents their perspectives and experiences. Triangulation involves the use of multiple and different sources, methods and perspectives to illuminate the research problem and its outcomes. This study undertakes a multiple triangulation approach to examine policy documents, language textbooks, linguistic landscape and language learning trajectories relating to LLP for the Beijing Olympic Games. The technique enables me to project a multi-faceted, complex picture and produce an in-depth, rich understanding of the phenomenon under study.

Both text and talk are subject to multiple interpretations. Shardakova and Pavlenko (2004) point out that "different interpretations of texts come from different combinations of the properties of the text and the social positioning and knowledge of its interpreters" (p. 30). Qualitative researchers, particularly CDA analysts, aim to be self-reflexive and politically aware. Nightingale and Cromby (1999, p. 228) suggest that "reflexivity requires an awareness of the researcher's contribution to the construction of meanings throughout the research process, and an acknowledgment of the impossibility of remaining 'outside of' one's subject matter while conducting research." In analysing data, I reflect upon the ways in which my own values, experiences, interests, beliefs, political commitments, and social identities have shaped the research. As the investigator of the research, I have multiple identities as a Chinese EFL learner, an English educator, an international student and a global citizen, all which have informed the current research. As a Chinese EFL learner, I share the same experience of most English learners in China who have invested heavily in this language with aspirations to native-like fluency and upward social mobility, so that I am able to understand the desire for English among the Chinese and their dilemmas in English language learning. As a university English teacher in China who has been involved with teaching English as a foreign language for many years, I know the current circumstances and potential problems of English language education and the linguistic market in China. As a sociolinguistic researcher who worked for a doctorate degree in Australia within a multilingual society, I intend to raise a critical awareness of the spread of English among Chinese English learners, educators and policy makers and to suggest what lessons other countries can learn from China's experience. While conducting the research, I have been aware that the field of the current study is "inherently political and shaped by multiple ethical and political positions" (Nelson, Treichler, and Grossberg, 1992, p. 2). Meanwhile, I acknowledge that my own critical interpretation is not free from political and ethical values and is also subject to critical scrutiny.

Overall, this thesis adopts a context-sensitive critical approach to language policies, practices and ideologies embedded in the massive identity construction project of the two Beijing Olympics. By taking this approach, I hope to contribute to a richer understanding of the LPP for the Modern Olympic Games hosted in non-Anglophone countries.

3.4 Ethical considerations

As a qualitative researcher with human participants, I gave serious thought to ethical issues. In order to ensure an ethically responsible qualitative research process, three ethical principles are crucial to the conduct of human research: "beneficence," "respect," and "justice" (Sieber and Stanley, 1988, p. 53). The study involved four categories of participants: university students as Olympic volunteers, taxi driver, English teachers, and BOCOG administrative staff who were involved in official Olympic English training. Four strategies were used to safeguard the informants' rights through processes of data collection, analysis and presentation in this study: informed consent, confidentiality, anonymity, and non-traceability.

While conducting interviews and observations, informed consent was continuously sought. All participants received an information and consent form in their first language prior to interviewing or observation. Acknowledging that the informed consent process is "dynamic and continuous" (Madison, 2005, p. 114), I asked participants each time for their permission to conduct interviews or to make observations. At the beginning of interviews or observations, participants were fully informed of the aims of the current research, the purpose of the recording, how the data is processed, stored, and deleted, and who has access to the data. Most importantly, participants were made aware that their participation was voluntary and that they had the right to withdraw at any time during the study. In order to protect the anonymity and non-traceability of participants in the study, pseudonyms were assigned to all participating individuals and institutions. Aspects of interviewees' identities that could identify them, such as institutional affiliation, gender, age, residence, employment, and education background, are not being disclosed in any written reports of the research or in other forms of dissemination.

There is a particular ethical issue with regard to the political sensitivity of the Beijing Olympiad and BOCOG's confidentiality policy. Some participants, being Olympic volunteers and BOCOG staff, were required to sign confidentiality agreements with BOCOG and thus could not agree to interviews and observations before and at the time of the Games. In keeping with the spirit of "beneficence," "respect," and "justice" (Sieber and Stanley, 1988, p. 53), participants were approached with full understanding and respect. I always made adjustments according to participants' availability and avoided unnecessary risk or harm to them. Additionally, the study was mutually beneficial to participants, as I offered participants my personal English learning experience and advice for studying abroad, and I also assisted some participants with English translation.

Chapter 4
Beijing's commitment – international language environment

1 *The Beijing Olympic Action Plan*

The Beijing Municipal Government and the Beijing Organising Committee for the Games of the XXIX Olympiad (BOCOG) officially released the *Beijing Olympic Action Plan* (BOCOG, 2002) on July 13, 2002. Being a guideline document for both future social and economic development of Beijing and the preparation for the Olympic Games, the Plan embodies the concept of "development for Olympics; Olympics for development". It also serves as a landmark of the city's fast development represented by the preparation for the Olympic Games in the first decade of the 21st century.

The *Action Plan* consists of one overall plan and nine specific plans, which were implemented in three phases: the Preparatory Phase – December 2001 to June 2003; the Development Phase – July 2003 to June 2006; and the Pre-Games Operation Phase – July 2006 to the opening of the Games. The Plan sets out four major objectives for the preparation of the Olympic Games: (1) making the Games a great success in Olympic history; (2) speeding up the social and economic development of the city and of the country; (3) building up a new image of reform and opening-up for the capital, and (4) striving for a boom of sports in China.

The *Action Plan* is also the governmental guidance for the language planning and policy of the 2008 Beijing Olympic Games. As part of its overall strategic objectives, BOCOG pledged to stage "a best-ever Olympic Games in history" and hoped to run the 2008 Olympics in a manner that would not only promote "the modernisation of Beijing as well as the rest of the country" but also create "a new image for Beijing" (BOCOG, 2002). This new image would position Beijing as an "international city" which is "developing rapidly and opening wider to the outside world" (BOCOG, 2002). Ji Lin (2009, p. 5), Executive Deputy Mayor of the Beijing Municipal Government, believed "a city's international language environment reflects its levels of modernisation and internationalisation . . . Persistent work at improving Beijing's international language environment can contribute to the success of the Olympics and advance Beijing's modernisation." With regard to the construction of Beijing's "international language environment," the *Action Plan* (BOCOG, 2002) stipulated three aspects as tasks of top priority for the LPP of the Games: (1) the learning and popularisation of foreign languages; (2) the promotion of the proper use of Putonghua and Standard Chinese characters, and (3) the standardisation of bilingual/multilingual guiding signs. Foreign language learning and popularisation was seen as an essential element to create a language environment conducive to constructing the identity of Beijing as a successful Olympic host city by 2008, and as a modernised international city in the long run. A top-down language policy was formulated to promote the learning of foreign languages, predominantly English, as shown in the following excerpt.

I. Foreign Language Learning and Popularization
The Organizing Committee of the "Beijing Speaks to the World" Program will develop and implement the "Overall Plan for Citizens Speaking Foreign Languages (2003–2008)" before the end of 2002. The objective is to make most citizens capable of speaking one hundred sentences for everyday use in at least one foreign language by the end of 2007. Employees working in "window" industries, particularly those that may serve foreigners, shall be more vigorously trained in foreign languages. Over a period time [sic], rules shall be developed that will require employees to have a proficiency certificate before they can take up a job in certain industries or professions. Importance shall be attached to foreign language education in all schools, and measures shall be taken to improve the foreign language proficiency of all students. Programs that teach the relatively rare foreign languages should also be organized and given due emphasis.

The promotion and popularization of foreign languages will be strengthened. Newspapers, magazines, radio stations, TV stations and websites are all to increase foreign language programs or columns. The English-language paper *Beijing Today*, now a weekly publication, shall be published three times a week, starting from 2003, and it shall be made into a daily newspaper in 2005. The bilingual and multi-lingual programming capabilities at Beijing Radio and TV stations will be augmented. Beijing Telecom will set up a telephone translation number to serve foreign language learners and people relying on foreign languages for most of their communications.

BOCOG and the Beijing Municipal Government considered the provision of bilingual signs to be an important measure to promote the image of Beijing as an international city. Therefore, another focus of the work was the standardising of bilingual/multilingual signs displayed in public places frequented by Olympic visitors. Tasks and targets were set forth in the *Action Plan* (BOCOG, 2002) as follows:

III. Guiding Signs
Experts will be organized to conduct comprehensive research and systematic analysis in order to develop a set of standardized tourist guide systems for Beijing. The municipal Tourism Bureau shall examine the existing tourist guides, tourist maps, signs, pamphlets and their locations at various streets, key tourist sites and key tourist service facilities. The standardization of tourist information services shall be achieved by the end of 2005. Touch-screen e-guide facilities shall be made available at public locations frequented by tourists, and mobile information tellers shall be made available during the Olympic Games to provide

tourist information and guide services. Major roads, stations and stops, tourist sites and key cultural sites in Beijing shall have bilingual directional signs in both Chinese and English, and multi-lingual signs shall be available in certain special premises and stadiums. Before 2006, a system to examine foreign language signs shall be developed under leadership of the "Beijing Speaks to the World" Program Organizing Committee [The name of this program was changed to "the Beijing Speaks Foreign Languages Program" in 2002]. Starting from 2002, simplified icons shall be adopted and promoted with reference to international norms in order to gradually change the current situation in which guiding signs now are in words only and without any types of indicators. Bilingual electronic stop reporting systems shall be promoted at appropriate times among the city's bus and metro systems. Braille and sign language services shall be given due emphasis.

As it was only the third time that the Olympic Summer Games had been held in Asia, an early focus by both local Olympic organisers and the IOC emerged on whether the "language environment" of the Olympic host city could stand the severe linguistic challenge of the Olympics. Even though the Beijing Olympic organisers had made strong commitments to raise Beijing's overall foreign language level, the international community still held serious doubts about the 2008 Olympics being hosted by an Asian socialist country. A Xinhua Agency research project (Chinese International Communication Research Centre, 2006) revealed 47 per cent of surveyed foreign journalists worried that the foreign language level of Beijing would be an obstacle for their work in the host city. IOC president Jacques Rogge was reported as saying that while he was confident that Beijing would stage a distinctive and best-ever Olympic Games in history, he expressed concern about the issues of qualified personnel and Beijing's language environment (Hu, 2007). Faced with these concerns, the Chinese government made its commitment to the world in the *Olympic Action Plan* (BOCOG, 2002): "By 2008, information services will be inexpensive, rich in content, free of language barrier, and personalized and available for anyone, at anytime and anywhere." The concerns about language environment and language services both in China and abroad gave the foreign language popularisation campaign in Beijing added urgency. In the seven years leading up to the Beijing Olympic Games, the Beijing Municipal Government and the Olympic authority had taken four major measures to implement the top-down foreign language popularisation campaign and construct "the international language environment": first, the founding of the Beijing Speaks Foreign Languages Programme (language policy making and enforcing mechanism); second, the launch of the Beijing English Testing System (language testing mechanism); third, the initiation of the Official Language Services Suppliers (language service mechanism); and, fourth, the promotion of English language learning and teaching celebrities (role model and identification mechanism).

2 The Action Plan of the BSFLP

The Beijing Speaks Foreign Languages Programme (BSFLP) was launched in 2002 and was one of the city-wide foreign language popularisation projects directly managed by the Beijing Municipal Government. The BSFLP grew out of the Citizens' English Speaking Programme which was initiated in 2000 as part of the bidding effort for the 2008 Olympic Games. Members of the Organising Committee of BSFLP included mayor, deputy mayor, directors of various municipal government departments, and heads of 18 districts and counties. Ever since its founding, the Organising Committee of BSFLP had closely cooperated with BOCOG to create a "good language environment" in the city. The BSFLP Organising Committee enlisted 35 domestic and foreign specialists from the United States, Britain and Singapore to form the consulting group. The aim of the BSFLP, as stated by Liu Yang, deputy director of the BSFLP Organising Committee Office, was to "encourage Beijing inhabitants to learn and speak English and turn Beijing into the international city it was always supposed to be" (Stanway, 2008). According to Liu Yang, the Chinese Government was the only government that had made a promise to eliminate language barriers during the Olympics, and Beijing had been doing its best in this regard (Stanway, 2008). The following introduces the overall objectives and working procedures of the programme as well as important aspects of the LPP of the Games including foreign language popularisation, language services in window industries, signage standardisation, technology-supported language services and foreign language service market.[7]

2.1 Overall objectives

In 2003, the Organising Committee of the BSFLP (2003) published its first five-year *Action Plan* (2003–2008) as a more comprehensive and explicit plan for the LPP of the Beijing Olympic Games. The *Action Plan* set three main overall objectives: 1) the 5-million foreign language speaking population; 2) the standardisation of bilingual signs; 3) foreign language services in window industries.[8]

---

[7] The following contents of the *Action Plan of the BFLSP* are my translation.
[8] "Window industry" in Chinese discourses mainly refers to government departments and service trades that concern foreign affairs.

The city's foreign language speaking population shall rise to 5 million, accounting for 35 per cent of the city's total population by 2008, bilingual street signs in public places shall be standardised, foreign language services shall be accessible in the window industry in key areas, foreign language service facilities shall be systematised, and foreign language service volunteers shall be institutionalised; thus a favourable international environment can be created for the successful holding of the Beijing 2008 Olympics, and Beijing's commitment to significantly improve the city's international communicative competence can be fulfilled. By 2020, the overall foreign language level and comprehensive quality of citizens will be improved in essence, forming a first-class cultural environment suitable for foreigners to work, study and live in Beijing, and the city's international communicative competence will be significantly enhanced, providing a reliable guarantee for the formation of the basic framework of Beijing's modern international metropolis.

2.2 Working procedures

In order to achieve these overall objectives, the Organising Committee of the BSFLP (2003) planned to implement the *Action Plan* and construct the "international language environment" in three phases:

Phase 1 (2003): The main work in 2003 is to strengthen the organisational and institutional construction of the BSFLP so as to form an effective working mode; encourage foreign language learning activities among Beijing citizens; continue to expand the bilingual and multilingual teaching pilot projects; gradually standardise the language used by various government departments and service industries and bilingual signs displayed in key cultural sites, neighbourhoods, and tourist areas. Information centres for domestic and foreign tourists will be set up in the main neighbourhoods. The volunteer teams of foreign language services will be set up initially.

Phase 2 (2004–2006): From 2004 to 2006, the focus will be on promoting foreign language learning activities so as to improve the overall foreign language proficiency of Beijing citizens; implement bilingual education in qualified schools; provide essential foreign language services in window industry and service industry; set up standardised bilingual signs in business and cultural sites, main neighbourhoods and tourist attractions of the city; build information centres; expand and train the volunteer team of the BSFLP, and basically solve the language difficulties for foreigners in Beijing.

Phase 3 (2007–2008): From 2007 to 2008, the Beijing English Testing System will be fully implemented so as to standardise Beijing citizens' foreign language learning activities; standardised bilingual signs shall be used in all business and cultural sites, main neighbourhoods and tourist attractions of the city; information centres shall be constructed extensively; the city's foreign language TV and radio stations shall begin to broadcast and foreign language newspapers shall be circulated; the volunteer team of the BSFLP shall accumulate more language service experience in practice so as to ensure the success of the 2008 Olympic Games.

2.3 Governmental planning for foreign language popularisation

In the *Action Plan*, the Organising Committee of the BSFLP (2003) attached equal importance to both formal education and social education to improve the quantity and quality of Beijing's foreign language-speaking population. The teaching of foreign languages, predominantly English, was encouraged in educational institutions from kindergarten through to graduate school. Meanwhile, various social resources were required to be integrated into the provision of different types of foreign language training for Beijing citizens.

1. Formal Foreign Language Education
    1) Reform foreign language teaching methods in schools. Draw on successful international experience to explore the reform of foreign language teaching methods and examination systems. Adopt advanced teaching methods and actively carry out bilingual and multilingual teaching reform experiments. Gradually offer foreign language courses in kindergartens, encourage primary and secondary schools to carry out foreign language teaching experiments, systematically carry out foreign language education from preschool education to tertiary education to improve foreign language competence among students, and build a foreign language education system that meets the requirement of an international metropolis.
    2) Develop a group of sophisticated foreign language teachers. Make plans for training and recruiting foreign language teachers. Strengthen the training of foreign language teachers in primary and secondary schools. Update their pedagogical theories and improve their foreign language teaching skills. Create favourable conditions to attract qualified foreign teachers to participate in foreign language teaching.
    3) Enrich foreign language teaching content. Add content about traditional Chinese culture and local conditions and customs of foreign countries to foreign language teaching. Improve students' overall quality through strengthening the education of China's conditions and customs and cultivating open-minded cultural awareness and international outlook.
2. Social Foreign Language Training
    1) Carry out various forms of social foreign language training. Give full play to Beijing's unique advantages in foreign language education, integrate various social resources including colleges and universities, training institutions and professional translation companies, and actively cooperate with overseas training institutions to train senior foreign language personnel as planned. The forms of foreign language training for Beijing citizens can be diversified according to local conditions. Give full play to the advantages of various resources, and carry out large-scale public activities which the government promotes, enterprises participate in, and citizens benefit from.
    2) Cultivate high-quality interdisciplinary talents. Open up high-level foreign language training and researching channels such as overseas study, professional training and overseas advanced foreign language training. Put the stress on cultivating government officials and business leaders who can directly communicate with foreign experts and professional institutions.

3) Improve the foreign language proficiency of Beijing citizens in daily communication. Foreign language training for Beijing citizens, especially those with low foreign language level, shall focus on improving their oral foreign language competence in daily communication.
4) Strengthen the training of professionals of less commonly taught languages. With the aim of serving the 2008 Olympic Games, build a talent bank of professionals of less commonly taught languages based on the training of students majoring in less commonly taught languages in foreign language institutes.

2.4 Governmental planning for language services in window industries

Besides the overall objectives, the *Action Plan for the BSFLP* (Organising Committee of the BSFLP, 2003) also set specific foreign language learning and testing plans and objectives for Beijing residents from different walks of life. Civil servants were requested to take the lead in English language learning and testing. Meanwhile, great importance was accorded to "employees working in 'window industries' (those that may serve foreigners)", such as police officers, taxi drivers, bus drivers and attendants, subway staff, hotel workers, and employees in commercial sectors.

> Civil Servant: Civil servants in Beijing shall grasp common conversational English and elementary English for civil services within three years (2003–2006). Civil servants are generally required to grasp more than 100 commonly used English sentences. Civil servants under 40 years old with a bachelor's degree or above are required to grasp more than 300 commonly used English sentences, and can basically communicate and work in English. Before 2008, 1000 civil servants with a higher level of English will be selected for intensive training for no less than three months, so that they can basically reach the level of international communication.
>
> Staff in the Public Security Department: 80% of the police under 40 years old should pass an elementary oral English test at the national or municipal level, and have certain listening and speaking ability in English. 6000 police officers with a higher English level who have certain English listening, speaking, reading and writing abilities need to pass an intermediate oral English test at the national or municipal level. 300 police officers as top English learners who have high English listening, speaking, reading and writing abilities need to pass an advanced oral English test at the national or municipal level. 200 police officers who speak French, Russian, Japanese, Arabic and other foreign languages need to pass an advanced level test in another foreign language, and can basically meet the requirements of interpretation in dealing with foreign affairs.
>
> Staff in the Transportation Department: By 2008, 60% of the city's 80,000 taxi drivers shall pass the test of *300 English Sentences for Beijing Taxi Drivers*. 80% of them shall pass the test of *100 English Sentences for Beijing Taxi Drivers*. All bus drivers and attendants shall pass the test of *100 English Sentences for Bus attendants*. 80% of subway employees shall pass the test of *300 English Sentences for Passenger Service Workers*.

Staff in the Tourist Industry: Successfully complete the "Tourist and Hotel English Level Examination". By 2008, employees with English certificates shall account for 90% of the total number of certified employees in five-star hotel, 80% in four-star hotels and 60% in three-star hotels. The standard language service level of employees in tourist hotels, restaurants and tourist attractions will be evaluated.

Staff in the Retail Industry: Closely relating to business practice and industry characteristics, cultivate a group of front-line employees who can provide foreign language services and improve the comprehensive quality of employees in the commercial industry. Adopting *Beijing Business Service English Training Textbook* as the teaching material, actively promote the Multi-level Business English Test. Incorporate the Multi-level Business English Test into the national assessment of vocational skills. Require 60% of front-line employees under 40 years old including salespersons, restaurant waiters, hotel receptionists, room attendants, beauticians, hairdressers and photographers to pass the test. Promote foreign language speaking activities for retail workers, so as to make shopping in English accessible.

2.5 Governmental planning for signage standardisation

In the *Action Plan* (Organising Committee of the BSFLP, 2003), the standardisation of Chinese-English bilingual signs in public places and facilities was regarded as an important aspect of constructing Beijing's "international language environment" and a key factor for enhancing the city's level of internationalisation. At the request of the Beijing Municipal Government, a series of local standards for the English translations of public signs were promulgated and a Chinglish-reporting system was established before the Beijing Olympics, which I will discuss in more detail in Chapter 7.

1) Formulate the local standards of public signs in Beijing. Use international generic standards for reference, widely consult Chinese and foreign language experts for advice, compile a manual for bilingual signage, and standardise the language used in public places and facilities. Promote the local standards of public signs through the official websites of the Beijing Municipal Government (www.beijing.gov.cn) and the BSFLP (www.bjenglish.org.cn) as well as other news media, making it convenient for relevant departments and ordinary citizens to check, learn and use.
2) Gradually standardise bilingual signs and notices. Give full play to the role of Chinese and foreign experts to gradually set up, rectify and standardise the graphics, characters and bilingual information on road signs displayed in public places and facilities such as major tourist attractions (spots), cultural venues, commercial facilities, Olympic venues, transportation lines, highways, streets, stations, subways and airports in accordance with generic international standards. Set up a bilingual signage supervision committee, open a hotline for "picking up mistakes in English signs", and give full play to the public's manpower to correct and supervise existing bilingual signs.

2.6 Governmental planning for foreign language popularisation in mass media

Another focus for constructing Beijing's international language environment was on the mass media. According to the *Action Plan for the BSFLP* (Organising Committee of the BSFLP, 2003), two aspects of work were emphasised: 1) foreign language TV and radio programmes; 2) foreign language books and newspapers.

1) Broadcast foreign language TV and radio programmes. Edit foreign language programmes for Beijing citizens, and produce foreign language teaching programmes in collaboration with foreign language education experts and foreign language training institutions. Set up foreign language channels in Beijing TV station and Beijing People's radio station, and gradually add bilingual programmes in other channels to assist the citizens in learning a foreign language and understanding foreign culture. Encourage TV and radio stations in all districts and counties to increase the broadcasting frequency of foreign language teaching programmes.
2) Publish and distribute foreign language books and newspapers. Organise colleges, universities and publishing institutions to compile and update a batch of teaching materials and audio-visual products for Beijing citizens and people in different industries. Publish bilingual books on specific subjects to meet the needs of international talents, and increase the publication and circulation of foreign language learning books and newspapers. Increase the circulation of bilingual manuals of conversational Chinese for foreigners studying Chinese in Beijing. Foreign language columns shall be set up in major newspapers and magazines. Publish foreign language newspapers to showcase Beijing and involve Beijing citizens in learning foreign languages. The circulation and coverage of foreign language newspapers shall be increased.

2.7 Governmental planning for technology-supported language services

In addition to bilingual signs and media and publications in foreign languages, various technology-supported language services, such as the multilingual service hotline, bilingual information navigation system, bilingual travel website, tourist information centre, and telephone translation, were also important measures for constructing an "international language environment" and improving "Beijing's internationalisation level" (Organising Committee of the BSFLP, 2003).

1) Set up bilingual information electronic service systems. Multilingual service hotlines, Chinese-English bilingual information navigation system and inquiry telephones shall be set up in the city's comprehensive service centres, administrative departments and service units concerning foreign affairs to provide convenient information services for foreigners' work and life in Beijing. Consult foreigners for their suggestions and opinions on building Beijing into a modern international metropolis.

2) Improve bilingual websites for living and travelling in Beijing. Build bilingual travel websites as portal websites for promoting Beijing on the basis of existing tourist service websites. Provide information inquiry services to facilitate the shopping, entertainment, catering, leisure and tourist activities of citizens and foreigners in Beijing and visitors from home and abroad.
3) Build a network of Beijing tourist information centres. Drawing on the successful experience of international tourist cities, set up more tourist information centres in addition to the 20 existing ones to provide free bilingual information services in the places tourists often visit, such as parks, tourist attractions, museums, exhibition halls, hotels, airports and stations. The tourist information centres where conditions permit can provide multilingual services to meet the diversified needs of domestic and foreign tourists. Tourist information centres can provide multilingual print materials including travel brochures, scenic spot introductions, maps, timetables, and books and magazines that promote Chinese culture.
4) Set up a bilingual hotline for the taxi business. Install a translation service hotline telephone in all taxis to provide multilingual services. Improve the foreign language service level of the taxi business so as to solve the travelling problems of foreigners.

2.8 Governmental planning for regulating foreign language service market

Since the start of the 21st century, globalisation and the development of information technology have greatly promoted the prosperity of the language services market, and ushered in a period of rapid development for China's language services industry. At the same time, the language services industry has also faced many problems and challenges, such as a lack of standards for language services and accreditation of language service providers. The *Action Plan for the BSFLP* (Organising Committee of the BSFLP, 2003) made plans in this regard.

1) Standardise the language used in foreign language publications. Strictly implement the language censorship system and the editor responsibility system in publishing foreign language books. Fundamentally standardise the language used in foreign language publications and ensure the quality of these publications.
2) Standardise bilingual content on websites. Formulate relevant language standards and use them as reference to standardise the language used on bilingual websites of various publishers, window industries, large enterprises and institutions. Standardise the bilingual content of government affairs on the official portal of the People's Government of Beijing Municipality (www.beijing.gov.cn). Add Chinese-English bilingual content on the websites of all commissions, bureaus, district and counties.
3) Standardise the foreign language service market. Actively promote the establishment of the association of translators, foreign language training institutions and other intermediary organisations. Regulate translation companies and foreign language training market through self-regulation.

2.9 Governmental planning for public foreign language activities

In order to mobilise the general public to participate in foreign language learning and achieve the overall aim of a "5 million foreign language speaking population", the *Action Plan for the BSFLP* (Organising Committee of the BSFLP, 2003) planned a series of public foreign language teaching activities and various forms of competitions.

1) Carry out a series of public foreign language lectures by Chinese and foreign language experts in a planned way. In accordance with the principle of "organising elaborately, increasing languages, enriching contents and forming brands," we shall continue to organise public lectures and other activities, and form a batch of excellent language service products by 2008.
2) Carry out a series of foreign language competitions. Regularly hold a series of competition activities, such as citizens' English TV competition, English speech competition for middle school students, business English TV competition, Chinese singing foreign songs TV competition, English for specific purpose TV competition, children's English competition, etc. On the basis of the existing competitions, we should open up new competitions, introduce new forms and more languages in competitions, and make the competitions livelier and richer in content. All districts, counties and industries shall hold various forms of foreign language competitions according to their won characteristics.
3) Carry out popular and interesting foreign language popularisation activities. Continue to hold "Foreign Language Week in May" and "Foreign Language Park Party in October" every year. Increase the participation of the citizens and make foreign language popularisation activities into excellent programmes. Various districts and counties can carry out foreign language and culture popularisation activities through various channels such as garden fairs and temple fairs. Encourage communities and neighbourhoods where conditions permit to open "foreign language corners" and "foreign language teahouses."
4) Carry out foreign language proficiency test. Formulate unified standards of foreign language proficiency test for the citizens in cooperation with authoritative foreign language testing institutions at home and abroad. Encourage the citizens to actively participate in the testing of foreign language proficiency and constantly improve their language proficiency.

2.10 Governmental planning for foreign language volunteers

Last but not least, the Organising Committee of the BSFLP (2003) made plans for recruiting volunteers from home and abroad who were committed to public services and had foreign language skills to carry out a variety of voluntary services. Olympic volunteers are the group of people who are most likely to participate in intercultural exchanges with foreign athletes, coaches, officials and visitors. Their foreign language proficiency directly reflects the host city's intercultural communicative competence and international image.

1) Set up a team of volunteers for the BSFLP. Recruit volunteers from the general public, mainly colleges and universities, in 2003. Build a database of volunteers to reserve a certain amount of foreign language talents, so as to prepare for the 2008 Olympic Games and large-scale international events.
2) Promote Beijing citizens' foreign languages popularisation activities. Organise volunteers to carry out various English teaching activities in communities, neighbourhoods, window industries and government departments. Consolidate the initial achievements of the BSFLP, keep up the enthusiasm of the citizens, window industry practitioners and government officials in learning foreign languages, and further improve their foreign language level and international communication awareness.
3) Participate in various large-scale international activities. Provide volunteers opportunities to practice in the annual "China Beijing International Hi-Tech Expo", "Beijing International Tourism and Culture Festival" and other large-scale activities, so as to enhance China's international service capacity.
4) Strengthen volunteer training. Volunteers can have an in-depth understanding of international communicative etiquette and knowledge about customs, dining habits, religion, and culture of most countries through lectures and social practice, thus improving their comprehensive quality. Convene international symposiums, organise special groups to observe the 2004 Athens Olympic Games and other activities, carry out international exchange of volunteers, and build a first-class volunteer team that meets international standards.

Rules and regulations are the most commonly used devices by those in authority that directly affect and create de facto language practices and thereby turn ideology into practice, in private as well as in public domains (Shohamy, 2006, p. 59). In the construction of Beijing's "international language environment," the BSFLP was the language policy making and enforcing mechanism used by the authority to maximise its control over language behaviours by enforcing rules and regulations on language learning and use.

2.11 The implementation and outcome of the *Action Plan*

In their preparation for the Beijing Olympics, the BSFLP Organising Committee and relevant government departments had made concerted efforts to raise the English proficiency of Beijing citizens. Both formal education and social education were given equal stress. In the *Action Plan* the Organising Committee (2003) proposed to implement English Education from early preschool to tertiary level in Beijing. Since 2001, the teaching of English had been promoted nationwide to Grade 3 in primary schools in cities and townships in response to a policy statement issued by MOE (2001a). In 2004, Beijing Municipal Education Commission

(2004) issued a work plan to further lower the threshold of Beijing's compulsory English education to Grade 1 in primary schools. In fact, English is almost a compulsory subject in Beijing's kindergartens as a growing number of parents want their children better equipped for the future (China Education and Research Network, 2001a). In addition to being taught at all levels of education, English was also officially promoted through content-based English language teaching, widely known in China as "Chinese–English bilingual education" (双语教学 *shuangyu jiaoxue*). In 2001, the Education Ministry (2001b) issued an official guideline on enhancing the quality of college education, requiring that at least 5–10% of all the courses on a university curriculum should be taught in English within three years. Under this guideline, adopting English textbooks became a new trend in Beijing's universities. More and more universities began running courses that used English textbooks for non-English-major students, especially for those majoring in computing, management and economics (China Education and Research network, 2001b).

In addition to school education, the Organising Committee of the BSFLP integrated various social resources in popularising English. They encouraged collaborations between tertiary institutions, language training institutions, translation companies and foreign organisations to conduct various forms of foreign language training for Beijing citizens. According to official statistics (Official Website of the Beijing 2008 Olympic Games, 2007c), the BSFLP involved more than one million Beijing citizens in various public English learning activities before the 2008 Olympic Games, including free community lectures, training courses, TV contests, park festivals, foreign film screenings, and computer-assisted autonomous study. By the end of 2007, the Organising Committee of BSFLP had established a volunteer team and organised six English language park festivals, 701 community-level English training centres and 433 community English corners[9] where local residents practiced English with one another (Deng, 2009; Stanway, 2008). Many television contests sponsored by the BSFLP were held between 2002 and 2008, including "Contest on Residents' Daily English," "Chinese Sing Foreign Songs Contest" and "Business English Contest" (Zhang, 2009). Foreign language learning books, including *Beijing Residents English Speaking Handbook*, *100 English Sentences for Beijingers* and *300 English Sentences for Beijingers*, were published during this preparation period. The Organising Committee also

---

[9] The phrase "English corner" commonly refers to a public location in China where Chinese English learners gather together regularly to improve their oral English skills. On the English corner day, some popular English corners are often visited by hundreds of students and professionals. People can be seen giving speeches in English or leading open discussions.

made concerted efforts with Beijing universities and the media to expand the circulation of English newspapers and periodicals.

Another focus of the BSFLP's work was on improving the English proficiency of civil servants and service sector employees in Beijing. Plans and objectives were formulated in various government departments and service industries to ensure "obstacle-free" English language services for the Beijing Olympics. The BSFLP Organising Committee claimed more than 60,000 civil servants had passed relative English proficiency tests by 2006 (Foreign Affairs Office of the Beijing Municipal Government, 2008b). According to the *Beijing Daily* (Jia, 2007), a more stringent policy was to require over 90,000 Beijing taxi drivers to pass an English proficiency test to keep their driver's license. Those who did not pass the English examination at the end of their training might not be allowed to work during the Games. Learning English became part of the daily routine for Beijing civil servants and service sector employees in their preparation for the 2008 Olympic Games and, more importantly, became a central aspect of their job security. English proficiency thus emerged as being closely tied to occupational and economic utility in the Beijing Olympic context. By imposing strict English training and testing requirements on Beijing citizens, especially personnel in service sectors, the *Action Plan for the BSFLP* perpetuated the supremacy and power of English and consequently served to exclude those without the required English proficiency from accessing equal social rights.

In addition to improving English proficiency among Beijing citizens, English standardisation was another important theme of the BSFLP. Beijing took the lead nationwide in standardising English signs at tourist and cultural sites, medical treatment facilities, stadiums and other public places, developing local standards for English translations of public signs, organisation names, professional titles, restaurant menus, service facilities, and more. A system to report Chinglish was developed under the leadership of the BSFLP Organising Committee. Bilingual/multilingual tourist websites and information hotlines were all required to be improved to service foreign visitors. At least 830,000 nonstandard English signs in public sites were replaced with standardised ones as part of the city's preparations and English menus in 1,300 restaurants and catering enterprises located on main roads were standardised (Foreign Affairs Office of the Beijing Municipal Government, 2008b). I will elaborate in greater detail in Chapter 7 the bilingual signage standardisation campaign that sought to eliminate Chinglish and otherwise amend the linguistic landscape to fit Beijing's role as the Olympic host city in 2008.

3 The Beijing English Testing System (2006–2013)

Beijing's Olympic English popularisation campaign was pushed even further by the launch of the Beijing English Testing System (BETS) in 2006. The BETS was cooperatively launched by the Organising Committee of BSFLP, the Foreign Affairs Office of the Beijing Municipal People's Government and Cambridge ESOL, with the Beijing Education Examinations Authority made responsible for its administration. The authority described the exam as an important Beijing Municipal Government measure to "prompt local residents to learn and speak English and improve Beijing's image as an international metropolis in preparation for the upcoming 29th Olympic Games in Beijing" (Xinhua, 2006). All Beijing citizens who lived and worked in Beijing, regardless of their age, gender, profession, schooling background, nationality and residence, were called upon to enrol in this examination (Xinhua, 2006).

BETS was divided into three levels, namely BETS-1, BETS-2 and BETS-3, to test local residents' abilities to listen, speak, read and write in English. The test had been conducted twice a year in Beijing since 2006 and continued to be offered in the post-Olympic period until 2013. Beijing citizens passing BETS were able to obtain two certificates per level, jointly issued by the Organising Committee of the BSFLP, the Foreign Affairs Office, the ESOL Examinations of Cambridge Assessment and the Beijing Education Examinations Authority, along with a badge saying "I can speak English" (Zhang, 2009). The Organising Committee of the BSFLP encouraged Beijing citizens to wear this badge in order to assist foreign visitors more effectively. The Beijing Education Examinations Authority asserted that the two certificates could be used as internationally recognised references both for Chinese government departments and businesses to recruit employees and for Beijingers to prove their English proficiency when they applied to study abroad (Xinhua, 2006). In these official discourses 'foreign visitors' were imagined as a homogenous community in which English was the default language they spoke. The danger of this language ideology lies in that it ignored the large number of inbound non-English speaking foreign visitors and led directly to the shortage of multilingual professionals at Games time.

The BETS certificate has in fact not been as internationally recognised as the Chinese authority initially asserted. However, it became the key to a host of opportunities in Beijing, such as Olympic volunteer recruitment, career opportunities in public or private sectors, eligibility for professional promotion, and government-sponsored studying abroad programmes. BETS proved to be popular with Beijing English learners, especially those who work in the service sector including the public security, transportation, sanitation, postal, local taxation and banking industries. Foreign affairs offices of districts and counties promoted

BETS on governmental websites and posters. In preparation for the Olympics, the Beijing Municipal Government (2007a) required 2 percent of service sector personnel to pass BETS-1 in 2007. Approved by the Beijing Municipal Government (Foreign Affairs Office of the Beijing Municipal Government, 2007c), BETS had been incorporated into Beijing's existing vocational qualification system, serving as a gatekeeper of professional accession and promotion. Major local government departments and enterprises such as the Beijing Health Bureau, Beijing Post Office and China National Offshore Oil Corp. all adopted BETS into their human resource training system (Cambridge ESOL, 2010). In these departments and enterprises, employees who held a BETS certificate were enlisted into a talent pool of personnel given priority in professional promotion and study abroad programmes. BETS had also been incorporated into the curriculum system of Beijing Olympic model schools such as Beijing No. 65 Middle School and Beijing No. 25 Middle School (Cambridge ESOL, 2010). By the end of 2009, BETS had been held eight times and 42,851 people had taken the test (Zhang, 2009, p. 21).

Shohamy (2006, p. 93) contends that language tests are a powerful mechanism for manipulating language and creating de facto language policies, especially in terms of deciding the priority of specific languages in society and education. Mandating testing in specific languages contains a direct message from policy makers about "language priorities and the marginalisation of other languages" (Shohamy, 2006, p.106). Test takers are usually not aware of the effects of tests in imposing de facto language policies and perpetuating ideological agendas of those in power, therefore they tend to comply with decisions made through the tests (Shohamy, 2006, pp.93, 106). By incorporating BETS into Beijing's existing vocational qualification system and school curricula, the Beijing Municipal Government intentionally used this language test as a powerful language policy device to manipulate language realities by diverting the focus of learning to English and perpetuating the power of English, while homogenising and suppressing language diversity. After the Games, as a continuing government project, BETS was pushed further and into more fields to involve more Beijing citizens in learning English. Given the power of BETS and other English proficiency tests, the supremacy of English over other foreign languages in Beijing is maintained.

4 Olympic language services providers

In Olympic Games prior to 2008, language services were undertaken mainly by foreign language experts and volunteers temporarily recruited from the host country and abroad. The biggest problem with this language service model is that the quality of language services is uneven due to the lack of professional translators and interpreters and of an effective management system. In addition, although there were some translation companies involved in the language services of the Olympic Games in the past, there was no precedent for such large-scale language services to be outsourced to institutions, organisations or companies. The 2008 Olympic Games were an extraordinary event, posing significant challenges to China's language services. After doing a lot of research on Olympic language services, BOCOG finally persuaded the IOC to agree to nominate language service providers for the first time at the 29th Beijing Olympic Games. Faced with the complex linguistic challenges of the Olympic Games, BOCOG initiated a set of language service provider categories and outsourced various kinds of language services to schools and universities, training institutions, foreign language media, translation and IT companies (see Table 3).

Table 3: Olympic language service categories and providers.

Language Service Category	Language Service Provider
Translation and Interpretation Service Supplier	Yuan-pei Translation
Language Training Service Suppliers	1. EF English First Co., Ltd.
	2. Aifly Education & Technology Co., Ltd.
Language Training Base	Beijing New Chinese Education
Language Training Media	English Learners' Lighthouse Newspaper
Multilingual Services Supplier	1. CapInfo Limited Company
	2. Beijing Olympic Multilingual Service Centre

4.1 Translation and interpretation service supplier

Being an essential component of services for the Beijing 2008 Olympic Games, translation services play an important role. About 1,500 translators and interpreters were needed inside and outside the Olympic venues. They were expected to translate nearly one million words of news into 10 languages[10] every day. Yuan-pei Translation was appointed the Official Translation and Interpretation

---

[10] The 10 languages were claimed by BOCOG to be the world's most widely spoken languages besides Chinese, identified as English, French, Russian, German, Japanese, Arabic, Spanish, Portuguese, Italian and Korean.

Supplier of the Beijing 2008 Olympic Games on December 30 2006, defeating many competitors willing to offer a sponsorship fee of more than 100 million yuan, as among them EF education, which was the language services provider of the 2004 Athens Olympic Games. This was the first time in Olympic history that a private enterprise was entrusted with the translation and interpretation services for the Games. According to the requirements of BOCOG, the main responsibility of the Translation and Interpretation Supplier was to recruit qualified overseas and domestic professional interpreters and conduct the necessary training to ensure that the interpreters could complete the required language service work.

As a pioneering Chinese translation company, Yuan-pei Translation had established sophisticated translation service mechanisms, including 24-step workflow, five-stage quality control and three-stage examination – all innovations in the undertaking of foreign language services. Moreover, Yuan-pei Translation had developed an innovative quality system, which was not just unique in the translation industry in China but featured strict workflow control, rigorous quality control and a systematic quality system. During the Beijing Olympic Games, Yuan-pei Translation provided interpretation and translation services for 14 units including the Chinese sports delegation, the Chinese Olympic Committee, BOCOG, the Olympic Sailing Committee, the IOC and the Olympic Broadcasting Company.

The Olympic Games brought great direct economic benefits to Yuan-pei Translation. "The actual expenditure of the oral and written language services for the Beijing Olympic Games must be more than 150 million yuan," said Jiang Xiaolin, general manager of Yuan-pei Translation (Ma, 2008), claiming that the "Olympic programme will help Yuan-pei translation achieve the target of 250 million yuan in sales revenue in 2008." The sales volume of Yuan-pei Translation in 2006 was 30 million yuan, with a net profit margin of 28%. In 2009, the brand value of Yuan-pei translation reached 210 million yuan, making it the most valuable brand in China's translation industry. For Jiang Xiaolin, winning the Olympics was just the beginning. "Sponsoring the Olympics to make Yuan-pei an international brand is the most cost-effective business." He hoped to use the brand effect of Olympic language services provider to position Yuan-pei translation as a global language services provider.

In the process of providing translation and interpretation services for the Olympic Games, Yuan-pei Translation encountered two major problems: one was the shortage of multilingual talents, the other was the issue of language services in emergency situations. The Olympic Games are a global event, and a large number of documents needed to be translated from English to French, Arabic and other commonly used world languages. However, China's education system in the past did not put enough emphasis on the cultivation of multilingual talents (Ma, 2008). Even though Yuan-pei Translation offered a handsome salary, there was still a dearth of professional interpreters and translators of foreign languages other than English at the Games time. Language access for emergency response was a more complicated challenge encountered by Yuanpei. The Beijing Olympic Games involved more than 80 official languages of 205 participating countries and regions, whereas Chinese universities only had teaching programmes in 44 foreign languages at that time. Due to the shortage of translators and interpreters of LCTLs, emergency support mechanisms were exceptionally important. There is great uncertainty in competitive Games: when an unseeded player who speaks an LCTL wins a medal and then gives a press conference, an interpreter needs to be in place immediately. Moreover, language services for the Olympic Games require a large number of standby personnel. If the originally assigned interpreter suddenly falls ill and is unable to work, standby personnel should immediately take his/her place to ensure the completion of the language service work.

The Beijing Olympics provided significant impetus to the education and training of translators and interpreters. In 2007, the professional degree Masters in Translation and Interpretation (MTI) was approved by the Academic Degrees Committee of the State Council, which was a significant milestone in the education and training of language professionals. Additionally, the Games made outstanding contributions to upgrading the traditional translation industry to the language services industry, promoting the transformation of its service flow from "small workshop" to "industrialisation," and integrating the combination of the Internet, modern communication technology, software technology and language services.

4.2 Language training service suppliers

The initiation of the Official Language Training Services Suppliers of the Beijing 2008 Olympic Games aimed at the provision of specialised English training for professionals directly involved in the 2008 Olympics. In March 2007, EF English First Co., Ltd. (EF) and Aifly Education & Technology Co., Ltd. (Aifly) were selected as Official Language Training Services Suppliers of the Beijing 2008 Olympic Games. EF had sponsored several major international sporting events in the past, including the Seoul 1988 Olympic Games (English First, 2011a). However, the Beijing 2008 Olympics marked the first time in Olympic history that 'language training services supplier' was officially considered to be an independent sponsorship category. The Beijing Olympic Committee proclaimed that the initiation of the new sponsorship category was "one of the most important decisions in ensuring the success of the Beijing Olympics" (Aifly Education Technology Company, 2008). Bill Fisher, CEO of EF, asserted that "[t]he Olympics are a great chance for China to starting talking to the world, and English is the tool for making it" (Official Website of the Beijing 2008 Olympic Games, 2007b). In language training services, English was given added utility and symbolic value as it was tied to the Olympic success.

From a business perspective, the introduction of the language training services supplier category was a win-win strategy for both BOCOG and the successful bidders. By selling the sponsorship right of the Beijing Olympic Games, BOCOG was able not only to appoint professional English training institutions to deliver its massive English training service but also to earn an entry price of 16 million yuan from each language services supplier (Official Website of the Beijing 2008 Olympic Games, 2005a). Actual bidding prices were much higher. In return, EF and Aifly received benefits such as the right to use the emblem and logo of the Beijing Olympics and BOCOG in their advertising and marketing, priority in advertising on TV and outdoors at the time of the Games, and priority in sponsoring Olympics-themed cultural activities and the torch relay. Both EF and Aifly used a series of marketing techniques to maximise their sponsorship. Although it is difficult to make a quantitative analysis of the benefits that the Olympics brought to suppliers, the enhancement of brand image and reputation of suppliers is likely to be considerable. Obviously, for EF and Aifly, winning the sponsorship gave them a substantial edge in competing with their 50,000 counterparts in the English language teaching business for a larger share of the multibillion-dollar English training industry in China. I will now describe these two official language services suppliers in more detail.

4.2.1 English First: "Native speaker superiority"

Founded by Bertil Hult in 1965 in Switzerland, EF Education First grew to become the largest private education company in the world by the first decade of the 21st century (English First, 2010a). EF English First is a subsidiary of EF Education First that specialises in English language training, educational travel, and cultural exchange. EF English First (EF) entered China in 1994 as the first foreign private language school. In the 1990s, the English training market in China was monopolised by domestic English language schools led by big names such as *New Oriental* and Li Yang's *Crazy English*. Targeting high-end clients, EF did not achieve significant market penetration in China when it first entered the market. Nonetheless, with an influx of foreign language schools spearheaded by EF since the 1990s, "native teacher" quickly become the buzzword for the English training market in China. With the continuous growth of foreign language schools, the ideology of "native speaker superiority" has been explicitly stated and extensively publicised by foreign language schools on their websites, advertisements and promotional materials. Meanwhile, Kirkpatrick (2000) additionally observed a strong preference for "native speaker standard" held by the Chinese MOE and by Chinese professionals in ELT.

In 2007, English First (2007) was entrusted with the task of providing English training services to 100 athletes, 120 Chinese competition judges, 250 translators and interpreters, 300 venue staff, and over 4,000 BOCOG staff. English First (2007) asserted that the aim of its Olympic English training programme was to prepare their clients with "adequate English skills to act more effectively as Olympic hosts." Because EF targeted high-end clients involved with the management of the Beijing Olympics, my Olympic volunteer interviewees did not get access to EF English training.

EF's successful bid for its role as official language training services supplier of the Beijing Olympic Games demonstrates the acceptance of the idea of "native speaker superiority" by the Chinese government and professionals in reference to English language teaching. In the bid, EF defeated major competitors including China's largest private English education provider, *New Oriental,* and another well-known foreign private English education provider, *Wall Street English School.* English First (2007) claimed that its competitive advantages over other language training providers in the bid for the Olympic language training services supplier role derived from its past experience as the sponsor of several major international sporting events and customised training programmes based on its EnglishTown system, which "differentiated EF from other language training providers and has made EF the industry leader." In its advertising discourses, the ideologies of internationalism, professionalism and "native speaker superiority" were used by EF as its unique selling proposition.

The EnglishTown System combines teacher-led classes with online iLab sessions and the chance to practice English socially in its Life Club (English First, 2007). Based on this system, English First (2008a) carried out its Olympic English training programmes, including a 3-month intensive training camp, 3,000 online training courses, 200 English learning workshops, and other interactive activities such as a speech competition and the Life Club during the year after its successful bid. What the EnglishTown system vigorously promotes, as the slogans and images in an illustration on EF's website (see Photograph 7) clearly show, is an English immersion programme enabling Chinese learners to learn and practice communication with, native teachers – who also happen to be White. Furthermore, EF (2011c) asserts on its website: "All our native teachers are qualified to teach English . . . With weekly training we believe our teachers are the best in China." The assumed "superiority" of "native-speaker" over "non-native speaker" in EF's discourse reinforces a narrow definition of pedagogical expertise, one in which a great deal of prestige is given to native-like pronunciation and fluency. In this way, "native speakers" are discursively constructed as "best English teachers" who hold the position of authority. Clamorously advocating the "native speaker superiority," EF (2010b) advertises itself as "the world's leading English expert."

Photograph 7: EF's EnglishTown System. http://www.ef.com.cn/englishfirst/englishstudy/olympics.aspx?lng=en3 (accessed 31 March 2011).

In addition to "native speaker superiority," EF vigorously promotes "the alchemy of English" (Kachru, 1986) in its advertising discourses. The term "alchemy" captures the attitudes to the status and functions of English in EF's discourses well.

In EF's official self-introductory film, competence in English signifies "an added potential for material and social gain and advantage" (Kachru, 1986, p.1).

> 英语打开机会的大门，提供交际的机会，带你走向成功。全球有超过 20 亿的人正在应用英语进行交际。决胜职场、留学海外、轻松开拓新生活。　　　　　(English First, 2008b)
>
> [English is the key to the door of opportunities. English proficiency offers opportunity for intercultural exchanges and leads you to success. There are 2 billion people communicating in English. English helps you win in the job market, study abroad, and create a new life easily.]

The brand effect of the Olympics helped EF rapidly occupy the high-end market and develop into one of the largest and most recognised English training brands in China. Since EF's cooperation with BOCOG, many major companies such as Beijing Daily, Lenovo, CNOOC, Huatai Insurance, Huawei, FedEx, and McDonalds also selected EF as their preferred English training service provider (English First, 2010c). In the year of 2007, EF opened 20 new schools across China at the speed of one school every three weeks. By 2008, EF had established 100 English training schools in more than 50 cities throughout Mainland China, with over 1,000 English teachers and 1,000 administrative personnel (English First, 2010c). The 2008 Beijing Olympic sponsorship became a touchstone for EF's booming business in the highly competitive English training market in China.

Since the Beijing Olympics, EF has more proactively participated in sport sponsorship. In 2009, EF was appointed as the only official language services supplier for the 2010 Guangzhou Asian Games and assisted the Organising Committee (GAGOC) in training over 60,000 volunteers and GAGOC staff in the run-up to that sporting event (English First, 2007). In the same year, the Brazilian government announced that EF was selected as the official provider of language courses for the *Olá, Turista* [*Hello, Tourist*] project to train approximately 80,000 tourism trade professionals for the 2014 World Cup to be hosted in Brazil (English First, 2009b). In 2011, EF was appointed as Official Supplier to the XXII Olympic and XI Paralympic Winter Games in Sochi, Russia, in the category of language training services (English First, 2009a). The company provided English training for almost 70,000 participants, including volunteers and employees of the Sochi 2014 Organising Committee and professionals such as clerks, receptionists, waiters, tour guides, cabdrivers and phone operators (English First, 2011b). This massive English training programme demonstrated "an enormous desire in Russia to learn English – the global lingua franca" (English First, 2011b), according to Philip Hult, the EF CEO. Just like China, as an "expanding circle" country where English has not played an official or institutional role, Russia also desires the Olympic Games and English for the same reason:

as an expression of development, modernity, internationalisation, progress, and prestige. The company's role as Olympic language training services supplier has quickly expanded. After the Sochi Olympic Games, it was also selected as the language training service supplier for the PyeongChang 2018 Winter Olympics and the 2020 Tokyo Olympics[11] and the 2022 Beijing Winter Olympics. EF's sponsorship history has deepened the connection between English and sport. In the era of globalisation, through sponsorship of English training institutions, international sporting events of ever-increasing size and participant numbers have greatly accelerated the global spread of English and further strengthened the dominance of English.

4.2.2 Aifly: The Crazy English method

In contrast to EF, Aifly is a domestic English training provider. Aifly Education & Technology Co. (Aifly) was co-founded in 1997 by Huaqi Information Digital Technology Co., Ltd., a leading Chinese digital product group company, and Li Yang Culture & Education Development Co., Ltd., one of China's most well-known private English training providers. In contrast to EF which used the ideologies of internationalism, professionalism and native speaker superiority as their unique selling proposition, Aifly drew on Li Yang's Crazy English teaching methods and teaching force. University students who constituted the main body of Olympic volunteers were the most important potential clients for many private language schools. Consequently, the realm of official language training sponsorship became a battlefield for Aifly and other bidders. The founding of Aifly itself was directly related to the Beijing Olympic Games. The past experience of Li Yang Crazy English School in delivering mass English lectures helped Aifly stand successful in the bid for the official Olympic language services supplier. In March 2007, Aifly was entrusted by BOCOG with providing English training for 100,000 Olympic volunteers in Beijing and co-host cities at the time of the Games. It was not until the Olympic volunteer recruitment plan was finalised by BOCOG at the end of 2007 that Aifly was able to launch its English training programme. Given the limited time, scale, and complexity of the training programme, Aifly created a multimodal library to support traditional one-on-one interaction, small group classes, intensive Crazy English training camps, online Aiflyworld programmes, television learning programmes, and exchange programmes (Aifly Education Technology Company, 2008). Although providing English language training to an enormous number of Olympic volunteers within

---

11 The Tokyo 2020 Olympic and Paralympic Games have been postponed until 2021 because of the worldwide coronavirus pandemic, although the Games will keep the name "Tokyo 2020."

a year seemed to be "mission impossible" for all English education providers, Aifly (2008) claimed it fulfilled this mission successfully.

Aifly's language training services were based on Li Yang's Crazy English method. Significantly, the patriotic theme ran through the Crazy English method. Such patriotism was in total conformity with the socio-politics of the Beijing Olympics: to foster patriotism among Chinese citizens and promote Chinese culture through English. With proactive support from the Chinese government, Aifly was granted the permission to teach English to gatherings as large as 30,000 at historically and politically significant locations such as the National Stadium, Forbidden City (see Photograph 8), Marco Polo Bridge, and the Great Wall (Woodward, 2008, p. 54). The government also permitted Aifly to broadcast and publish the Crazy English method and its theories in lectures, in books, and online. Aifly's clients included officials in government departments and sport associations, soldiers of the Chinese People's Liberation Army (PLA), Olympic volunteers and employees in enterprises and companies, as well as school and university students. Before the Beijing Olympics, Aifly had been invited to give mass English lectures to

Photograph 8: Crazy English mass lecture in the Forbidden City. Retrieved March 31, 2011 from http://www.ywenglish.com/dispnews.asp?id=17.

78 government departments, committees, bureaus and offices, including the Ministry of Water Resources, *China Daily*, Lenovo, Bank of China, China Mobile, Air China, Beijing Capital International Airport, General Administration of Sport of China, national sports teams and the volunteers of the Eleventh World Championship of Woman's Softball (Aifly Education Technology Company, 2007a).

Ideologically, English was equated with "*the* international language" and always associated with "the power of alchemy" (Kachru, 1986) in Aifly's discourses. A good example can be found in the speech of Nathaniel Jones, CEO of Aifly, given at the press conference announcing the language training services suppliers of the Beijing Olympic Games:

> The Olympic Games are a chance for China to communicate the friendliness and hospitality of Chinese people to the world and learning to communicate that message in *a visitor's native language* will make all the difference. For Aifly this is an unparalleled opportunity and responsibility for us to achieve our goal – *Making English language training accessible, enjoyable, and life changing for everyone in China.*
> (Official Website of the Beijing 2008 Olympic Games, 2007a [italics added])

The speech makes a number of assumptions, including that China's communication to "the world" takes place with visitors whose "native language" is English, and if Chinese learners grasp the visitors' "native language" they obtain "life changing" capital equally accessible for everyone. In addition, the speech implies that English learning experience with Aifly is not a story of hardship but enjoyment. It is not difficult to imagine how such a remark could whip up intense desire for English competence among many Olympic volunteers who aspired to a better life while serving their country. The intersection between patriotism, the acquisition of symbolic capital, and English learning did not play out only in the discourses of official language training services supplier *Aifly* but also in the use of English language learning and teaching (ELLT) celebrities in the Olympic English popularisation campaign. In Section 5, I will examine two of those ELLT celebrities, *Aifly* founder and guru Li Yang and Policeman Liu Wenli.

4.3 Multilingual service suppliers

Beijing's commitment of information services for the 2008 Olympic Games is "inexpensive, rich in content, free of language barrier, and personalized and available for anyone, at anytime and anywhere" (BOCOG, 2002). The Olympic Multilingual Service Centre and the Multilingual Service System developed by CapInfo were the two strategies that Beijing adopted to fulfil its commitment.

4.3.1 The Olympic multilingual service centre

As one of the leading foreign studies universities in China, Beijing Foreign Studies University (BFSU) played a crucial role in the Olympic language services. BFSU and the International Relations Department (IRD) of BOCOG co-launched the Multi-lingual Service Centre (MSC) for the Beijing Olympic Games on 7 July 2008, a month before the opening ceremony. The Centre aimed to provide "barrier-free" interpretation and translation in 44 languages, almost all the languages used by Olympic participants, and was expected to create a legacy for communities: a permanent institution for BFSU to continue to provide language services and to facilitate its multi-language teaching.

The MSC operated five programmes for Olympic language services, with a multilingual switchboard programme plus specific programmes for volunteers, interpreters, language service venue managers, and observers. The staff of the Olympic multilingual service centre were mainly from BFSU, including 500 volunteer students and 300 volunteer teachers as well as paid professionals. The Multilingual Switchboard was an idea borrowed from Sydney 2000 and established specially for IOC and BOCOG officials, Olympic athletes and delegates. It offered telephone interpreting in 44 languages, including around-the-clock lines in 10 languages (English, French, Russian, German, Japanese, Arabic, Spanish, Portuguese, Italian and Korean) and 18-hour lines in 34 languages, even covering some LCTLs such as Icelandic, Sinhala and Hausa. The switchboard helped with on-site language obstacles that could not be handled immediately in competition venues, non-competition venues and service venues. For example, the language services venue manager (LSVM)[12] was given switchboard cards in different languages. If a Russian athlete was in trouble and could not find a Russian-Chinese interpreter on spot, he/she could turn to the LSVM. Using the phone card for the Russian category, the LSVM would dial the operator speaking Russian, and the operator would interpret for the LSVM and the athlete. If the venue staff or interpreters met technical problems, they could also turn to the LSVM for Switchboard help. Around 300 BFSU volunteer teachers together with international students served as operators for the Multilingual Switchboard. During the Olympics (24 July – 28 August 2008) and the Paralympics (30 August – 16 September), the Multilingual Switchboard received and responded to more than 3,000 calls: 2095 for the Olympics, of which 471 were in Spanish (accounting for 22.5%), 438 in Russian (21%), and 424 in French (20.2%); and 852 calls for the Paralympics (Wang and Zhang, 2008).

---

[12] Each venue had a designated person in charge of language services during the Beijing Games.

In the volunteer programme, 2,500 BFSU undergraduate and postgraduate students served as volunteer interpreters and were deployed in 31 competition venues and several non-competition venues (Wang and Zhang, 2008). Of these, 567 acted as Olympic Family Assistants (OFA) – taking care of IOC officials, VIPs and officials from Olympic committees across the world. They were majoring in 13 foreign languages: English, French, German, Spanish, Portuguese, Italian, Russian, Dutch, Polish, Arabic, Japanese, Korean, and Thai. Their clients included IOC president Jacques Rogge, IOC Honorary President Juan Antonio Samaranch, former US president George W. Bush, and former German chancellor Gerhard Schroder, among others. Their jobs included language assistance, transportation arrangement and daily programme coordination. During the Games, those students not only escorted the guests to competition venues, press conferences and diplomatic occasions, but also helped them and their spouses with daily life – airport pick-up and see-off, tour guiding, health care, legal issues, and so forth. Prior to the Games, BFSU had carried out numerous training programmes for its students and the volunteers from other universities and institutions. BFSU students, equipped with good linguistic competence, had been given extended training on culture, history, economy, politics and other pertinent matters. In addition, as one of the training bases for Beijing Olympic volunteers, the University extended English language training programmes to nearly 30,000 volunteers and hosted English language tests for more than 10,000 volunteer drivers. In addition, the University trained 609 volunteers (551 from BFSU) for the International Relations Department of BOCOG (Wang and Zhang, 2008).

The interpreter programme consisted of the Olympic News Service (ONS) team and multilingual emergency response team. ONS was the official news release channel within the organising committee. The first language of ONS was English. The language service office of the International Relations Department of BOCOG undertook the task of translating information and news from English into Chinese and French. In line with the principle of translation into the native language, French translation was undertaken by foreigners and Chinese translation was undertaken by domestic translators. The translation tasks of pre-Games information included: the biographies of athletes, coaches, referees, officials and horses; the information of national and regional Olympic Committees; historical achievements, such as the results of major events in Olympic history; background information on events, competitions and individual sports federations; the agendas of the IOC, BOCOG, sponsors and cultural activities; the agenda of press conferences; and information about venues, registration, accommodation, transportation, and meteorology. The translation tasks of Games-time news included the forecasts of sports events (analysis and forecasts of the main events and of daily competitions before the game or event); the review of sports events (the review of the main events and daily competitions after the game or event); impromptu speeches (of athletes and coaches shortly after the game or event); summaries of the main contents of press conferences; the extended lists of contestants (information on athletes in the main sports events, including their biographies); media reports (important reports related to media interviews); comprehensive news (news articles other than the above-mentioned established types, covering important events related to the Olympic Games); official news of the International Sports Federation; and other Games-time news and updates of some pre-Games information.

The multilingual emergency response team served as the backup force for language services before and during the games. Its main task was to assist the Olympic family before and during the Olympic Games to respond to urgent and unplanned multilingual translation and interpretation needs. The multilingual emergency response team provided professional interpretation services for urgent language needs such as press conferences, meetings and escort events at various venues, including simultaneous interpreting and consecutive interpretation services in English, French, Spanish, Russian, German, Japanese, Korean, Arabic and Chinese. Emergency interpretation tasks were supposed to be reported to the team at least one day in advance, providing relevant information such as time, place, language and number of people. The translation service of the multilingual emergency response team mainly involved English translation of the meeting minutes of the head of delegation, important documents and letters of BOCOG leaders, press conferences and other press releases. In principle, tasks with a translation requirement of more than 3000 words were to be submitted at least three days in advance; tasks with a translation requirement of more than 5000 words at least five days in advance; and tasks with a translation requirement of more than 10000 words at least one week in advance.

Due to the large demand for language services in various venues during the Olympic Games and the difficulty of management, the language services venue manager programme was carried out to assist the management of language services and undertake translation and interpretation services for leaders and VIPs in some venues. BFSU sent 24 graduate students to each venue (whether competition or non-competition) to be deputy language service manager. A deputy language service manager belonged to the respective venue team, which was directly led by the language service manager, and received the appropriate training at the venue. The working time, training and services of the 24 deputy managers varied from venue to venue.

Apart from achievements, there were areas that merited reflection and improvement. For example, English-Chinese interpreters account for a majority of all interpreters in China, and English has often ended being the default language in significant international events held there. Other foreign languages, including French, the other working language of the IOC, were all considered to be 小语种 *Xiao Yu Zhong* [minor languages] in Chinese educational discourses and thus not given due attention in personnel training for multilingual services. Multilingual personnel were obviously insufficient for Beijing 2008, leading to the consequence that some sports events only provided Chinese-English interpretation. Of the 562 BFSU volunteers for the Olympic Family Assistants Programme, 415 were English-Chinese interpreters, while only 54 volunteers had majored in French (Wang and Zhang, 2008). The number of students speaking foreign languages other than English and French was much smaller. Although the Graduate School of Translation and Interpretation (GSTI) of BFSU had already been conducting the multilingual interpretation course for one year, the students of this course still used English when taking part in the OFA Programme at Games time. The tennis venue, for example, was only equipped with Chinese-English interpreters due to insufficient multilingual personnel. That meant all foreign coaches and players had to listen to and answer the questions in English. However, some of them were not proficient in spoken English, which caused communication obstacles. Therefore, Beijing 2008 presented China with the challenge of how to strengthen its multilingual services for increasingly frequent international mega-events in the future.

4.3.2 Technology-supported multilingual services

At the time of previous Olympic bids, intelligent multilingual services, very different from the language services that are completed manually, had not yet appeared. The 2008 Beijing Olympic Games carried out intelligent language translation service via the Multilingual Service System developed by CapInfo Company Ltd. CapInfo is a state-controlled IT company founded in 1998, whose fundamental mission was to provide digital services for major digitalisation projects in Beijing. The company was a sponsor of the bidding campaign for the 2008 Olympic Games in Beijing and the application integrator of the Olympic website, providing network service to BOCOG. CapInfo was committed to provide timely, convenient and comprehensive multilingual information services for the Beijing 2008 Olympic Games through its Multilingual Service System. A total of 150 million yuan was invested by CapInfo, the Ministry of Science and Technology, Beijing Municipal Government, and the Science and Technology Committee of 2008 Olympic Games in five years of research on speech recognition, machine translation, text-to-speech synthesis and application software. The Multilingual Service System implemented intelligent language translation services by integrating speech recognition, machine translation, text-to-speech synthesis and other technologies. Through the system, Olympic information and city information were provided in eight languages including Chinese, English, French, Russian, Spanish, Japanese, Korean, and Arabic. The spectators, registered members and tourists were able to access multilingual services through application terminals such as the official website of the Beijing Olympic Games, call centre, mobile phone, personal computer, and digital information kiosk (see Figure 3). Foreign visitors could use their native language to make a request for information through mobile phones, networks, and other application terminals; any such request would be converted into Chinese to yield the corresponding Chinese information, which would in turn be converted into a result displayed in the native language of the request's initiator. This kind of intelligent multilingual information service did much to solve limitations on the supply of the human and material resources needed by manual translation and it improved the efficiency of multilingual services. The Multilingual Service System became a new mode of technology-supported language services, which provided a new direction for the language services industry.

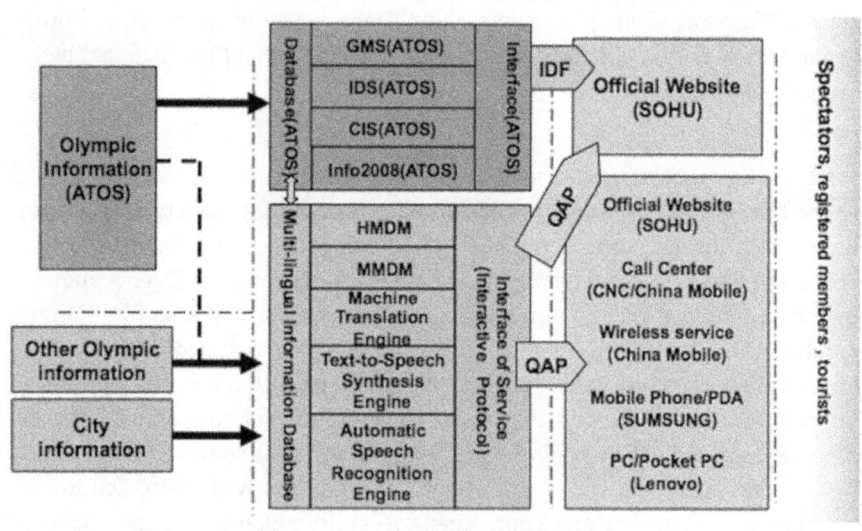

Figure 3: Distribution platforms (voice and/or web and/or terminals in city).

Besides the Multilingual Service System, another technology-supported language service is worth mentioning. Before the Games started, the GSTI of BFSU had attempted to provide remote interpreting for the Beijing Olympics (Wang and Zhang, 2008). GSTI, together with a well-known manufacturer of video communication products, explored the feasibility of converting a video conference system into equipment dedicated to distance interpreting. The new equipment would have been installed in the MSC and connected to several venues during Games time, enabling interpreters to stay in the MSC while interpreting for conferences in different venues. That innovative concept interested BOCOG leaders. When Mr. Liu Qi, President of BOCOG, inspected BFSU, he attended the demonstration given by GSTI on operating the interpretation system and was impressed by it. Although the concept did not become reality due to time pressures, the demonstration was a good attempt and conducive to the trend of technological advancement of interpretation services.

5 English language learning and teaching celebrities

In addition to the official English popularisation campaign, the celebrity effects of officially-endorsed model English learners was another important and influential factor in the spread of English in Beijing and the rest of the country. The way in which people acquire social values and behaviours from celebrities is a concern of mass media research. As a mass-media phenomenon, celebrities are created by the media and dependent on public attention (Fraser and Brown, 2002). On the other hand, celebrities have enormous social influence. In media-saturated countries "celebrity" and "success" have become virtually synonymous; and thus celebrities often become role models "whose values, beliefs, and behaviour are likely to be adopted by others within their sphere of influence" (Fraser and Brown, 2002). Previous studies (e.g., Bandura, 1986; Basil, 1996; Fraser and Brown, 2002) have suggested that identification is a mediator of celebrity effects. Identification is the process of social influence by which individuals adopt the values and behaviours of a celebrity (Fraser and Brown, 2002, p. 187). Bandura (1986) found that a person who identifies with a celebrity is more likely to adopt behaviours that are displayed by the celebrity. In this section, I would like to borrow the concept of "celebrity" to explain how celebrity identification has led Chinese people to identify with English language learning and teaching (ELLT) celebrities' perceived values and copy their language learning behaviours.

Just as proficiency in English was perceived as a cornerstone of further development for the nation, so too was it seen as a valuable asset for individuals. The English fever phenomenon in China gave rise to many celebrities who played an exemplary role in ELLT. In this research, "ELLT celebrities" refers to ordinary Chinese citizens who were made famous because of their English language learning achievements and who became widely recognised English language learning role-models through high exposure in the mass media. When the preparation for the Beijing Olympics was fully under way, two Chinese

English learners were accorded the role of official English language learning role models and given celebrity status by extensive media attention: the founder of *Crazy English* Li Yang and multilingual policeman Liu Wenli. Through the ubiquitous reach of radio, television, print media, and the Internet, both of them had gained legions of followers. Their "success stories" were widely publicised in the media, and were used as a tool to further motivate the Chinese people to learn English. As I will discuss below, both Li Yang and Liu Wenli also benefitted from the Olympic English popularisation campaign, successfully converting the symbolic capital of English into social and economic capital in their lives.

5.1 Crazy English founder Li Yang: English learning as an act of patriotism

Li Yang, founder of *Crazy English*, a popular but highly controversial English learning method in China, had been an ELLT celebrity long before the Beijing Olympic Games. As a successful English learner and English training magnate in China, he probably tops the list of Chinese English language learning celebrities and has exerted tremendous influence on the population's English language learning practices and desires. Born in 1969, Li Yang studied for a mechanical engineering major in Lanzhou University when he was confronted with the need to pass college English tests. That motivated him to develop what he called "a language cracking system" – *Crazy English* (CRIENGLISH, 2007). It took Li Yang only a few years to give up mechanical engineering and turn his radical method into one of China's most well-known brands of English training and a multi-million-yuan business. The Crazy English method relies on three core principles: "speak as loudly as possible," "speak as quickly as possible" and "speak as clearly as possible" (Bolton, 2002, p. 195). In Crazy English lectures, Li Yang encourages students to shout out motivational English expressions loudly, quickly and repeatedly with hand gestures that are supposed to stress the pronunciation. Central to the Crazy English method is the belief that these practices are instrumental in breaking down a common barrier faced by Chinese learners of English, namely, their fear of "losing face," a self-perceived obstacle of Chinese EFL learners in communication with "native English speakers" (Woodward, 2008, p. 28). "This is a new method for Asian people, who are shy and introverted," Li Yang proclaimed, "my method can give people confidence very quickly. I try to simplify English for common people. I became an idol and a celebrity for Chinese young people because of this content" (Independent News, 2009). In many of his public appearances, Li Yang spoke about his own earlier difficulties in mastering English, urging his devotees to follow his example of self-improvement, and exhorting his audiences to engage in mass recitations of English slogans such as "I enjoy losing face!", "Welcome setbacks!", "Relish suffering!" and "Seek success!" (Bolton, 2002, p. 195). In a radio broadcast that is heard at the beginning of a Chinese documentary film about *Crazy English* produced and directed by Zhang Yuan, Li Yang explains his theories of success as follows:

> Hello everybody! My name is Li Yang. This probably sounds strange. People have asked if I've fabricated my hardships. My parents, classmates and teacher will testify that I lacked confidence. I didn't know where to end up. I had an inferiority complex, felt ignorant. I didn't feel capable of anything. I was always telling myself to be determined: I'll start tomorrow! I'll start tomorrow! Everyone wants to succeed, I want to serve as an example. My Crazy English consists of many philosophies of life and success . . . Money is no longer a problem. In one day, I could make 20 to 30 grand, 30 to 40 grand. That time is past. I've moved onto another stage. Once I've accomplished something, it becomes dull. I think I've found a bigger goal. To tell thousands of people about my process of struggle. Everyone needs to do his work well. Because Chinese people lack confidence. Chinese people need to put their noses to the grindstone.
> (Excerpt of Li Yang's self-introduction in English as cited in Bolton, 2002, p. 195)

Styling himself as a conqueror, Li Yang tries to create a connection between his own success story and his audience's desires and ambitions. In this archetypal story of personal achievement he transformed himself from a nobody who "lacked confidence," "had an inferiority complex" and "didn't feel capable of anything" to a somebody for whom "money is no longer a problem" and, indeed, no longer even of significance as he is now pursuing "a bigger goal" beyond monetary gain. In his message, the value of English as an inherent aspect of success and self-transformation is highlighted and taken for granted. In Li Yang's lectures English becomes some sort of magic wand that will allow devotees to achieve successes that would normally be considered out of the reach of average Chinese people, such as "making money internationally." In a lecture to Tsinghua University students, for instance, he told the audience that it is possible to earn 30,000 US dollars per hour teaching English in Japan in companies such as Sony (Bolton, 2002). In Li's discourse, English proficiency is always tied up with accomplishment, self-confidence, self-value, pleasure, money, and success. Through encouraging self-confidence and promising material rewards through its rags-to-riches narrative, the Crazy English method aroused intense English desire among millions of Chinese learners. Despite the rhetoric, the pedagogical success of the method has been questioned, as discussed in Chapter 5 Section 2.3 (see also Woodward, 2008).

Compared with other ELLT celebrities, Li Yang claims that he has "moved to another stage" with regard to the promotion of English learning – one where

English language learning has become not only a means of self-transformation but also a facet of Chinese patriotism. The *Crazy English* philosophy contains "a sharp and focused nationalism" (Bolton, 2002, p. 196), which can be captured in Li Yang's personal motto: "激发爱国主义热情，弘扬民族精神；攻克英语，振兴中华 [stimulating patriotism, advocating national spirits, conquering English, revitalizing China]" (Wikipedia, 2009). Li Yang believes that English learning is a most important step to raise China to the position of a global power. Li's books, which sell in the millions across China, always contain patriotic slogans (see Photograph 9) such as "Conquer English to make China stronger!" "Help 300 million Chinese speak good English" and "Make the voice of China be widely heard throughout the world" (Independent News, 2009). "I want [the Chinese] to use English and spread Chinese as a world language . . . Mastering English and therefore enriching our country is an act of patriotism" (Yamane, 2005 cited in Woodward, 2008, p. 34).

Photograph 9: Poster for Li Yang Crazy English. Retrieved on March 31, 2011 from http://www.bjcrazyenglish.com/.

The ideology of the Crazy English philosophy that advocates learning English for national benefits is rooted in the slogan of 洋务运动 *yangwu yundong* [the Self Strengthening Movement] which had been gradually launched between 1861 to 1894 in China: "师夷长技以制夷 *Shiyi changji yi zhiyi* [learning advanced technologies from Western barbarians in order to fight against them]." The idea became the major source of the campaign of learning from the West during the late Qing dynasty. Li alludes to this slogan in his own lectures, in which he often urges students to go abroad to learn from the West and bring that knowledge and experience back to serve China. Li Yang's *Crazy English* philosophy fits in neatly with the Confucian dichotomy of learning functions: Western learning for 用 *yong* [external utility] and Chinese learning for 体 *ti* [internal essence]. The principle of "中学为体；西学为用 *zhongxue wei ti; xixue wei yong* [Chinese learning for essence; Western learning for utility]" was based on the belief that Western learning (this, of course, includes foreign languages, predominantly English) could be imported for practical purposes without their cultural essence being involved, hence Chinese cultural essence could be kept intact by Chinese learning (Gao, 2009, p. 63).

Li Yang's *Crazy English* philosophy fits well with the socio-politics of the Beijing Olympics and propelled him to enormous prominence in the Games. In 2005, the General Administration of Sport of China appointed Li Yang as "General Coach of National Team Athletes." In the next year, he was appointed as "Olympic Ambassador" as well as the "General Coach of 1.5 million Olympics Volunteers" by BOCOG and as an expert consultant by the Olympic training working group of the Beijing Municipal Government. As the general coach of Olympic volunteers and founder of the *Crazy English* movement, Li Yang was described as a patriotic teacher. In one of Li's mass English lectures before the Olympics, over 20,000 college students were exhilarated in reciting repeatedly after him, "I will make my country proud!" (Aifly Education Technology Company, 2007b). Through active cooperation with the Beijing Olympic organisers, Li Yang's status as an ELLT celebrity was increasingly elevated, and his philosophy in English language teaching gained legitimacy. Rising from ordinary person to social hero, he became the fulfilment of personal self-transformation through English. For millions of Beijingers and Chinese who identified with Li Yang, learning English was a patriotic act for the success of the 2008 Olympics and the development of the Chinese nation. Li Yang's celebrity effect not only contributed to the swift expansion of his own English teaching business, but also heightened the symbolic meaning of English in China as a valuable asset, which consequently aroused a growing desire for English.

5.2 Multilingual policeman Liu Wenli: English learning as empowerment

In contrast to Li Yang, who had long been a celebrity in China before the Beijing Olympics, police officer Liu Wenli, who taught himself 13 foreign languages in preparation for the Games, was more of an instant English learning celebrity whose fame was directly embedded in China's Olympic English fever. Born in 1967, Liu Wenli started to learn English in the 1990s when he was a support service worker in a Beijing suburban police station. In 1995, the United Nations convened the Fourth World Conference on Women in Beijing. Liu Wenli worked on the front line of public security during the conference. A failed cross-cultural encounter motivated him to learn English and become "the first English speaking policeman" (Li, 2008). As an adult English learner with only high-school education, Liu Wenli taught himself English through rote-memorising English words and expressions, practising English with other Chinese learners in English corners, and striking up conversations with every foreigner he met on the streets (Li, 2008). Liu believes that "repetition" is the best method of foreign language learning: "There is no smarter way than repetition in language study. I've been doing just that for the past 13 years" (Cao, 2008).

Photograph 10: The banner reads: "Be devoted to public welfare and the Olympics; Set up a fine model of learning English." Retrieved on March 20, 2010 from http://bjliuwenli.blog.sohu.com.

Beijing's successful Olympic bid in 2001 set off an upsurge of English learning in various sectors in the capital city of China. After six years of assiduous study, Liu's English proficiency was greatly improved. In 2001, Beijing Municipal Public Security Bureau held an oral English contest to promote English learning. Liu Wenli, who was still a support service worker in a Beijing suburban police station at that time, won the contest. Soon after this, Liu was set up as an official model of English learning (see Photograph 10) and was dispatched to an important tourist destination in downtown Beijing in 2002. Liu described himself in a television interview as a "窗口岗位的窗口警察 [a model policeman at a model service post]" whose duty was to present Beijing's new image rather than catch criminals (BTV, 2008).

The promotion made Liu Wenli realise the material and symbolic value of foreign language learning in China in the context of the Beijing Olympics. Hence, Liu continued to learn French, German and another ten foreign languages at various levels. Famous for his language abilities, Policeman Liu was selected by BOCOG as a two-time Olympic torchbearer in the 2004 Athens Olympic torch relay and the 2008 Beijing Olympic torch relay. The success story of Policeman Liu was widely publicised on TV, radio and newspaper, by a range of foreign and domestic media that included the BBC, CNN, Reuters, NHK, CCTV, BTV, China Radio International, China Daily and the People's Daily. Many mainstream Internet media organs, like Sina, Sohu, 163.com and CCTV.com, created official blogs for Policeman Liu. In some media reports, Liu was discursively constructed as a civilian hero, someone known for great acts of courage or outstanding accomplishments with great moral virtue: for example, "linguist police officer," "English expert," "a man of self-discipline and perseverance."

Although Policeman Liu had not accumulated wealth in the form of an English teaching empire as Li Yang had, he was very conscious of the symbolic capital of English and his own celebrity status in China's English training market. In an interview, Liu told *Wuhan Evening Newspaper* (Li, 2008) that there were enormous business opportunities available to him.

记者：会 13 国外语，有没有给您带来什么物质上的收益？

[Reporter: Has grasping 13 foreign languages brought you any material benefits?]

刘文立： 目前还没有。我出名以后，曾经有一个英语学习机厂家找我，要我给他们代言，我只要对着镜头说一句："我刘文立英语这么好，多亏了某某学习机。"十几万就到手了，不过我拒绝了，因为我现在还是警察，不能做这事。可是再过 6 年，我就可以搞商业开发了。

[Liu Wenli: No, it hasn't. After I became famous, I was invited to be the spokesman of an English-learning electronic product. All that I was required to say for the payment of tens of thousands of yuan was one line: "Thanks to xxx English-learning machine, I, Liu Wenli, am excellent in English." Even so, I declined the invitation, because I am a police officer at present. I am not allowed to do so. In six years' time, I will be able to do business in English.]

记者：为什么？

[Reporter: Why?]

刘文立：6 年后我 48 岁，工龄满 30 年，可以退休。那时，我可以搞英语俱乐部、办培训班，当代言人、写书，一句话，我身上有巨大商机！

[Liu Wenli: I will turn 48 in 6 years. By that time, I may retire after 30 years of service. At that time, I will open English clubs and English training classes and be a celebrity spokesman. In a word, there are enormous business opportunities in me!]

Propelled by the unprecedented Olympic English fever, policeman Liu successfully transferred the linguistic capital of English into social, economic and other symbolic capital against the backdrop of the Beijing Olympic Games. In Liu's words, English and the Olympics have changed his life (Li, 2008). After Beijing won its bid to host the Olympics, he began to teach English to residents in his community. Liu Shuying is one of them: "He is a model for us to follow. To better help foreign guests, everybody is trying to learn English. Liu's diligence has inspired us. Everybody is working hard now" (Cao, 2008). Chen Guoying ran a bicycle shop in Liu Wenli's community: "Liu helped me make a bilingual signboard. That is the first one in the community. Of course, more shops have followed suit for Olympic guests' convenience" (Cao, 2008). Through extensive media publicity, Liu came to have a legion of followers and fans in China. Many Chinese adult EFL learners who had never received higher education, but desired for a better life, closely identified with him and regarded him as a role model who should be followed and emulated.

In addition to the Olympic foreign language popularisation campaign, the effect of officially endorsed ELLT celebrities was another important and influential factor in the spread of English in Beijing and the rest of the country. These two ELLT celebrities, the founder of *Crazy English* Li Yang and multilingual policeman Liu Wenli, were accorded the role of official English language learning role models and given celebrity status by extensive media attention. Through identification, they exerted great influence on Chinese learning English as an act of patriotism and self-transformation. Bourdieu (1991, p. 19) contends that the distribution of linguistic capital is related in specific ways to the distribution of other forms of capital (social, economic, cultural, and symbolic), which define the location of an individual within the social space. The highly regarded symbolic value of English is not purely imposed from the outside but, more often than not, constructed, reinforced and circulated internally in modern Chinese society. ELLT celebrities like Li Yang and Liu Wenli are all products of the contemporary Chinese society in which English is highly valued and capitalised. ELLT celebrities, who have a vested interest in China's English training market, are powerful in magnifying the linguistic capital of English and the spread of the desire for English in Chinese society. To date, very little research has explored the role of celebrities in promoting language ideologies among mass audiences, which ultimately shape behaviour (Fraser and Brown, 2002). Braudy (1986) suggests that we have ignored the importance of celebrities in shaping the values of society. In researching the prominent phenomenon of English fever in Expanding Circle countries such as China, we need a better understanding of how those marginalised economically or socially, and those who feel powerless, identify with ELLT celebrities and whether they model their English learning values and behaviours on them.

6 Summary

In countries with centralised systems such as China, decisions regarding language policies are made by central authorities and imposed by political entities in a top-down manner, usually with limited resistance as most local governments, schools and teachers comply. These policies are then reinforced by teaching practices, testing systems, and linguistic landscape. In the enactment and implementation of language policies, individuals or groups are subordinate to national interests and their linguistic choices are not free, but rather made available between predefined alternatives and their rights are, in fact, constrained (Tollefson, 1991). The chapter makes explicit BOCOG's (which represents the central Chinese government's) perception of foreign language proficiency (predominantly English) as a key factor contributing to the success of the 2008 Olympic Games, and details the multiple language planning strategies adopted by the Organising Committee of the BSFLP to improve the language environment of Beijing for the hosting of the Olympic Games. Additionally, it depicts the functioning of the BSFLP, BETS, private language training providers, technology-supported language services and English language learning and teaching celebrities in achieving the government's language planning goals. Foreign language policies (with English popularisation at the centre) in service to the Beijing Olympic Games were formulated in a top-down manner in a centralised system. That is, the authority organised relevant government agencies (for example, the Foreign Affairs Office of the Beijing Municipal People's Government) and a consulting group (composed of 35 domestic and international foreign language educationists) in policy making, but did not take into account the opinions and needs of grassroots sectors of the society, especially companies, organisations and institutions with foreign language requirements for their employees. Based on empirical data, I identify several ideological assumptions in official discourses – namely, native-speakerism, the alchemy of English, English as life-changing capital, English learning for *yong* (external utility), English learning as an act of patriotism, and the imagined community of native-speaker interlocutors – that misrepresent the changing sociolinguistic realities of the users of English as an international language. The status and value ascribed to English in the Olympic foreign language popularisation campaign reflects the general trend of China's English language education policies at the beginning of the 21st century. ELT was promoted as something that was "natural, neutral, and beneficial," with the purpose of sustaining economic development and enhancing international competitiveness. In official discourses, English proficiency was described as a catalyst for processes of modernisation, a supposed vehicle of internationalisation, and an effective guarantee for a successful Olympic Games, which eventually would benefit all levels of Chinese society. Chinese people, especially Beijing citizens, were urged to achieve personal success and contribute to the development of the host city as well as the country by learning English. Besides the existing educational, occupational, economic and symbolic values attached to English, learning English became virtually an act of patriotism in the Beijing Olympic context. In the official discourses, English had been used as a key in constructing the identity of China as a harmoniously developing modern nation-state, Beijing as an international Olympic city, and Chinese learners as patriotic global citizens. By underscoring the necessity of English education for cultivating patriotism and promoting Chinese culture, the Chinese government hoped to maintain a neutral and instrumentalist perspective in relation to English and took the learning and teaching of English as opportunities for Chinese learners to consolidate their native cultural identity. It can be argued that propaganda and ideologies about loyalty, patriotism, group membership and collective identity are strategies used by the state to maintain its control and promote its social, political and economic agendas. However, these official discourses prevailing in the Olympic foreign language popularisation campaign need to be critically examined and not assumed to be absolute truths. Fairclough (1989) asserts that discourse plays a particularly important role in exercising ideological control by consent. English education policies in China are the outcome of the state's allocation of the status and functions of English in accordance with its political and economic interests, and the standard and purpose of ELT is also manipulated by the state and its agencies to meet the needs of national development. It is crucial to note that the value and meaning of English in linguistic markets worldwide is not fixed and universal. The English ideologies embedded in these discourses should be best understood as a local, social and political construction in the Beijing Olympic context. In Chapter 5 I will discuss how and why English learning may not be rewarding to all Chinese learners. The effects of various language service measures and the assessment of Beijing's language environment will also be discussed in more detail in the following Chapter.

Chapter 5
Assessing Beijing's foreign language environment

Given the enormous size of the Olympic Games and the complexity of its participating members and events, any attempt at language management poses a very serious challenge. An important factor supporting China's language management in the Games is the strong authority of the central government in implementing its policy. In order to improve the overall foreign language level of Beijing citizens and enhance Beijing's international image in the preparation for the 2008 Olympic Games, the Organising Committee for the BSFLP carried out a series of activities in the host city, based on the *Action Plan for the Beijing Speaks Foreign Languages Programme (2003–2008)*. The national pride in hosting the Olympic Games greatly aroused the enthusiasm of Beijing citizens to learn and speak foreign languages. After five years of preparation, the Office of the Leading Group on Foreign Affairs of the Beijing Municipal Party Committee of the CPC, the Foreign Affairs Office of Beijing Municipal Government, and the Organising Committee of BSFLP commissioned the Datasea Market Research Company to conduct an assessment of Beijing's foreign language environment. On 1 August 2008, a week before the opening ceremony of the Beijing Olympic Games, the *Follow-up Survey and Analytical Report on Foreign Language Environment of Beijing* (Office of the Leading Group on Foreign Affairs of the Beijing Municipal Party Committee of the CPC et al. 2008) was officially released. In this chapter, I comment on 'Beijing's foreign language environment' in the run-up to the Beijing Olympic Games based on this official report and my research data.

1 Assessing foreign language speaking population in Beijing

1.1 The total number of foreign language speaking population in Beijing

Achieving a foreign language speaking population of 5 million in Beijing was the focus of the work of the BSFLP by 2008. The Organising Committee of BSFLP asserted that the number of people capable of speaking a foreign language had risen from 3.12 million in 2002 to 5.5 million in 2008 (Deng, 2009), accomplishing the target with regard to the construction of Beijing's "international language environment" in the 2003–2008 BSFLP *Action Plan*. However, the size of the foreign language speaking population actually depends on how it is defined. In the *Follow-up Survey and Analytical Report on Foreign Language Environment of Beijing* (Office of the Leading Group on Foreign Affairs of the Beijing Municipal Party Committee of the CPC et al. 2008), 'foreign language speaking population' is defined as those who can at least understand some simple foreign language articles, and those who can undertake simple communication in a foreign language. The report explains that the 'foreign language speaking population' includes people who have junior high school education and above and who have passed a certain foreign language proficiency test or achieved at least the low to intermediate level of a foreign language in self-assessment.[13] The permanent population of Beijing was 15.81 million in 2007 (Beijing Municipal Bureau of Statistics, 2007). According to the official definition, the size of Beijing's foreign language speaking population at the end of 2007 was 5.34 million, accounting for 35% of the permanent population, a marked increase of 12.4% over the corresponding total in 2002 (see Figure 4). Among them, there were 4.546 million people over 18 years old and 988,000 under 18 years old. The report explained that the size of the foreign language speaking population under 18 years old was estimated by summing the total number of students in secondary vocational schools, technical schools, general secondary schools, junior high schools, senior high schools and some primary schools as listed in *The Statistics of Students with Various Academic Degrees in the 2006 School Year*. Specifically, there were 77,000 students in senior vocational school, 52,000 in technical schools, 110,000 in technical secondary schools, 11,000 in adult secondary schools, 288,000 in junior high schools, and 259,000 in senior high schools, as well as 189,000 of the city's primary school students. The report claimed two fifths of primary school students were included in Beijing's foreign language population, as the foreign language level of primary school students had greatly improved in recent years. Obviously, the official definition and calculation of 'foreign language speaking population' is problematic. Given that China's examination-oriented education has long been criticised for producing 'deaf-mute English learners,' it is too optimistic to think that anyone who has junior high school education (let alone primary school education) or passed a certain foreign language proficiency test can be automatically recognised as a 'foreign language speaker' and thereby able to carry out effective intercultural communication in a foreign language.

---

13 In the official report, the self-assessment of foreign language proficiency is divided into four levels on the Likert scale: low, low to intermediate, intermediate to high, and advanced. The self-assessment of foreign language ability takes reading ability as the core and comprehensively evaluates listening, speaking, reading and writing ability.

Figure 4: Changes in the percentage of 'foreign language speaking population' in Beijing from 2002 to 2007.

1.2 Different levels of foreign language speaking population in Beijing

The Organising Committee of BSFLP divided Beijing's English speaking population into low-intermediate, intermediate-high and advanced levels. Among Beijing's 5,534,000 foreign language speaking population in 2007, there were 2,983,000 people who were at the low-intermediate foreign language level, 1,710,000 at the intermediate-high level, and 841,000 at the advanced level, accounting for 53.9%, 30.9% and 15.2% respectively (see Figure 5). A careful analysis of the calculation of these figures can reveal many problems. For example, the report claims there were 530,000 low-intermediate foreign language speakers who were under 18 years old. This figure was calculated by adding up the number of students in junior high schools and technical schools in 2007. Likewise, the number of intermediate-high level foreign language speakers under 18 years old was 458,000, which was obtained by adding up the number of students in high schools, vocational schools and technical secondary schools in 2007. This calculation method automatically links a person's foreign language proficiency with his or her academic qualification and ignores individual differences in foreign language ability, and therefore lacks validity.

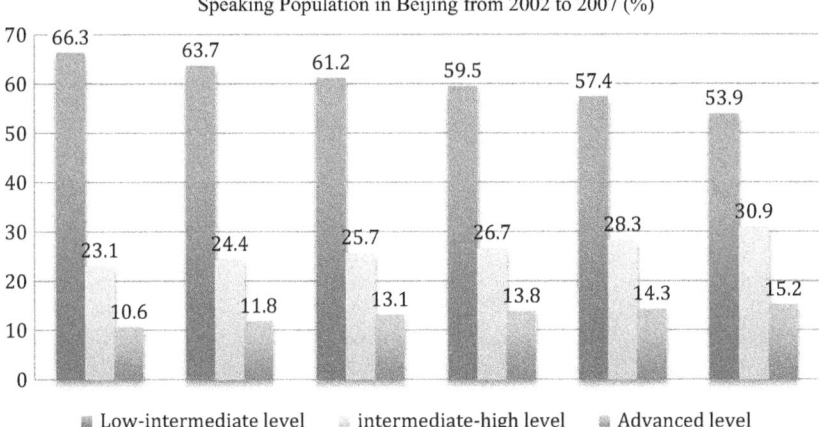

Figure 5: Changes in the proportion of different levels of officially recognised 'foreign language speaking population' in Beijing from 2002 to 2007.

1.3 Language distribution of foreign language speaking population in Beijing

According to the official report (Office of the Leading Group on Foreign Affairs of the Beijing Municipal Party Committee of the CPC et al. 2008), 74.2% of Beijing's officially recognised foreign language speaking population had learned only one foreign language in their life, and 90.5% of this group had learned English. English was the most widely studied language in Beijing before the Games. Of Beijing's English learners over 18 years old, 18.7% had taken a domestic or international standardised English examination. Among them, 10.8% had passed College English Test band four (CET-4) and 3.1% passed College English Test band six (CET-6). The majority of the people who had passed CET-6 were urban residents aged 18–34 who had college or higher education. In addition, 21.2% had studied Russian. Russian learners were mainly middle-aged and elderly people who generally had a low level of mastery and application of the language. Japanese was the most preferred second foreign language. In addition, there were also learners of other foreign languages such as French, Korean, German and Spanish in Beijing. These languages were categorised as 'minor languages' or less commonly taught languages (LCTLs) in China.

Although there was increased attention to teaching LOTE in this programme, the emphasis on teaching English to Beijing citizens had been intensified. The official view was that having a significant number of competent users of English in a whole range of professions, businesses, workplaces and enterprises was essential for the success of the Beijing Olympic Games and the sustained development of the country in this age of globalisation. As an active organiser and participant in the Olympic English popularisation campaign, Sun Lin,[14] manager of language services for the marathon contest, confirmed in my interview that the Chinese government had made its largest investment in popularising English rather than any other language. According to Sun, English enjoyed such a high status in China that the term "foreign language" had usually become equated with "English" in public discourses:

> Sun Lin: (. . .) 嗯，大部分［情况下］比如说，我说的就是提高公众的外语水平，基本上就是指英语。在社区里头也是，然后包括我们的服务人员，比如说交通服务人员啊、银行服务人员啊，基本上都是［学习］英语的。其他的语种的比较少。像我吧，因为外语吧，英语大家还有一些底子，要是说法语呀、西班牙语呀、用的机会不是特别多，而且底子也不好。
>
> [Sun Lin: (. . .) In most cases, for example, erm, when I say "improve public foreign language level", I refer to English. It's the same when I talk about foreign language learning of community residents and people in service sectors, erm, such as personnel in transportation sectors and banks, I mean learning English most of the time. In terms of foreign language, many Chinese learners like me have certain grounding in English. We don't have many opportunities to use [other foreign languages such as] French and Spanish. In addition, we have poor knowledge about those languages. (19-09-2008)]

The size of the officially identified foreign language speaking population is not enough to prove that Beijing has achieved an "international language environment." An adequate explanation of the "international language environment" which the Beijing authority claimed they had successfully constructed for the 2008 Olympic Games should take into consideration the sociolinguistic structure of long-term foreign residents and the Olympic visitors. In 2008, the number of foreigners staying in Beijing for longer than six months was 110,000 and most of those did not hail from an English speaking country but from South Korea (Xu, 2009). This number of long-term foreign residents represents 0.6% of Beijing's total population. It is argued that the number of foreigners residing in a city is an important index when judging the international level of a city (Xu, 2009). Compared to other major metropolitan cities such as London and New York, where foreigners accounted for 30% and 15.6% of the population respectively (Xu, 2009), the international component of Beijing's population is low. The *Beijing Statistical Yearbook 2009* (Beijing Municipal Bureau of Statistics, 2009) showed that there were 31,712 registered international students living in

---

14 Pseudonyms are used for all participating individuals and institutions throughout this dissertation.

Beijing in 2008. Their major source countries were Japan and South Korea, followed by the United States.

International tourists to Beijing also affect the "international language environment" of the city. According to Beijing Municipal Bureau of Statistics (2008), more than 3.8 million foreign tourists visited Beijing in 2007. These tourists came from diverse linguistic backgrounds, among which two neighbouring Asian countries, Japan and Korea, accounted for one fourth of the total number. In 2008, the Beijing Olympics did not benefit the host city's international tourism economy. According to the statistics released by Beijing Municipal Tourism Bureau (2008), Beijing received 356,000 overseas tourists in August 2008, a drop of 4.1 % compared with the same period in the prior year. During the month (July) prior to the Games' commencement, international travel to Beijing plummeted to 30% less than the previous year. In the month (September) after the Games, the tourism slump continued with international travel over 20% down. Table 4 shows the top ten tourist source countries to Beijing in August 2008. Compared with the same period in the previous year the number of tourists from four inner-circle English speaking countries (US, UK Australia and Canada) showed a significant increase in August 2008, accounting for 33.58% of the total number of inbound tourists. In contrast, the number of tourists from the six top non-English speaking tourist source countries (Japan, South Korea, Russia, Germany, France and Spain) dropped at varying degrees. In addition to the impact of visa restrictions during the Games, one possible

Table 4: Top ten tourist source countries to Beijing in August 2008.

Country of Origin	National Language	Number	Increased by %
Total foreign tourists		356,000	−4.1
1. United States	**English**	**68,304**	**37.76**
2. Japan	Japanese	40,652	−27.28
3. United Kingdom	**English**	**25,015**	**44.93**
4. South Korea	Korean	18,941	−58.92
5. Russia	Russian	17,067	−25.00
6. Germany	German	15,532	−5.56
7. France	French	14,216	−17.20
8. Australia	**English**	**14,912**	**37.68**
9. Canada	**English, French**	**11,324**	**19.10**
10. Spain	Spanish	6,837	−48.32

explanation is that the non-English speakers might have stayed away because they felt they were excluded from the Olympics. Even though the total number of non-English speaking tourists declined during the Games, it cannot be ignored that the Olympic visitors still came from diverse linguistic backgrounds. Ignoring this linguistically diverse background of international visitors in the foreign language popularisation campaign and granting English a superior status over other languages might have created various linguistic barriers. In fact, the Beijing Olympic organisers (Official Website of the Beijing 2008 Olympic Games, 2007) confirmed that Beijing would be short of advanced English speakers, multilingual speakers and speakers of foreign languages other than English.

The conception that equates "English" with "foreign language" or "international language" in Chinese discourses, as Sun Lin stated in Section 1.3, underlies the official definition of Beijing's foreign language speaking population and international language environment. The conception also explains the supremacy of English in China's foreign language education policy and in the Olympic popularisation campaign. Accordingly, Beijing's international language environment was one that was favourable to English speakers but not to speakers of LOTE. In Kubota's (2002) study on the impact of globalisation on foreign language education in Japan, she points out that the equation of "foreign language" with "English" reflects a discourse that "legitimates the global spread of English as natural, neutral and beneficial (Pennycook, 1994)" and a discourse of "colonialism that elevates English into the status of a 'marvellous tongue' (Pennycook, 1998)" (p. 20). The equation of English with foreign language leads to the assumption that English is the only viable language of choice for "Expanding Circle" countries like China to communicate to the linguistically and culturally diverse global community, helping to sustain the continued dominance of English in the world today. Moreover, ascribing English with superiority over other languages may make people lose sight of the linguistic and cultural diversity in local and global communities. Even though English is the dominant language of international tourism and communication, a favourable international language environment should accommodate the cultural and linguistic diversity that characterises the local and global context China is situated within.

2 Assessing Olympic foreign language popularisation

2.1 Beijing citizens' motivations towards foreign language learning

Studying motivation in language learning is well-established in the West from social-psychological perspectives (e.g., Brophy, 1999; Dörnyei 2005; Dörnyei and

Ushioda, 2009; Eccles and Wigfield, 2002; Gardner, 1985). In this book, I draw on Ryan and Deci's (2000) classification of intrinsic and extrinsic motivations to understand Beijing citizens' reasons and needs for studying a foreign language. An intrinsically motivated behaviour is activated and sustained for its own sake (e.g., joy, fun and interest in the activity itself) while an extrinsically motivated one is activated and sustained for 'separable' outcomes. According to the survey conducted by the Datasea Market Research Company in the official report (Office of the Leading Group on Foreign Affairs of the Beijing Municipal Party Committee of the CPC et al. 2008), even though 75.9% of respondents were motivated to learn a foreign language, only 7.7% claimed foreign languages were important in their work and life, and 5.1% were intrinsically motivated to learn foreign languages out of interest (see Figure 6). The majority of respondents said they were extrinsically motivated to learn foreign languages: 37.9% hoped to learn a foreign language because they wanted to contribute to the Beijing Olympic Games, and 25.5% to learn a foreign language for its utility value in enrolment and employment in China's formal linguistic market. However, 23.8% of respondents still claimed they were not motivated to learn any foreign language. Amongst that category, 18.8% felt foreign languages were no use to them at all, and 5% were forced to learn foreign languages for various reasons.

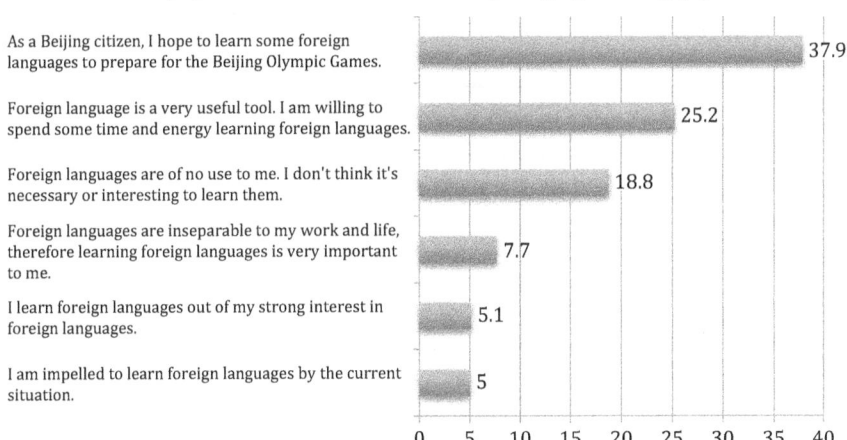

Figure 6: Beijing citizens' attitudes towards foreign language learning.

2.2 Outcomes of the Beijing speaks foreign language programme

In order to popularise and improve Beijing citizens' foreign language proficiency in the preparation for the Olympic Games, the Organising Committee for BSFLP organised a series of foreign language popularisation activities for Beijing citizens, such as an English TV Competition, English Speech Competition, Singing Foreign Songs TV Contest, and a series of lectures at Wangfujing Foreign Language Bookstore (see Table 5). According to the report (Office of the Leading Group on Foreign Affairs of the Beijing Municipal Party Committee of the CPC et al. 2008), 63.4% of the citizens heard about these activities. Despite the great efforts made to involve Beijing citizens in various foreign language learning activities, the willingness of the citizens to participate in those activities was not strong (see Figure 7). Apart from the 42.8% of respondents who showed interest in Chinese singing foreign songs contests, less than 20% were interested in participating in any other foreign language activities organised by the BSFLP. During the lead-up to the Olympics, the BSFLP's actions included the following:

Table 5: Foreign language popularisation activities of the BSFLP.

1	Held a series of "Greetings to the World" multilingual activities on campus – Students' French competition in Beijing
2	Held verification meetings on "English Translation of Menus in Beijing's Catering Industry"
3	Organised a series of public lectures on the BETS once a month in Beijing's universities
4	Organised a series of public lectures on "Learn Foreign Languages to Welcome the Olympic Games" once a month for Beijing citizens
5	Distributed free (trial) English newspaper *English lovers* to community residents
6	English speaking volunteers offered foreign language (English) classes to taxi drivers during the 500-day countdown to the Olympic Games
7	Organised a series of public lectures on the BSFLP for Beijing citizens once a month in bookstores
8	Established a working group on public English signs and regularly inspected English road signs
9	Carried out the "Let Youth Light up the Five Rings, Voluntarily Dedicate to the Olympic Games" activity in Wangfujing pedestrian street to recruit volunteers from Beijing municipal government agencies
10	Offered training courses on English signs to volunteers

Table 5 (continued)

11	Held the 2007 Amway – Beijing Citizens' Foreign Language Activities Week in Chaoyang Park
12	Jointly held the "I am hero" English Competition with Beijing TV station
13	Enrolled nearly 10,000 middle school students in "the Sixth Beijing Middle School Students' English Speech Contest"
14	Organised all trades, districts and counties to carry out inspection and correction of English signs in public places throughout the city
15	Launched a multilingual greetings online learning activity for citizens during the 400-day countdown to the Olympic Games
16	Launched a large-scale bilingual theme activity of "celebrating the anniversary of the Olympic Games, striving to be a bilingual journalist for the Olympic Games"
17	Organised middle school students throughout the city to participate in the finals of the "6th New Oriental Cup Middle School Students English Speech Competition" in Beijing
18	Organised 18 districts and counties in the city to participate in the activities of the "Third Beijing Family English Competition"
19	Held the "Sixth Beijing Citizens' Foreign Language Garden Fair" in Beijing Labour People's Cultural Palace. Nearly 80,000 citizens, dozens of foreign language education institutions and domestic and foreign media participated in the activity. At the same time, the "2007 World Language Challenge Competition" was successfully launched and "Excellent foreign language speaking communities" were selected in the garden fair.

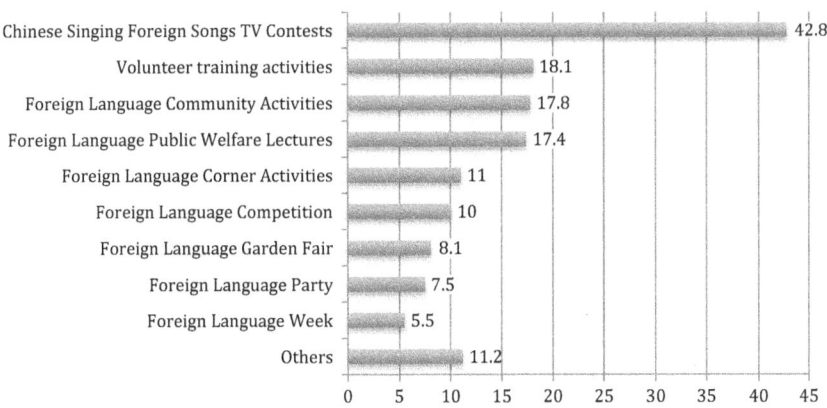

Figure 7: Interest in various foreign language popularisation activities.

2.3 Outcomes of Olympic foreign language training

According to the official report (Office of the Leading Group on Foreign Affairs of the Beijing Municipal Party Committee of the CPC et al. 2008), 33.1% of Beijing citizens had taken part in foreign language learning activities in 2007, mainly through self-studying of textbooks, or participating in foreign language learning activities at workplaces or in social organisations. Compared with 2006, the focus of foreign language learning continued to shift from listening to speaking ability. The main difficulties for Beijing citizens to learn a foreign language were lack of language environment and insufficient time, such that many had problems in persisting with their foreign language learning. Further, 50.6% of the respondents who had low foreign language proficiency said they had difficulties in learning the rudiments of a foreign language or did not know appropriate learning methods.

Participating in the Olympics gave many Chinese people, especially those who enthusiastically took part in the preparation and holding of the Olympic Games, a first experience of using English in real intercultural interactions. Olympic volunteer driver Hua Shuo admitted in my interview that his desire to practise English with foreigners was his main motivation to serve as an Olympic volunteer. However, for many Beijing citizens involved in the preparation for the Olympic Games, undergoing official English training did not guarantee their much-desired English proficiency and intercultural communicative competence. Taking English training of Olympic volunteers as an example, despite Aifly's assertion that it had fulfilled the job to train 100,000 Olympic volunteers, the actual participation rate and results were not as good as declared. In many cases, certificates of CET-4 and CET-6 were treated as sufficient evidence of English proficiency when recruiting Olympic volunteers, and consequently only those who held key management positions were assigned to participate in official English training. Of the 28 interview participants who were Olympic volunteers, only two attended English training from Aifly for the Olympic Games. Neither of those two interviewees considered Aifly's English training effective.

Zhao Chan, a media service volunteer from Tsinghua University, expressed his dissatisfaction with the outcomes of Aifly's training. Based on his own experience, Zhao found that his English proficiency had not improved by taking a Crazy English mass lecture of a few hours, the teaching method that Aifly had adopted for training Olympic volunteers and personnel in service sectors. A similar sense of dissatisfaction was expressed by Olympic volunteer Chen Zheng, a coordinating assistant of outdoor cultural and artistic activities in the big event group of the International Youth Camp, who attended a seven-day

Aifly immersion training camp before the Games with another 1,000 volunteers who were mainly selected from various Beijing universities. During the seven days of intensive English training, Chen Zheng and other camp members were required to undertake a great deal of English pronunciation (with gestures) and reciting drills. She said that the training made her aware of her "shortcomings" in English pronunciation and lack of reciting practice, but she denied that her English had truly improved after the training.

Zhang Jie: 你觉得参加这个英语培训营对你的英语有很大提高吗？

[Zhang Jie: Do you think your English proficiency has been greatly improved after attending this English training camp?]

Chen Zheng: 显然没有。但是就是［通过此次培训］确实能让自己认识到我们在学英语的时候有什么样的不足，以后注意。但是说在七天里面有很大的提高也不太现实。

[Chen Zheng: Certainly not. [Through the training] I did recognise my shortcomings in learning English. [I will] pay attention to them afterwards. However, it is not realistic to say my English has been greatly improved within seven days.]

Zhang Jie: 你通过培训看到了哪些学习方面的不足？

[Zhang Jie: What are the shortcomings that you recognised through the training?]

Chen Zheng: 主要就是发音上的一些问题。还有就是以前我在学英语的过程中不太背东西。然后他就就每天让我们背、背、背，每天背完这个背那个，一天到晚就是背，他认为你背下来了自然就会说了。

[Chen Zheng: Primarily, I have some problems with [English] pronunciation. And . . . I seldom recited when I was studying English. And then . . . he (the class lecturer) asked us to recite and recite and recite every day. We recited one thing after another. We've been reciting all day long. He believes that the more we recite the more naturally we can speak [in English] (21-09-2008)]

As requested by the BSFLP Organising Committee (see Chapter 4, Section 2.4 for details), voluntary English classes and proficiency tests were arranged for 80,000 Beijing taxi drivers. The authority required Beijing taxi drivers to pass an English proficiency test to keep their driver's license. Some statistics show that an average of 52 periods of English training were provided to Beijing taxi drivers by the time the Olympic Games opened in 2008 (Jia, 2007). However, since most Beijing taxi drivers speak little English and many skipped English classes, the taxi driver training courses did not work effectively (Associated Press, 2007). Almost all Beijing taxi drivers on duty during the 2008 Beijing Olympics passed designated English tests after training courses. Despite that, passing proficiency tests turned these Beijing taxi drivers into officially endorsed 'English speakers' on paper but did not actually bestow communicative competence on them. In reality, it was reported that the majority of them could not use English in practice (Xinhua, 2008b). Zhang Yonghui, a local taxi driver, told me that his taxi company had organised English training for two years and held regular English tests once every two weeks before the Beijing Olympics. In spite of his effort to learn English in his spare time, he said helplessly, "我英语不管用, 记不住, 和年纪有关。[My English does not work. I cannot remember English words due to my old age]" (08-08-2008). In his 50s at the time of this interview, Wang is a member of the "lost generation" who missed out on learning English during the Cultural Revolution, a historical period when English was politically undesirable and English classes were cancelled. Similarly, in a news report (Pallavi, 2007), Zhao, a 47-year-old taxi driver, moaned that despite having spent almost two years memorising his English phrase book, most foreigners did not understand his accent. "No one understands me when I speak English," he confessed mournfully, "After a while I just stopped trying and then I forgot everything I had learnt." Beijing citizens such as taxi drivers Wang and Zhao who were forced to "learn" English but failed to reach any significant English proficiency are certainly not likely to be in the minority. As is typical of rapidly expanding education systems, quantity came at the expense of quality in the massive English popularisation campaign in preparation for the Beijing Olympic Games. Language competence never comes easily, especially in an environment where a language is seldom used in everyday communication. The consensus in applied linguistics is that "language learning takes a long time and that the precise duration and final outcome as measured in proficiency level are almost impossible to predict as they depend on may factors, most of which are outside of the control of an individual language learner, such as age, level of education, aptitude, teaching programme, language proximity, or access to interactional opportunities" (Piller, 2016a, p. 46). The policy of requiring all Beijing citizens, regardless of their age, motivation, level of education and job responsibility, to pass English proficiency test for employment was not only problematic, but also unfair.

2.4 Use of foreign language media

Developing foreign language media is an important part of constructing Beijing's "international language environment" in the *Action Plan for the BSFLP* (2003). The needs in China for external propagation and internal foreign language popularisation had promoted the vigorous development of foreign language media, in particular, English media. Two aspects of work had been carried out: (1) foreign language TV and radio programmes; (2) foreign language books and newspapers. According to the official report (Office of the Leading Group on Foreign Affairs of the Beijing Municipal Party Committee of the CPC et al. 2008), China had set up 23 foreign language TV channels and 10 foreign language radio FM channels, and published 68 foreign language magazines and 49 foreign language newspapers by 2008.[15] These foreign language media were predominantly in English and covered a wide range of subjects including nature, society, humanities, science and technology, sports, and entertainment.

Despite the governmental efforts to popularise foreign languages (especially English) via mass media, most Beijing citizens claimed they had little access to foreign language media. As Table 6 shows, foreign language radio and TV programmes did not have high viewing rates, and the purchasing and utilisation rate of foreign language magazines and newspapers was very low. Only 0.9% and 2% of respondents said they read foreign language newspapers or books on a daily basis. Similarly, just 1.1% and 1.3% of respondents watched or listened to foreign language TV or radio programmes every day. In fact, the majority of Beijing citizens had virtually no access to any foreign language media. This proves that even in the capital of China, one of the country's most internationalised first-tier cities, neither English nor any other foreign language was a primary language that most people needed in their everyday life and work.

Table 6: The utilisation rate of foreign Language Media of Beijing Citizens (%).

	Newspapers	Books	Audio-visual Products	TV Programmes	Radio Programmes
Every day	0.9	2	2.3	1.1	1.3
At least once a week	2.5	3.1	3.8	2.1	1.5
At least once a month	2.4	1.7	4.2	3	0.9
Occasionally	10.5	9.9	16.5	20	11.5
Barely	83.7	83.4	73.2	73.7	84.9

---

15 See the *Follow-up Survey and Analytical Report on Foreign Language Environment of Beijing* (Office of the Leading Group on Foreign Affairs of the Beijing Municipal Party Committee of the CPC et al. 2008) for a list of foreign language TV and radio channels, magazines, and newspapers in China before the 2008 Beijing Olympic Games.

3 Assessing Beijing's foreign language environment

After six years of preparation, the Beijing Municipal Government claimed that the host city's "international language environment" had been "dramatically improved" through the city's English learning programmes and activities (Zhang, 2009). However, the official report (Office of the Leading Group on Foreign Affairs of the Beijing Municipal Party Committee of the CPC et al. 2008) suggests otherwise (see Figure 8). On a scale of zero to ten in a questionnaire survey, 30.2% of respondents rated Beijing 8–10 for its internationalisation level. The results showed 21.8% of respondents had a high appraisal of the popularisation of foreign languages in the window industries. However, 52.1% claimed that they had few opportunities to use foreign languages in their work and life, because people around them did not have high proficiency in foreign languages. More than half of the respondents said they had little access to learning foreign languages and the diversity of foreign language media and activities needed to be improved. Further, nearly half of the respondents were not satisfied with the standardisation of English signs in public places.

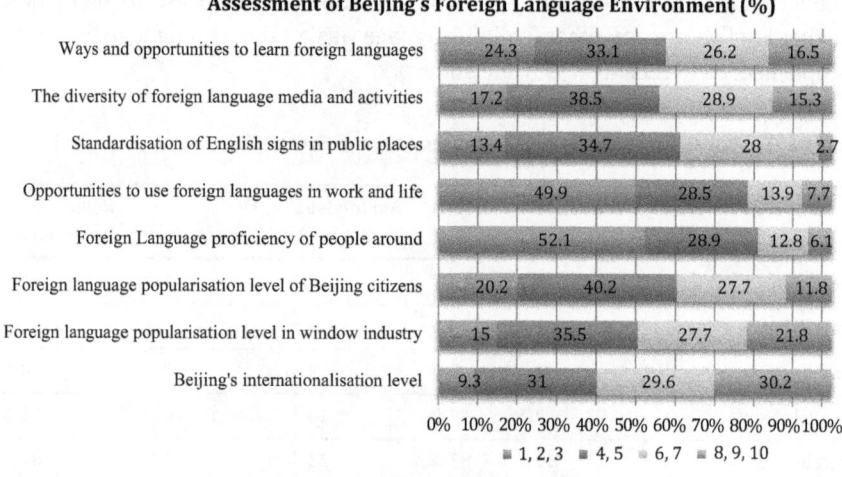

Figure 8: Assessment of Beijing's foreign language environment.

As Figure 9 shows, more than half the respondents were very satisfied or somewhat satisfied with English signs in tourist attractions, cultural museums, cultural and sports facilities, buses, subways and commercial sites. However, they thought that English signs in medical areas and sanitation facilities were unsatisfactory. These opinions are consistent with those of foreigners in Beijing. According to the

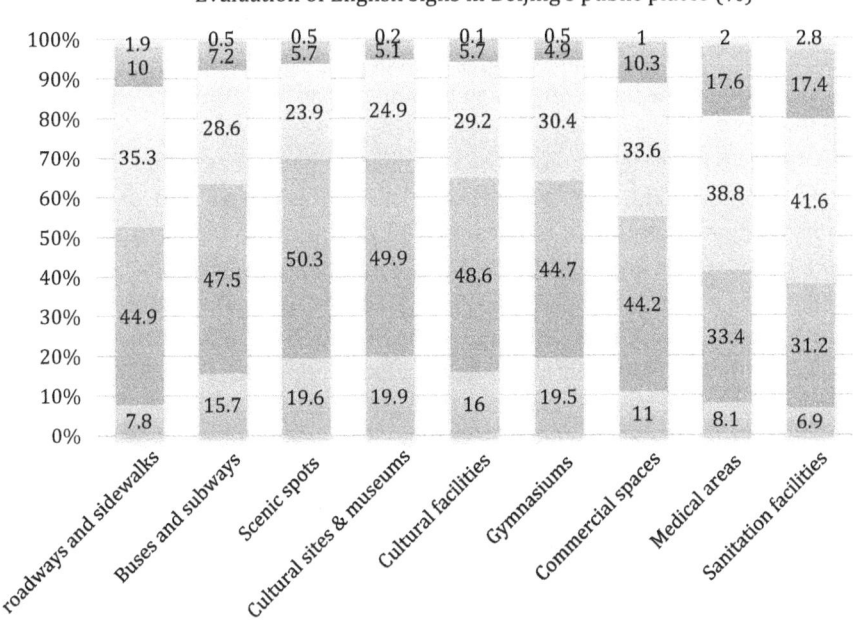

Figure 9: Evaluation of English signs in Beijing's public places.

report (Office of the Leading Group on Foreign Affairs of the Beijing Municipal Party Committee of the CPC et al. 2008), foreigners found road traffic signs, subway signs, and signs in tourist attractions the most standardised and useful. However, they also spotted spelling and grammatical mistakes on some English signs and suggested that more standardised Chinese-English bilingual signs should be added to public places such as buses and hospitals.

4 English fever in Olympic city identity construction

The intersection between English language learning and Olympic passion was well-captured in a 60 minutes documentary, *Mad About English*, which was released shortly before the Olympics. Directed by Singaporean Lian Pek, this documentary well captured the historical moment of China's Olympic English fever by faithfully recording how English impacted on five real-life characters in various stages of their lives. One of the most memorable images of this movie is tens of thousands of Chinese Olympic volunteers at the National Stadium yelling out in unison after Li Yang, the general coach of Olympic volunteers, "I can't stand my poor English! I want to change my life!" This intriguing documentary not only presents a vivid picture of China's Olympic English fever but also leaves us, once again, with the thought-provoking question: Why did the Chinese government and Chinese people desire English so fervently in the context of the Beijing Olympic Games?

"English fever" (cf. Krashen, 2003; Power 2005; Shim and Park, 2008), as a social phenomenon, refers to an overwhelming collective passion for and a concomitant heavy investment into learning English. English fever is also a prominent phenomenon in many other Asian countries, most notably Japan (Oda, 2007; Piller and Takahashi, 2006; Piller, Takahashi and Watanabe, 2010) and South Korea (Park, 2009; Piller, Takahashi and Watanabe, 2010; Shim and Park, 2008). Since China implemented its open door policy in 1978, English has firmly established its supremacy as the main foreign language in the education policies of China (e.g., Adamson, 2002, 2004; Chang, 2006; G. Hu, 2005; Y. Hu, 2008; Lam, 2002; McGuire, 1997). It is in the broad context of globalisation and China's drive for modernisation and internationalisation that "English fever" has been spreading across the nation in the last three decades. The status of English received a strong boost after China's entry into the World Trade Organisation (WTO) in 2001 and when Beijing was awarded the 2008 Olympic Games, also in 2001 (Bolton, 2002). The forces that propelled China towards its biggest international event in history have also driven the Chinese people to embrace English. Under the changing social, economic and political conditions both at home and abroad, the Beijing Olympics marked a pivotal period of identity construction at national, regional and individual levels. These different levels of identity construction were all somehow related to the learning and teaching of English, the *default* international language, an official language of the Olympic Movement and the dominant language in the age of the knowledge economy. English proficiency became an important component of desirable identities for China in its modernisation and internationalisation drive, and also for both Beijing as Olympic city and Chinese citizens of the 21st century. In China's official discourses, especially those that accelerated the spread of English in the context of the Olympics, English is portrayed primarily as a necessary instrument which can facilitate access to modern scientific and technological advances as well as economic development, and secondarily as a vehicle to promote international communication both for the society and the individual.

Like other aspects of the urban transformation geared towards the Beijing Olympics, the government-led planning and decision-making system has made the English popularisation campaign within the host city and across the country very efficient. The Beijing Olympics spurred an English learning frenzy, which involved over 4,000 athletes, judges, BOCOG staff, 1.5 million Olympic volunteers and several million Beijing residents as learners of English. In a similar vein to Korea's approach in the 1986 Asian Games and the 1988 Seoul Olympic Games, the Chinese government promoted the 2008 Olympiad as "a call for citizens to gain a global mindset and to be equipped with important characteristics of globality, one of which is the ability to speak English" (Shim and Park, 2008, p. 144). In collectivist societies like China, people from birth onwards are integrated into strong, cohesive in-groups (such as race, class or state) and taught to prioritise the good of the society over the welfare of the individual. When the enthusiasm of patriotism was mobilised by the Chinese government representing the state, the spirit of collectivism added moral value to English learning. As a result, Beijing citizens from various walks of life and age groups were encouraged to express their patriotism and glorify the whole nation by learning English. Before the Olympics, the domestic press had been packed with stories about patriotic senior citizens, chefs and police officers learning their ABCs in an effort to do their bit for the games. For Beijing citizens, learning English was not only 'beneficial' but also a patriotic act. A 2008 survey in Beijing showed 86.39% of participants planned to take part in English training (Liu, 2008). The Olympics became the powerful driving force for the spread of English in the Olympic host city and the rest of China. The growing popularity of English training was found across all age groups. As a result, China's English education market has been booming. In 2008, Chinese learners of English totalled 350 million (Liu, 2008), and that number had risen to 400 million in July 2010, accounting for about one-third of China's population (He, 2010). According to sources from the National Education Development Statistical Bulletin (Ministry of Education of PRC, 2011), China's training market had an estimated market value of 300 billion yuan ($44 billion) in 2010. Of that total, the English training market was estimated to reach 30 billion yuan ($4.4 billion). Statistics show that there were more than 50,000 organisations or companies that offered English lessons outside school in China, competing for a share of the lucrative English cake before the Beijing Olympiad (Research in China, 2008).

5 Questioning the instrumentalist view of English

In spite of the powerful role of language education policies (LEP) in determining language practices and manipulating language ideologies, Shohamy (2006, p. 91) points out that there is very little research on the actual effect and consequences of LEPs. In this section, I will look into my interview participants' English learning trajectories as consequences of China's English education policies implemented in response to the state's political agenda at the beginning of this century.

Through case studies, I intend to shed light on how the instrumentalist view of English circulated and naturalised in official discourses impacted on Chinese learners' language beliefs and language practices.

5.1 High expectation vs. low practicability

The Beijing Olympics not only gave many Chinese people a strong incentive to learn English but also an optimistic prospect of English language use in post-Olympics China. The instrumentalist view of English reinforced by the Beijing Olympic English popularisation campaign gave rise to the "need" for English for personal advancement amongst many of my interview participants. An argument that is often cited in discussions around English is the one that English has a high use value in the workplace and that students will "need" English to be successful in the labour market (Piller, 2007). For many interview participants in this study, what motivated them to learn English was primarily a view of their job prospects. The belief that learning English could help people gain advantages in employment was accepted by many as a matter of course. Kong Pei, for instance, was a senior undergraduate student in tourist management from a third-tier university in Wuhan. At the time of the Games, he was recruited as an Olympic volunteer driver for the Table Tennis Stadium at Peking University. Before his participation in the Beijing Olympics, Kong Pei admitted that he had not realised "the real importance of English" due to lack of exposure to the language and limited occasions to use it outside the classroom. The Olympic experience changed his understanding of his employment prospects after his graduation.

> Kong Pei: 我有几个姐姐他们现在已经参加工作了嘛，我也马上要找工作了。她们就跟我讲说，如果你的外语水平好的话，首先这就是一个门槛。即使以后你讲外语－讲英语的机会很少，但是确实这就是一种优势。特别是一些好的工作，还有一些层次比较高的工作比如说经理啊，他们可能就会用英语来跟你面试。如果你连这一关你都过不了的话，那对于工作来说就不用谈可以找到一个岗位了。

> [Kong Pei: I have several elder sisters who have already taken up jobs. And I'm also going to look for a job soon. They told me . . . high foreign language proficiency, in the first place, plays a gate-keeping role in seeking a job. Even if later on probably you have very little chance of speaking a foreign language – speaking English, high English proficiency is indeed an advantage. While applying for good jobs, especially those senior positions such as manager, well, candidates will be interviewed by employers in English. If you cannot even pass it, getting a job will be out of the question. (27-09-2008)]

The successful staging of the Beijing Olympics impacted on the way many Chinese people understand the future of China and their own possibilities in that future. For Olympic volunteer driver Chao Feixiang, English was an "absolute essential" not only for an "increasingly open China" but more importantly for his own desired identity as "a successful manager or director" after his graduation from university.

> Chao Feixiang: (. . .) 现在就是说我们国家越来越开放。很多外资企业、外国人都进到我们国家。我觉得在一个公司或者一个企业里面，比如说一个成功的经理人或者一个主管，他所涉及到的不仅仅是他的专业领域，文化、政治、经济、甚至语言这一块他都要涉及到。因为你所接触的人群可能是外国人，而且英语作为国际上的通用语言，所以我觉得英语是非常有必要的。尽管在平时工作当中没有可能用到，但是对于一个主管或者是一个经理人的话，在以后绝对是有机会用到的。因为你熟悉了语言，你就可以跟别人沟通，然后可以学些别人的一些先进思想或者方法什么的。对以后的话，我觉得是非常有必要的。

> [Chao Feixiang: (. . .) Nowadays, just like . . . our country is becoming increasingly open. A large number of foreign enterprises and foreigners have entered into China. And I think- In my opinion, in a company or an enterprise, take a successful manager or director for instance, what he may be involved with is not only professional knowledge but also cultural, political, economic and even linguistic knowledge. Because whom he will come into contact with may be foreigners, and English is said to be a common language in the international community. In this regard, I think English is an absolute essential. >> . . . >> Even though [English] may be << . . . << of no use in daily work, for a director or manager, [English] will definitely be useful in the future. (. . .) I think [English] is an absolute essential for the FUTURE. (27-09-2008)]

With a more optimistic view of international mobility in post-Olympic China, some of my interview participants, especially those who were educationally more advanced and enjoyed better social resources, came to believe in English as a defining measure of life's potential in Chinese society and beyond. In 2008, Zhao Chan was a second-year student in a successive postgraduate and doctoral programme at a leading Chinese university located in Beijing. During the Olympics, he worked with a group of "native English speakers" from Australia and the US as Olympic volunteers for the media operation at the Main Press Centre. Zhao Chan's Olympic volunteering experience confirmed his belief in the instrumentality of English for "highly educated people" like himself.

> Zhao Chan: (. . .) 毕竟现在这个世界是一个西方价值观主导的世界。你要融入这个世界中，就必须学习英语，因为英语是一个世界性的语言 (. . .) 特别是我的同学英语好的人有很多，他们会有很好的机会，不管是工作的机会还是交流的机会。英语好的人会获得更多的信息，或者是你出国发展你的国际事业，针对你个人的发展都有好处。我现在做的这个科研，绝大多数文献都是英语的，所以我觉得英语对一些文化水平高的人，还有那些科研人员和高级商务人员，包括像政府部门他们需要交流的时候，都是非常重要的。

> [Zhao Chan: (. . .) After all, this is a world dominated by Western values. If you want to integrate into the world, you have to learn English, as English is a world language (. . .) Particularly, many of my fellow students have high English proficiency. They have better access to information. Alternatively, if you want to go abroad and develop your international career,

[English] is beneficial for your personal advancement. In my case, most of the literature for my current research project is in English. So I think English is critically important for highly educated people like research fellows and senior business personnel, as well as [civil servants working with] government departments involved with international communication. (22-09-2008)]

The need for English for employment opportunities and career advancement was also deeply felt by Chinese learners of foreign languages other than English. Qin Si was an Olympic volunteer with the VIP accompanying and Spanish language service. However, she did not start to learn Spanish, a 'minor foreign language (*xiao yuzhong*)' in China, until she was admitted to the Spanish programme in her university. From primary Grade 3, she had been a learner of English for ten years. Even though Spanish majors in her university usually had good job prospects, Qin Si continued to study English. In four years of college, she regularly attended College English classes and passed CET-4. In the interview, Qin Si said she still could barely speak English, and thus expressed her concerns given the need for English for job applications.

> Qin Si: 我听以前找工作的人说，作为XX高校的，用人单位不太怀疑你的专业能力。而且他们有的人，是一个上上届的学生自己说，他说他已经是系里面最差的了，他虽然最差可是他出去找工作，还是要比其他学校的要好 (. . .) 但是他说用人单位会考一下你的英语，他们也会考英语，找工作面试的时候，他们会组织讨论什么的，最后他们让你用英语总结你的表现，或者说用英语做一些自我介绍啊什么的。

> [Qin Si: I heard from those job seekers that . . . as graduates from XX University, employers wouldn't doubt your academic capability. And there is someone, a student graduated the year before last year; he said he was academically the poorest student in the department. Despite this, he could get better job offers than those graduated from other universities (. . .) But he said employers might test your English proficiency, they would test English proficiency. While interviewing job applicants, they would organise a discussion or something else. At the end, they would let you summarise your performance in English, or let you, say, do a self-introduction in English. (22-09-2008)]

For many Chinese learners of English such as Kong Pei, Chao Feixiang, Zhao Chan and Qin Si, mastering English was a central part of their seemingly boundless aspirations, a path to a more interesting and lucrative career and a tool to engage with the rest of the world in a way that their parents could never imagine. However, these language ideologies are too often assumed to reflect reality without critical examination of the facts. Takahashi (2011) stresses that the ideology of English should be best understood as "a local, social and political construction in a given country and community." What has not been realised is that individual learners of English themselves participate in the construction of their perceived social reality of English. Worldwide, researchers have long recognised that the spread of English manifests itself differently in different contexts. Even though it is generally believed that English proficiency gives better access to symbolic resources (such as education, social status) and material resources (economic enhancement, career advancement), the value and power of English is by no means inherent and universal.

In contrast to this pervasive argument of the need for English, emerging research evidence shows that English as linguistic capital may not be all that rewarding in terms of career or educational advancement (Piller, Takahashi and Watanabe, 2010, Zhang, 2011). Chinese learners of English have always been struggling with low exposure and practicability of English outside the classroom relative to their heavy investment in English language learning (Zhao and Campbell, 1995; Yang, 2003). A study in 2005 pointed out that 90 percent of occupations in China's job market had nothing to do with English (Zhang, 2005). That is to say, no more than 20 percent of university graduates needed English to different levels in their workplaces. Due to the low practicability of English in Chinese society, especially in the job market, what seemed to really matter is not actual English competence but the proof of possessing it, mostly by university degrees and English test certificates. Given an average of twelve years of compulsory English education from primary grade 3 to undergraduate programmes, the English-centric education policies similar to those of many other non-Anglophone countries (Piller & Cho, 2013) had caused a huge waste of human, material and financial resources.

5.2 Problems and dilemmas of English language learning

Although my interview participants generally held positive views of English as a "neutral and beneficial" instrument for personal advancement, the mandatory learning of English could pose serious problems of educational equity and dilemmas of learner identity for them.

5.2.1 Absence of spontaneous motivation

All the Olympic volunteers I interviewed were university students of the same age cohort (20–25 years old in 2008). Except for a minority student who did not start learning English until university, most of the respondents started their English learning from Junior Secondary Grade 1, whereas a few who had better access to ELT resources in their home cities started at the primary school level. As English was part of compulsory education and *Gaokao* (National College Entrance Examination) for most participants, they reported that they did not have the choice and could not afford the time to study a LOTE as well. In actual practice, it is most likely that parents made decisions for their children regarding language choice in foreign language education. The Chinese education system's favouring of English over other foreign languages and the requirement of English proficiency test certificates in much of the job market both constituted a socialised and institutionalised motivation but not a spontaneous motivation to study English among Chinese learners.

Zhang Jie: 你是有意识地自主选择学习英语的吗？

[Zhang Jie: Did you consciously choose to learn English as a foreign language?]

Chen Zheng: (. . .)我家里人比较倾向于让我出国。其实算是父母的选择吧，不是我自己选的。那时候我也不知道为什么要学英语。(. . .)这也是一个教育导向问题。因为高考啊、报考学校啊，像现在一些高校啊包括研究生招生，小语种［考生］都会有限制。(. . .)然后你找工作的时候，(. . .)你像在我们北方，我家在辽宁，我们那边的日企、韩企，也有一些德国来的企业比较多。像德国来的企业，你不会德语可以但是你要会英语。但是像日韩的那种企业，他们就会喜欢要日语生和韩语生这样。也会有一些不同的选择方向吧。但是现在就是越来越多的考试它没事考你一下英语，它就限制在英语上。我觉得这是一个教育导向问题。

[Chen Zheng: (. . .) My parents were inclined to send me abroad. Actually, it was my parents' choice instead of my own. At that time I didn't know why I should study English. (. . .) This is also a matter of educational orientation. Because like *Gaokao* and university application . . . like when some universities and graduate schools recruit applicants, there are restrictions for those who learn foreign languages other than English. (. . .) Then, when you are job searching (. . .) like in the north, my hometown is in Liaoning Province, there are many Japanese, Korean enterprises and also a few German enterprises. In German enterprises, it's OK not to speak German as long as you speak English. But Japanese and Korean enterprises prefer to recruit Japanese and Korean speakers. There are also different choices. But there are more and more occasions where English is tested. English is the restriction. I think this is a problem of educational orientation. (21-09-2008)]

5.2.2 "Too much time, too low efficiency"

English language learning is mostly presented as a story of hardship. In a speech addressing the 1996 conference on foreign language education, Vice Premier of the State Council, Li Lanqing (1997), stated that the most serious and pervasive problem with English language teaching in China was that it took too much time but achieved fairly low efficiency. The English learning trajectory of Ji Haiqiang, a senior university student in Beijing and Olympic volunteer of hotel service, speaks for itself. Ji Haiqiang grew up in an intellectual family in Guilin, a prefecture-level city situated in southern China. Having commenced learning English in primary grade 3, he had a head start in academic success over most of his peers who only started learning English in secondary school. After primary school, Ji Haiqiang was admitted to a highly competitive local secondary school, with a curriculum that placed a particular emphasis on foreign language training. Compared to regular secondary schools, English education was more intensive in this foreign language secondary school and English classes were conducted by local and foreign teachers with overseas language textbooks and a variety of creative programmes. However, things were completely different when Ji was promoted to senior secondary grade 2. The English education in his grade became examination oriented. According to him, all training for fostering English communicative capability halted and all they had to do in English classes was take simulated tests. English learning was no longer enjoyable for him, and instead became a great pressure with the sole aim of doing well in the *gaokao*. After Ji was admitted to an undergraduate programme in sociology in a Beijing university, he continued to spend most of his time learning English, however the quality of college English teaching was a huge disappointment to him. After years of continuous and heavy investment in the language, Ji's self-assessment was that he had only acquired the ability to pass exams instead of a communicative competence in English.

Zhang Jie: 你怎么评价你的英语能力？

[Zhang Jie: How do you evaluate your proficiency in English?]

Ji Haiqiang: 我觉得考试能力有，但是真正的实际应用能力 . . . 我觉得，就我们班来说，怎么说呢，举个例子吧，老师上英语课时(. . .)他点的是［成绩］比较好的人，我看，在我心目中是英语不错的人。站起来一句话都说不完整(. . .)叙述一件事情，一件简单的事情都叙述不出来。但是你让他考试，他肯定能考挺高的分。但是真的要他说，他说不出来，一句话都说不出来。

[Ji Haiqiang: I think I have the ability to pass examinations, but in terms of a true communicative competence in [English] . . . I think, as far as my class is concerned, how can I put it, let me give you an example. When in English class (. . .), the teacher always chooses academically better students [to answer questions]. In my view, these students are good at English. [However], [they] can't even finish a complete sentence [in English] when they were asked to stand up and answer a question in class. [They] can't give an account of a thing . . . a simple thing. But if you test them, they can sure get a fairly high score. But really, [they] can't speak [English], even a sentence. (03-08-2008)]

5.2.3 The *ti-yong* tension in learning English

Despite the official emphasis on personal choice, benefits, neutrality and complementarity of English language learning, some interview participants reported that English learning had negatively affected their L1 competence and their cultural identities. In 2008, Xu Jian was a senior student in an undergraduate programme in English interpreting at a leading foreign language university in Beijing. At the time of the Olympics, she was recruited by BOCOG as an Olympic volunteer with VIP accompanying and (English) language services after screening and training. Xu Jian grew up in Changchun, a provincial capital in the northeast of China. After she finished her secondary education in a foreign language school, she was exempted from *Gaokao* and recommended for admission to university. While Xu Jian was visibly proud of her English proficiency, she considered it "a sad fact" that her competence in Chinese had been negatively affected by her English thinking pattern.

Language learning is a site of identity construction and negotiation (Norton, 2000). Language learners' understanding of their identities in the target language affect their agency, motivation, investment, and resistance in the learning of the language. My interview with Wei Ru, a Chinese ethnic minority student, reveals that identity conflicts in learning English had been painfully felt by some ethnic minority students. When I met Wei Ru in Beijing in August 2008, she was a senior undergraduate student majoring in ethnology in a Beijing university. During the Beijing Olympics, BOCOG entrusted her university with voluntary work for the International Youth Camp. Hence, Wei Ru was recruited as a coordinating assistant for outdoor cultural and artistic activities in the big event group of the International Youth Camp. It was her responsibility to assist with outdoor transportation services for members of the international youth camp. Wei Ru is a member of the Chinese segment of the Nanai people. Owing to historical reasons, the Nanai are a cross-national ethnic group with populations in both China and Russia. After the founding of the People's Republic of China, Chinese Nanais were officially recognised as the "Hezhe nationality" (赫哲族 *Hezhe-zu*), one of the smallest ethnic minority groups in China. The Hezhe people have their own language which belongs to the Manchu-Tungusic language family (Bradley, 2006). Despite the loss of practical daily communicative use of the ethnic language, Wei Ru still nominated the Hezhe language as her mother tongue and held on to her Hezhe ethnic identity. Because of her ethnic affinity with the Nanai of Russia, Wei Ru also strongly identified with the Russian language. Like many fellow students in her hometown – a small county in Heilongjiang Province that borders Russia, Wei Ru started to learn Russian as a preferred foreign language subject from grade one in junior high schools. With a very high standard of Russian language teaching and abundant exposure to the Russian language in the locality, many local high school graduates including Wei Ru acquired high levels of proficiency in Russian. Russian used to be an advantageous subject for many local students in *Gaokao*. However, the government's desire for China to play a much bigger role in the global economy under the prospect of China's double success in 2001 of winning the bid to host the 2008 Olympic Games and joining the WTO resulted in a grand expansion of English language education in the first decade of the 21st century. In 2001, MOE (2001a) issued a policy statement entitled *Ministry of Education Guidelines for Vigorously Promoting the Teaching of English in Primary Schools*, requiring a lowering of the threshold of compulsory English education from the first year of junior high school to Grade 3 in elementary school. This national language-in-education policy has led to rapid expansion in English language education in China at the beginning of the 21st century.

Before sitting the *Gaokao* in 2004, Wei Ru and other high school graduate students were required to list their university programme preferences as a prerequisite for admission to higher education. The predicament facing learners of Russian was that there was only a limited range of undergraduate programmes available for them to apply to. Many undergraduate programmes only admitted high school graduates with English as their test subject in *Gaokao* (Huang 2009). Facing the same dilemma, Wei Ru and her fellow students had to make the same painful choices between Russian and English. Unlike some of her classmates who chose to repeat a year to cram English in order to make it into a prestigious college and a preferred major, Wei Ru insisted on learning Russian and became a *Gaokao* candidate of Russian. Wei Ru did not share the widespread sense of the importance and utility of English and felt little motivation to study English. For her, obtaining a good command of Russian was more rewarding and would bring more tangible benefits than being able to speak English in the locality.

> Wei Ru: (. . .) 当时我们班有很多同学为了学英语，就蹲了一年。但是我们家就考虑［我］学习挺好的，没必要为了一个语言，就是没有意识到这个语言－因为我们家是县城嘛，就比较偏远，就没有想过英语－因为我们那儿打交道的都是俄罗斯人，俄罗斯人特别多，就根本没有想过什么［学］英语。走出来才发现英语这么重要。从来没有想过，也根本没有意识到。所以我当时也没有蹲级啊怎么样，就一直学着俄语。
>
> [. . . Many fellow students in my class repeated a grade for studying English. But my family thought there was no point in [repeating a grade] solely for learning a language, since I was doing very well at school. I was just not aware that this language [is so predominant elsewhere] – because my hometown is in a remote county, and we dealt with Russian people all the time. There were a great number of Russian people in our county, thus I had never thought of learning English. I've never thought about and didn't realise English is so important elsewhere until I left [my hometown]. So, I didn't repeat a grade and went on learning Russian. (21-09-2008)]

In 2004, Wei Ru was admitted to a preparatory programme in a university for nationalities in Beijing due to the restrictions facing Gaokao candidates of Russian.

In 2001, MOE (2001b) issued a policy to require that at least 5–10 percent of all the courses on a university curriculum should be taught in English within three years. In 2004, MOE issued the *University undergraduate education evaluation programme* (2004), attempting to ensure that the percentage of English-Chinese medium courses should be no less than 10 percent of a university curriculum. The document also stipulates that English textbooks should be adopted in English-Chinese bilingual classes and the percentage of time allocated to teaching in English should be no less than 50 percent of the total classroom hours. As English was a compulsory part of the university curriculum for all non-English majors at her university, Wei Ru was forced to give up Russian learning and became a marginalised student in college English education (Zhang, 2011). The need to learn English had been largely imposed on her by various governmental, institutional and societal forces. In fact, English language education did not empower Wei Ru but presented her with a formidable obstacle to education, employment, and other activities requiring English proficiency. For Wei Ru, the English culture was represented by the Anglo-American culture and thus the English language was perceived to embody values undesirable and antithetical to her native culture and her affiliation to the Russian language. Therefore, the undesirable and powerless identities in English severely affected Wei Ru's agency and investment in English language learning. She responded to the learning of English with resistance.

> Wei Ru: (. . .)我就觉得中国人常说学了外语是为了能和别的国家的交流, 但是我觉得现在英语对我来说, 其实不太愿意学, 心理［动机］比较弱。如果想学早就有条件, 早就可以去报班啊去学, 但是我心里特别地犯抵触。可能因为从小一直受俄罗斯影响吧, 我特别 — 你像有些同学特别想出国嘛, 我不是因为 — 对外我总是说因为语言嘛, 但是我心里边特别排斥, 就是英美那些国家的人, 我特别不喜欢外国人, 我真的特别不喜欢。可能从小受环境影响吧, 就是对中国人和俄罗斯人感觉都比较亲切, 但就对那种美国啊、英国啊, 大家都比较喜欢去的那些国家, 我特别不喜欢。我想给我多少钱让我去我也不会去。
>
> [(. . .) Chinese people always say we should study foreign languages to communicate with other countries, but personally, I'm RELUCTANT to study English. Psychologically, I have no desire to learn English. I've LONG had the conditions to learn it if I really wanted to. I could have attended English classes. But I have a VERY strong resistance to studying English, probably because I have been influenced by Russia since childhood. I particularly – Some of my classmates desire to go abroad, but I don't – When asked, I always say I don't want to go abroad because of my poor English, but in fact I particularly resist those English speaking people such as Americans and Britons. I really dislike them very much. Probably, due to the influence from my childhood environment, I feel a special affinity for both Chinese and Russians. However, speaking of USA, UK and those English-speaking countries which others desire to go to, I dislike them very much. I think I'll never go to those countries, NO MATTER HOW MUCH MONEY I would be given. (21-09-2008)]

Viewing China's widely-publicised English desire in the run up to the Olympics makes it too easy to assume that Chinese learners of English were all motivated to learn it for instrumental or integrative purposes, regardless of their diverse socio-economic, ethnic and linguistic backgrounds. However, the reality is that not all Chinese students were motivated to learn English for a real application of the language or integrating into Western culture. The English learning trajectories discussed above show that English language learning is a complex, contextualised and fluid experience, which is embedded in the institutionalised discourses about English, and is closely linked with the learner's sense of who they are and who they want to be in the future. The spread of English in China has been neither a purely neutral nor universally beneficial process; rather, it has resulted in unequal resource allocation between mainstream society and disadvantaged groups. After a review of the empirical evidence of the benefits of English for individuals internationally, Tollefson (2000) argues that the spread of English is intimately linked with political decisions that benefit some groups at the expense of others. Interview participant Xu Jian commented on the status quo of English language education in China: "在我理解中英语在中国就像贫富两级分化一样。[In my view English language education in China is the same as the polarisation between the poor and the wealthy.]" (22-09-2008). English resources are not as equally accessible and beneficial for all Chinese people as portrayed in the advertisements of English language schools such as Aifly and EF. In the Beijing Olympic context, English proficiency was advantageous for stakeholders who shared a vested interest in the English training industry. While benefitting a few, the analysis of Wei Ru's English learning trajectory finds that English-centric language policies may result in serious disadvantages to those who lack equal access to English teaching resources, including members of minority ethnic groups whose cultural and personal dispositions favour LOTE but who had the need to learn English imposed on them. Based on the statistics released by MOE (2009), there were more than 100 million full-time secondary students learning a foreign language nationwide in 2008. Of these students, more than 95% were studying English as a compulsory school subject. Given the fact that approximately 60 percent of China's population resides in rural areas where English teaching resources are scarce, it is certain that a proportion of students have been and will be disadvantaged by the policy (Hu, 2007).

6 Rethinking the language factor in global city formation

Global city status has become a goal pursued by many metropolitan governments in developing countries. What lies behind the global city aspiration is the governments' competition for power, wealth, and influence on the international stage. Before the Beijing Olympics, Beijing had announced ambitious measures to make the city a top global city, and had undergone dramatic transformation (Wei and Yu, 2006). The municipal government considered the "international language environment" an important guarantee for making Beijing a global city and had carried out a massive foreign language popularisation campaign to this end. What underlay the foreign language popularisation campaign in the preparation for the Beijing Olympic Games was the state-directed language ideology that foreign language proficiency, especially English proficiency, was an important indicator in world/global city formation. A revisit to this language ideology requires us to look back at what makes a 'world/global city' and what role language plays in its measurement.

6.1 The concept and assessment of world/global city

Since the 1960s, world/global city research has been rapidly growing. Most of the published literature focuses on conceptualising and ranking world/global cities in the global economy. Global/world city research originates in Hall's (1966) assertion that "there are certain great cities in which a quite disproportionate part of the world's most important business is conducted' (p. 7). He predicted that '[t]he economic life of the world will be concentrated into a few major information centres', namely, London, Paris, Randstad Holland, Rhine-Ruhr, Moscow, New York, Tokyo (1966, p. 240). Following Hall, John Friedman and Goetz Wolf in their seminal study of world city formation (1982) argued that within the context of the new international division of labour associated with post-1970s capitalism, world cities were increasingly understood as playing a role in gluing the world economic system together. Friedmann (1986) went on to outline his famous 'World City Hierarchy' that classified thirty world cities as either primary or secondary in either the core or the semi-periphery of the world economy: of those, only nine core cities (London, Paris, Rotterdam, Frankfurt, Zurich, New York, Chicago, Los Angeles, Tokyo) and two semi-peripheral cities (São Paulo, Singapore) were classified as primary. The term 'global city' gained wider academic currency through Sassen's (1991) work in which she elaborated on cities as "basing points" in the context of globalising financial and producer services economies. She envisioned a poly-nodal world economic system with New York, London, and Tokyo cemented as the 'primary loci' of globalisation. Other than world/global cities, Ng and Hills (2003) argue that in the era of globalisation cities should aspire to be great cities. Great cities are places with an enlightened mode of governance; where technological and economic advancement sustain global and local development, thereby enriching socio-economic, human, cultural and environmental capital.

Assessment of the performance of world/global cities is an indispensable part of the growing world/global city literature, since it is critical for understanding their position in globalisation and provides useful information to policymakers, urban planners and the general public. Various indexes and ranking have been proposed for measuring cities around the world. For example, Reed (1981, 1989) was the first to analyse world cities using the indicator-based method. He studied 76 cities in more than 40 countries through the assessment of 9 financial indicators and 41 indicators related to culture, economy, geography and politics. In the World City Hypothesis, Friedmann (1986) adopted a hierarchical approach, ranking cities according to seven interrelated selection criteria including major financial centre, headquarters for transnational corporations, international institutions, rapid growth of business services sector, important manufacturing centre, major transportation node, and population size. Informed by the conceptual framework of 'Great cities', Ng and Hills (2003) present a comparative study of five Asian world cities benchmarked against 57 indicators involving enlightened governance, innovative technological and economic activities promoting global and local development, and human, social, cultural and environmental capital. Hussain, Zaidi, and Rozenblat (2018) present a city ranking based on diversity, strength and network centrality to assess the cities' importance in the world.

Besides rankings reported in academic papers, there are also numerous rankings published for the general public that have attracted wide attention. The Economist Intelligence Unit (www.eiu.com/topic/liveability) annually releases the Global Liveability Index ranking 140 cities worldwide based on the quality of stability, healthcare, culture and environment, education, and infrastructure. The consulting firm Mercer (mobilityexchange.mercer.com) publishes an annual Quality of Living Index for expatriate employees in prevalent assignment locations around the world that ranks over 200 cities based on safety, education, culture and environment among other factors. The IESE Cities in Motion Index, prepared by IESE Business School (www.iese.edu/faculty-research/cities-in-motion/), ranks 174 cities based on nine main dimensions including human capital, social cohesion, economy, public management, governance, environment, mobility and transportation, urban planning, international outreach, and technology. The Global Power City Index (GPCI), developed by the Mori

Memorial Foundation (www.mori-m-foundation.or.jp), evaluates and ranks 48 major cities of the world according to their comprehensive power through measuring 70 indicators of 6 urban functions including economy, research and development, cultural interaction, liveability, environment, and accessibility. The Global City Index is designed by the consulting firm A.T. Kearney, Foreign Policy journal and the Chicago Council on Global Affairs (www.atkearney.com), and ranks global cities according to 27 metrics across five dimensions: business activity, human capital, information exchange, cultural experience and political engagement.

So far, international scholars' assessment of world/global cities has gradually changed from the recognition orientation of existing world/global cities to the planning orientation of future world/global city formation. In the early studies, the assessment of world/global cities mainly adopted economic indicators. With the intensification of globalisation, there was a shift to pulling social, political, cultural, infrastructure and other aspects of urban performance into the measurement matrix alongside the economic and financial factors. Since the 21st century, an increasing number of world/global city studies also include innovation and sustainable development in the assessment index system. It is worth noting that few city indexes and rankings take foreign language proficiency of the citizens as a dimension to evaluate a city's global standing, even though language competence serves a fundamental role in education, human capital, knowledge economy and intercultural communication. The ranking results of various indexes prove that there is no single correct path a city should tread to become global, and that English is not the necessary condition and means to achieve that end. In the 2008 Global City Index (Foreign Policy, Kearney and Chicago Council on Global Affairs, 2008), for example, no city dominated all dimensions of the index. The 60 cities included in this index represent a broad cross section of the world's centres of politics, commerce, culture, and communication (see Table 7). In the top ten global cities, Paris (No. 3), Tokyo (No. 4), Seoul (No. 9) are not in English speaking countries, yet Paris led the world in information exchange and Tokyo came second in business activity. Beijing's successful Olympic spectacle earned it much international respect. In the index, Beijing emerged as the No. 12 global city overall, ahead of other national capitals such as Brussels (13), Berlin (17) and Moscow (19). The city was the highest-ranking megacity from a developing country in that year. Clearly, limited English proficiency did not prevent Beijing, the capital of a socialist developing country and transitional economy, from joining the ranks of global metropolises. In their analysis of five Chinese global cities (Beijing, Hong Kong, Shanghai, Guangzhou, Shenzhen), Chubarov and Brooker (2013) challenged a 'globalist perspective'

Table 7: The 2008 Global Cities Index.[16]

Ranking	City	Dimension				
		Business Activity	Human Capital	Information Exchange	Cultural Experience	Political Engagement
1	New York	1	1	4	3	2
2	London	4	2	3	1	5
3	Paris	3	11	1	2	4
4	Tokyo	2	6	7	7	6
5	Hong Kong	5	5	6	26	40
6	Los Angeles	15	4	11	5	17
7	Singapore	6	7	15	37	16
8	Chicago	12	3	24	20	20
9	Seoul	7	35	5	10	19
10	Toronto	26	10	18	4	24
11	Washington	35	17	10	14	1
12	**Beijing**	9	22	28	19	7
13	Brussels	19	34	2	32	3
14	Madrid	14	18	9	24	33
15	San Francisco	27	12	22	23	29
16	Sydney	17	8	27	36	43
17	Berlin	28	29	12	8	14
18	Vienna	13	31	29	11	9
19	Moscow	23	15	33	6	39
20	Shanghai	8	25	42	35	18

which posits 'global city' formation is a uniform process whereby cities all end up striving to be, or resembling, London, New York and Tokyo. By adopting a functional approach sensitive to the specific political, economic, socio-cultural functions of individual cities, they argued that these Chinese megacities prove

---

16 The 2008 Global City Index developed by A.T. Kearney, Foreign Policy journal and the Chicago Council ranked 60 major cities of the world. Here I only quote the ranking of the top 20 cities.

that there are multiple pathways to global city formation in a non-Western, non-capitalist context.

Interestingly, among a range of rankings of world/global cities published to the general public, the international English training institution EF English First, the official language training service supplier for seven Olympic Games,[17] started to publish its English Proficiency Index (EPI) in 2011. The 2019 EF EPI (EF Education First, 2019a) evaluates 2.3 million test takers from 100 countries and regions. According to the index, Europe has the highest EPI average score (56.71), followed by Asia (53), Latin America (50.34), Africa (50.28) and the Middle East (44.60). The countries with the highest English proficiency are clustered in Scandinavia, while at the other end of the spectrum many Middle East countries have the lowest English proficiency (see Table 8). France (No. 31),

Table 8: EPI ranking of countries and regions.

Very High		High		Moderate		Low		Very Low	
1	Netherlands	15	Hungary	30	Costa Rica	47	Belarus	70	UAE
2	Sweden	16	Romania	31	France	48	Russia	71	Bangladesh
3	Norway	17	Serbia	32	Latvia	49	Ukraine	72	Maldives
4	Denmark	18	Kenya	33	Hong Kong (China)	50	Albania	73	Venezuela
5	Singapore	19	Switzerland	34	India	51	Bolivia	74	Thailand
6	South Africa	20	Philippines	35	Spain	52	Vietnam	75	Jordan
7	Finland	21	Lithuania	36	Italy	53	**Japan**	76	Morocco
8	Austria	22	Greece	37	South Korea	54	Pakistan	77	Egypt
9	Luxembourg	23	Czech Republic	38	Taiwan (China)	55	Bahrain	78	Sri Lanka
10	Germany	24	Bulgaria	39	Uruguay	56	Georgia	79	Turkey
11	Poland	25	Slovakia	**40**	**China**	57	Honduras	80	Qatar

---

17 Since 1988, EF has provided language training services to Olympic Games seven times, namely, for the 1988 Seoul Olympics, 2008 Beijing Olympic and Paralympic Games, 2014 Sochi Winter Olympics, Rio de Janeiro 2016 Summer Olympics, PyeongChang 2018 Winter Olympics, Special Olympics World Games Abu Dhabi 2019 and the 2020 Tokyo Olympics (postponed until 2021).

Table 8 (continued)

Very High	High	Moderate	Low	Very Low
12 Portugal	26 Malaysia	41 Macau (China)	58 Peru	81 Ecuador
13 Belgium	27 Argentina	42 Chile	59 Brazil	82 Syria
14 Croatia	28 Estonia	43 Cuba	60 El Salvador	83 Cameroon
	29 Nigeria	44 Dominican Republic	61 Indonesia	84 Kuwait
		45 Paraguay	62 Nicaragua	85 Azerbaijan
		46 Guatemala	63 Ethiopia	86 Myanmar
			64 Panama	87 Sudan
			65 Tunisia	88 Mongolia
			66 Nepal	89 Afghanistan
			67 Mexico	90 Algeria
			68 Colombia	91 Angola
			69 Iran	92 Oman
				93 Kazakhstan
				94 Cambodia
				95 Uzbekistan
				96 Ivory Coast
				97 Iraq
				98 Saudi Arabia
				99 Kyrgyzstan
				100 Libya

Spain (No. 35), South Korea (No. 37) and China (No. 40) are all classified in the moderate English proficiency band. Russia (No. 48) and Japan (No.53) are recognised as countries with low English proficiency. Turning to city scores, Amsterdam ranks the highest in English proficiency of the 100 surveyed cities. Paris, Tokyo and Seoul, the three non-English speaking top ten global cities in the 2019 Global City Index, scored 60.28, 52.58, and 57.14 respectively in EF EPI. Beijing, which scored 55.68 in EPI, falls behind Paris and Seoul, but is ahead of Tokyo in English proficiency. Based on these statistics, EF English First (2019a) claims that English proficiency is "positively correlated" with scientific innovation, human and economic development, global connectedness, democracy, even power and gender equality. The report (EF Education First, 2019a) suggests that countries or cities "where people speak the best English" are like to have greater global talent competitiveness, more cutting-edge scientific research, higher gross domestic product, net income and labour productivity, and lower power distance, and therefore tend to be "wealthier, more open, and more internationally minded" (p. 18). More surprisingly, the report (EF Education First, 2019a) underscores that "there is a very strong correlation between English proficiency and the Good Country Index, a composite measure of how much a country currently contributes to humanity as a whole (p. 18)." As the official language training service suppliers of seven past and upcoming Olympics Games, EF's remarks on the intrinsic 'value' of English clearly have an impact on the language policy of the Olympic host countries and the general public who invest heavily in English learning. These comments regarding English concur with the triumphalist descriptions of English as an international language (e.g., Crystal, 1997; Hanson, 1997) which uncritically endorse the ideology of English as the language of science, technology, modernisation and internationalisation in the academia. In this view, monolingualism in English and cultural homogenisation were presented as inevitable and desirable in a globalising world, and ignored the underlying political, cultural, and ethical questions surrounding this phenomenon. Piller (2016a) criticised the ideology which equates academic excellence with the production of knowledge in English. She (2019) argues that the close association between English and academic excellence has resulted in diminishing the authority of academic knowledge in LOTE. In fact, the academic authority in English is achieved by the use of English as the dominant medium of contemporary academic communication rather than by some "inherent attributes" as described in EF's report. We must be on guard against using English proficiency as a scale to evaluate a country's contribution to humanity. This linguistic evolutionism and social Darwinism will provide moral justification of racial discrimination against and cultural assimilation of non-English speaking groups.

A comparative study between the 2019 Global City Index and the 2019 EF EPI will find that there is no causal relation between the English proficiency of a city and its standing in the world. The dominance and 'value' of English proficiency in today's world should be understood as a sociocultural and historical construct rather than reflecting some essentialist attributes of the language. If English proficiency predicts global competiveness as the EF report claims, then the current world would be simply stratified into three levels of "globalness" in line with Kachru's (1985, 1992) three-circle model of World Englishes. In this imagined world, the inner circle countries[18] in which English acts as a first or native language would naturally nurture the "perfect" global cities. However, in the 2019 EF EPI only Berlin and Brussels, which are among the top 20 cities with "the best English proficiency", made the top 20 in the Global Cities Index (GCI) of that year (see Table 9). The A. T. Kearney 2019 Global Cities Report (Kearney, 2019) reveals a world in flux and reinforces the notion that no city has a lock on being the most global city. The results (Kearney, 2019) show that even though New York, London, Paris, Tokyo, and Hong Kong maintain their decade-long dominance as the top five cities in the Global Cities Index, a fundamental shift in the world city system is underway. North America and Europe are wrestling with political uncertainty and rising nationalism, which is raising questions about their long-range prospects. London and other key European cities have experienced a slowdown in business activity. In general, performance across all the leading European cities has stalled since 2018. Weakening human capital scores are fuelling this inertia, as the most qualified and diverse talent look elsewhere for opportunities or simply stay home. This is happening across top European cities, including London, Brussels, and Berlin. At the same time, the strength of China's economy and improved openness in the Middle East are propelling cities in these emerging regions toward greater prominence on the global stage. Over the past 40 years, China has made remarkable achievements in the growth and development of its cities. The urbanisation rate rose from 18 percent in 1978 to 60 percent in 2018, and the country's urban population grew from 170 million to 830 million (Kearney, 2019, p. 9). China proves that its urban areas continue to improve their liveability, become more citizen-centric, and close in on the world's leading cities. Beijing ranks No. 9 in the 2019 GCI, moving three places forward from 2008. In fact, the average Index scores of Chinese cities have grown three times faster than that of the North American cities, and in the Global Cities Outlook rank, the Chinese cities improved 3.4 times faster than European cities (Kearney, 2019, p. 8). Business activity remains the largest contributor to the Index scores. But strides that Chinese cities have made in human capital and information exchange have significantly accelerated their progress.

---

18 The countries located in the Inner Circle include United Kingdom, United States, Australia, New Zealand, Ireland, Anglophone Canada, South Africa, and some Caribbean territories.

Table 9: The Cross reference between 2018–2019 GCI and 2019 EF EPI.

2019	2018	Δ	GCI Ranking	2019	EF EPI Ranking
1	1	–	New York	1	Amsterdam
2	2	–	London	2	Stockholm
3	3	–	Paris	3	Copenhagen
4	4	–	Tokyo	4	Helsinki
5	5	–	Hong Kong	5	Oslo
6	7	+1	Singapore	6	Vienna
7	6	–1	Los Angeles	7	**Berlin**
8	8	–	Chicago	8	Mumbai
9	9	–	Beijing	9	Hamburg
10	11	+1	Washington, DC	10	Warsaw
11	15	+4	Sydney	11	Lisbon
12	10	–2	Brussels	12	Bucharest
13	12	–1	Seoul	13	Budapest
14	16	+2	Berlin	14	Zagreb
15	13	–2	Madrid	15	Davao City
16	17	+1	Melbourne	16	Manila
17	18	+1	Toronto	17	Porto
18	14	–4	Moscow	18	**Brussels**
19	19	–	Shanghai	19	Kuala Lumpur
20	22	+2	Amsterdam	20	New Delhi

6.2 English and China's global city aspiration

Chubarov and Brooker (2013) reviewed a body of 'global city' research in Chinese language literature and identified three waves of global city studies in China. The earliest studies of 'world city (*Shijie Chengshi*)' and 'global city (*Quanqiu Chengshi*)' in mainland China dated back to the beginning of the 1990s when major cities were undergoing rapid transformation from socialist cities with manufacturing and residence functions to becoming trade, exchange and consumption cities in a new era of Chinese modernity and global engagement. A second wave of studies coincided with China's successful bid to host the Olympic Games and accession to the WTO in 2001 and further internationalisation of the Chinese economy. Xue (2003) outlined multiple criteria blocked in four groups (economic power, social development, infrastructure, international contacts) to measure globalising Chinese cities. The third and most recent wave of studies were prompted by the decision of the Chinese state to promote Beijing as a world city in tandem with its status as Olympic host city (Xu, 2011).

In the early 1990s, the Development Research Centre of Shanghai Municipal People's Government (www.fzzx.sh.gov.cn) developed an assessment index for measuring global cities (Office of the Leading Group on Foreign Affairs of the Beijing Municipal Party Committee of the CPC et al. 2008). This index distinguishes three levels of global cities, namely, elementary, intermediate and advanced, based on a set of economic, financial and demographic indicators (see Table 10). Notably, the proportion of English speaking citizens in the local population was regarded as a dimension to evaluate global cities. Specifically, an elementary global city is supposed to be one in which no less than 40% of its population has communicative competence in English. This could be where BOCOG's requirement of 5 million foreign language (predominantly English) speaking citizens (35% of Beijing's total population) originated.

Table 10: The DRC global city assessment index.

Indicator	Unit	Elementary	Intermediate	Advanced
Per capita GDP	USD	>5000	>10000	>20000
Primary industry value added as a proportion of GDP	%	>60	>68	>73
Per capita annual income	USD	4000	7000	15000
Per capita electricity consumption	Kilowatt-hour	2000	3000	4000
No. of vehicles per 10,000 people	(vehicle)	1000	1500	2000
No. of telephone per 10,000 people	(telephone)	3000	4000	5000
The proportion of foreign nationals in the local population	%	0.6	1.0	2.0
The proportion of inbound tourists in the local population	%	40	70	100
The proportion of English speaking citizens in the local population	%	40	60	80

Table 10 (continued)

Indicator	Unit	Elementary	Intermediate	Advanced
Exchange rate of international major currency	%	100	100	100
Exports of local products as a share of GDP	%	40	60	100
Total imports as a share of GDP	%	30	50	80
Trading volume of foreign exchange market	Billion USD	150	300	600
Foreign direct investment as a share of local investment	%	10	20	30

Against the background of China's internationalisation drive, English is often tied up with multiple terminologies, used in various commentaries, such as "global competitiveness," "global citizenship," "global mindset," and "intercultural competence." English is taken for granted as the language of internationalisation of nation-states. However, the connection between English and global city formation is assumed rather than proven. This assumed connection is not only problematic, but also harmful to the world's cultural diversity and language maintenance. This assumption can misguide policy makers into believing that a city's global competiveness is delivered via English, so as to neglect the importance of national languages and LCTLs in language-in-education planning and national development strategies, and eventually perpetuate English hegemony. Over the past three decades, China has been opening its doors to the outside world and changing from a 'domestically-focused country' into an 'internationally-oriented country' (Li, 2010). The foreign language needs of 'domestically-focused countries' were mainly confined to a few dominant languages in the fields of diplomacy, military affairs, security and translation. In contrast, 'internationally-oriented countries' have much more extensive demands for foreign language capacity, as these countries have closer social and economic ties with the rest of the world and undertake more international obligations. In the third wave of China's global/world city studies, a group of sociolinguists (e.g., Dai, 2011; Li, 2015; Wen, Su and Jian, 2011; Yang, 2015; Zhao, 2016) put forward the concept of 'national language capacity' as an important constituent of the nation's comprehensive power. These scholars see language resources as both soft power and hard power of a country. They recognised that an English-only approach to foreign language education is a limitation to the building of national language capacity in line with the interests of a national development strategy. China is a country with the largest foreign language learning population but poor foreign language resources (Li, 2011). The urgent task of China's foreign language planning is to improve its multilingual competence based on an assessment of the country's foreign language talent pool and national demand for foreign languages.

7 Summary

China has been in the grip of 'English fever,' a phenomenon that took root and spread throughout the country three decades ago and became white-hot in the process of the identity construction of Beijing as the host city of the 2008 Olympics. The Beijing Olympic Games became a powerful driving force for the spread of English in Beijing and the rest of China through an Olympic foreign language popularisation programme. What underlay the Chinese government's intensified emphasis on learning English was a conception which equates 'English' with 'foreign language' and 'English proficiency' with 'global competence.' Consequently, the figure of 5 million for Beijing's foreign language speaking population was just a huge number with low proficiency. This officially identified 'foreign language speaking population' does not justify the claim that the Olympic host city has overall high foreign language proficiency and accordingly an "international language environment." As a direct result, Beijing was short of advanced English speakers, multilingual speakers and speakers of foreign languages other than English at the time of the Games. Most significantly, regulations such as the requirement for employees in service sectors in Beijing to pass English tests for employment have maintained the hegemony of English and perpetuated the differentiation of the "haves" from the "have-nots." Intercultural competence in the form of English worked to the advantage of those who had it, in terms of increased networking opportunities, accelerated promotion or enhanced access to information. Lack of proficiency in English, on the other hand, denied other individuals access to those same resources.

Language policy informs practical language teaching and language use in education and other crucial spheres of public life and involves the choice of what languages are to be used and how they are made legitimate by the state. In Shohamy's (2006, p. xvi) expanded view of LP, the language textbook is in fact an effective "language policy tool" or "mechanism" which is created as a consequence of overt policy statements and used to perpetuate language practices. Given the direct effects of textbooks on language practice, in the next chapter I will examine two official Olympic English textbooks to shed light on a different perspective on the LPP for the 2008 Beijing Olympics.

Chapter 6
Imagined communities and identity options in Beijing Olympic English textbooks

This chapter explores the imagined communities and identity options constructed in two Olympic English training materials by conducting linguistic and semiotic analyses of the multimodal meaning-making resources in the textbooks. It is organised as follows: I first introduce the theoretical rationale underpinning studies of identity construction in language textbooks; this entails reference to feminism, poststructuralism, critical discourse analysis and critical pedagogy. After this, I elaborate on the respective content, form, and pedagogical goals of the two sampled English textbooks and the rationale for selecting them as my data. In the subsequent sections, three imagined communities (targeted learners, imagined interlocutors, and Beijing as an Olympic city) are examined. Overall, I will show that the two textbooks offer biased, stereotyped and oversimplified identity options to targeted Chinese learners. Moreover, the two textbooks attempt to construct a harmonious imagined community without even suggesting that cross-cultural communication might also fail. These discursive constructions have the potential to negatively impact learners' language learning trajectories.

1 Identity options in language textbooks

The study of identity constructions in foreign and second language (FL/SL) textbooks is emerging as a new research direction, informed and prompted by feminist and poststructuralist reconceptualisation of language education (e.g., Blackledge and Pavlenko, 2004; Block, 2003, 2007; Cummins, 1994; Norton, 2000; Noton and Toohey, 2002; Pavlenko, 2001, 2002) and new developments in critical pedagogy (e.g., Apple, 1990, 1992, 1996; Giroux, 1988, 1989). In response to second-wave feminism, the 1970s and 1980s witnessed a flurry of content (such as portrayal of the two genders with respect to their visibility, occupation, personality, relations and roles they play) and linguistic (grammatical features which denote discrimination against one of the two genders) analyses of gender representation in language textbooks. These textbook analyses found abundant evidence of gender bias against women in general in terms of "exclusion," "subordination," "distortion," and "degradation" (Sunderland et al. 2000). In the early 1990s, third-wave feminism arose as a challenge to the essentialist definition of gender and the overemphasis on the experiences of upper-middle-class White women. Under the drive of the third wave of the feminist movement, a poststructuralist interpretation of gender and sexuality has gradually been embraced by educational theorists and practitioners. In the field of second language acquisition (SLA), Norton's (1995) call for "a comprehensive theory of social identity" (p. 12) triggered a far-reaching reconceptualisation of identity. As a result, the past two decades have seen an increasing research interest in identity and language learning from a poststructuralist perspective. The scholarship on identity and language learning is also informed by critical pedagogy. Critical pedagogy takes as a central concern the issue of power in the teaching and learning context. It is widely acknowledged that textbooks play a vital role in defining what and whose knowledge is valued and taught. Being the most common pedagogic device of formal education, textbooks are never neutral knowledge but rather "embodiments of a larger process of cultural politics" (Apple, 1992, p. 1). According to Apple (1992), textbooks signify particular constructions of reality and embody legitimate knowledge and culture by enfranchising one group's cultural capital and disenfranchising another's. That is to say, what counts as "legitimate" or "truthful" knowledge – what is included in textbooks – is the result of complex power relations and struggles among identifiable class, race, gender, and religious groups (Apple, 1992, 1996).

Grounded in feminist and poststructuralist theory and critical pedagogy, several researchers (see Shardakova and Pavlenko, 2004, for an overview) have expanded the focus of inquiry in language textbook research by considering a range of social identities and students' perceptions of the identity options offered to them. An extension of scholarly interest in identity and investment in language learning relates to the imagined communities that language learners aspire to when they learn an additional language (Norton and Gao, 2008). In particular, Shardakova and Pavlenko (2004), introduced a new analytical approach to identity options in language textbooks. In their study of two popular beginning Russian textbooks, two sets of identity options were examined: imagined learners (targeted implicitly by the texts) and imagined interlocutors (invoked explicitly). In doing so, they ask a wide range of identity questions, encompassing those of gender, race, class, ethnicity, religious affiliation, (dis)ability, sexuality, and other identities. Their study elaborated how the main characters of the two Russian textbooks were portrayed as able-bodied White middle-class educated young men and members of the international elite, while Russian interlocutors were typically depicted as White middle-class speakers of Standard Russian. Such identity options are unlikely to be pertinent for Russians with African or Asian heritage, or for members of many Russian-speaking ethnic minorities. This previous study suggests that language textbooks may offer oversimplified, stereotyped and biased identity options to targeted FL/SL learners. The oversimplifications, stereotypes and biases in language textbooks may deprive the learners of important means of self-representation and at times even self-defence. They may also negatively affect the learners' degree of engagement with the target language and culture, and the development of their intercultural competence (Shardakova and Pavlenko, 2004).

Adopting Shardakova and Pavlenko's (2004) analytical approach, the current chapter aims to investigate how language textbooks, through their content and form, legitimise particular knowledge about the world and validate certain identity repertoires, and how such identity repertoires in turn structure learners' access to linguistic resources and interactional opportunities in the target language. Specifically, I ask the following research questions:
1) Which learners are targeted implicitly as Chinese interlocutors in the multimodal texts and who is excluded?
2) What types of interlocutors are made salient and who is left out in the multimodal texts?
3) How is the interaction between Chinese and foreign interlocutors depicted?
4) Which English varieties are promoted?
5) What linguistic and cultural ideologies underlie the production of the texts?

As language textbooks are direct consequences of overt language policies, they not only reflect language ideologies embedded in explicit language policies but also serve as an effective mechanism of manipulating language behaviours and ensuring that language ideologies are turned into practices. In the implementation of the LPP for the Beijing Olympic Games, language textbooks served as an important language policy device. By answering the above questions, I try to add a new dimension, which is different from the ones in previous data analysis chapters, to the global research question about the ways language policies and language ideologies were tied to identity construction in the 2008 Beijing Olympic context.

2 A Conversational English Reader

By the time the bell sounded for the 2008 Beijing Olympic Games, China's Olympic English popularisation campaign had been in full swing for six years. The campaign not only boosted the multibillion-dollar English training industry but also gave a great impetus to the flourishing of ELT publications. Various domestic and overseas ELT materials had flooded the Chinese book market by the Olympic year (21st Century, 2008). On 4 August 2008, I visited Wangfujing Bookstore, one of the biggest bookstores in Beijing. This six-floor bookstore had a wide variety of EFL teaching materials, simulated English test papers, reference books, and a special collection of Olympic English training materials. These Olympic English training materials fell into two general categories: (1) English textbooks for general communicative purposes targeting Beijing residents, such as *Beijing Residents English Speaking Handbook, 100 English Sentences for Beijingers, 300 English Sentences for Beijingers* and *1,000 Olympic English Sentences*; and (2) English textbooks for specific purposes directed at professionals in various sectors, such as *English for civil servants, Olympic security English, Police English, Tourist English, Hotel English*.

I purchased a selection of the plethora of English training materials available in the Wangfujing bookstore and later selected two titles from the *Beijing Olympic Games Training Series* for further analysis: *A Conversational English Reader (Elementary)* (BOCOG and Beijing Municipal Education Commission, 2007a) and *A Conversational English Reader (Advanced)* (BOCOG and Beijing Municipal Education Commission, 2007b). These two textbooks were selected based on three criteria.

Firstly, the two versions of *A Conversational English Reader* constituted the first official English-language training material regarding Olympic language services in China (Official Website of the Beijing 2008 Olympic Games, 2008). This pair of readers were compiled and published under the direction and auspices of the Beijing Municipal Education Commission and BOCOG. They were used as manuals to teach targeted Chinese learners how to react to possible situations that could arise during the Olympic Games, with an additional focus on the Paralympics. In this sense, they represented officially authorised knowledge about the Olympics and English, especially how the image of Beijing as the Olympic host city should be projected in English. Therefore, it was interesting to examine what was considered "appropriate" and "correct" English language practices in the Beijing Olympic context.

Secondly, the volumes had a wider readership than others of this kind. The *Beijing Olympic Games Training Series* was a non-profit publication and consisted of a total of 13 books serving as essential training manuals for BOCOG staff, volunteers, contractors, domestic technical officers, personnel in the service sectors, students at primary, secondary and tertiary levels, Beijing citizens, and Chinese spectators (BOCOG and Beijing Municipal Education Commission, 2007a). Over 155,000 copies of each of the various training manuals had been distributed by 2008 (Official Website of the Beijing 2008 Olympic Games, 2008). In addition, statistics from *China Press and Publishing Journal* (2008) show that 2,064 copies of *A Conversational English Reader* (*Elementary*) and 1,725 copies of *A Conversational English Reader* (*Advanced*) were sold in the Beijing Books Building, the biggest bookstore in Beijing, within the two months of the Games (July-August, 2008). Additionally, the two *Readers* were widely distributed, especially to people who were likely to come into contact with foreigners during the Games. Overall, the two versions of *A Conversational English Reader* provide a particularly intriguing locus of inquiry, as the volumes represent the governmental guidelines pertaining to linguistic resources and communicative strategies that Chinese learners needed in order to deal with English-speaking visitors during the Games.

Last but not least, the *Readers* represent the shift of the pedagogical objective of ELT in line with the beginning of this new era. In order to meet the escalating demand for qualified personnel with a good command of communicative English, boosted by the prospects of further integration into the world system in the 21st century, the Chinese Education Ministry accelerated the development of the English education system towards a communicative stance (Nunan, 2003). Both *Readers* under study are composed of multimodal situational dialogues, with a clear emphasis on the productive use of English, especially speaking competence.

According to the editor of the *Elementary Reader*, the textbook targets personnel in service sectors and ordinary Beijing citizens who had received secondary education. In contrast, the *Advanced Reader* targets Olympic volunteers who are college students with a CET-4 certificate as well as BOCOG staff and contractors with an English level equivalent to CET-4. Table 11 provides an overview of the content and structure of the two *Readers*.

Table 11: Content and structure of the two *Readers*.

Textbook	Table of Contents	Features

The Elementary Reader	Unit 1 Being a Taxi Driver
	Unit 2 Serving at a Hotel
	Unit 3 Working in a Restaurant
	Unit 4 Giving Directions
	Unit 5 Talking to a Patient
	Unit 6 Selling at a Store
	Unit 7 Working for Public Transport
	Unit 8 Taking a Walk Downtown
	Unit 9 Meeting at a Competition Venue
	Unit 10 Serving as a Tour Guide
	Unit 11 Hosting at a High School
	Unit 12 Parting at a Farewell Meeting
		– Targeted learners:
		  – Personnel in service sectors
		  – Beijing citizens
		– Each unit contains:
		  – 4 dialogues (each is supplemented by a glossary and language tips)
		  – A list of related words and phrases
		  – An English passage of "Olympic tidbits"
		– 83 visual images in total:
		  – 48 cartoons
		  – 26 photos
		  – 8 illustrations
		  – 1 map
		– 96 primary interlocutors in dialogues:
		  – 48 Chinese characters
		  – 48 foreign characters

Table 11 (continued)

Textbook	Table of Contents	Features

The Advanced Reader	Unit 1 Reception Services
	Unit 2 Resident Services
	Unit 3 Competition Venue Services
	Unit 4 Spectator Services
	Unit 5 Media Services
	Unit 6 Leisure Time Services
	Unit 7 Gathering and Parting
		– Targeted learners:
		  – Olympic volunteers
		  – BOCOG staff
		  – Contractors
		– Each unit contains:
		  – 4 dialogues (each is supplemented by a glossary and language tips)
		  – A list of related words and phrases
		  – An English essay of "culture notes"
		– 101 visual images in total:
		  – 28 cartoons
		  – 56 photos
		  – 15 illustrations
		  – 2 maps
		– 74 primary interlocutors in dialogues:
		  – 34 Chinese characters
		  – 40 foreign characters

Given the different target groups, conversational topics in the *Elementary Reader* mainly concern public services for foreign visitors, whereas the *Advanced Reader* mainly involves Olympic volunteering work at various venues. The *Elementary Reader* contains twelve units and the *Advanced Reader* has seven units. Each unit consists of four independent situational dialogues on the same theme (supplemented by a glossary and language tips), as well as a list of related expressions and a supplementary reading attached at the end of each unit. The two *Readers* consist of multimodal meaning-making resources, combining verbal text, visual images and audio recordings. Both *Readers* have a range of characters and mixed-gender dialogues. Mixed-gender dialogues allow me to examine which identity options are offered for dominant roles and which are subordinated and devalued. My summary shows that 184 visual images of four different types (cartoon, photograph, illustration, map) are employed in the two textbooks. The cartoon presented before the verbal texts depicts the scene and main characters of each situational dialogue. The large number of images indicates the complementary language-image relation and the need to interpret the meanings construed through the co-deployment of textual and visual resources in the two *Readers*.

Multimodality is an evolving feature in ELT pedagogical contexts that has drawn substantial attention from educators and teachers. Despite the common adoption of multimodal resources in EFL textbooks, few studies are found at the in-depth discursive level (Zhang, 2005, p. 11 cited in Chen, 2010). In my analysis of verbal texts and visual images, I draw on CDA as an interpretive approach to link decisions of language choice and visual design to underlying ideologies, power relations and identity options. This chapter analyses three imagined communities: Chinese characters as targeted learners, foreign characters as imagined visitors, and Beijing as an Olympic city. Following Shardakova and Pavlenko (2004), my critical examination and interpretation of the two sets of identity options offered in the two *Readers* for Chinese and foreign characters was based on a numerical analysis of the occurrences of each identity category, including gender, professional occupation, socioeconomic class, race, citizenship, and ethnicity and a content analysis of texts as cross-cultural encounters between Chinese and foreign interlocutors in each category. The visual analysis for group identities only considers the visual presentation of characters involved in situational dialogues and portrayed in cartoons before verbal texts. Audio presentations of main characters are also examined in order to identify which variety of English is valued and promoted in the two *Readers*. In conducting my analysis, I take an intersectional approach (Piller and Takahashi, 2010) to examine how various categories, such as gender, race, class and other axes of identity, might intersect in contributing to social inequality. In doing so, I seek to illuminate which group of Chinese learners may be marginalised and disempowered in the process of learning English, and which group of foreign interlocutors become "unimaginable" as native speakers of English. In analysing the imagined community of Beijing constructed in the two *Readers*, I examine both the linguistic and visual representation of the host city through a content analysis of texts and photographs.

3 Imbalanced gender distribution

My analysis starts with the discursive construction of gender identities in the two *Readers*. Gender is one of the most salient identity options offered to characters in language textbooks. In the two *Readers*, gender intersects with other social identities such as professional occupation, socioeconomic class, race and ethnicity in empowering some groups but at the same time marginalising others in the imagined community of the Olympic city. Based on the analysis of gender representation (and under-representation), I am able to reveal the ways that gender ideologies are tied to English language practices in the imagined community of the Olympic host city Beijing. The gender distribution of primary characters in the two *Readers* are summarised in Tables 12 and 13 as follows:

Table 12: Gender distribution in the *Elementary Reader*.

Gender	Chinese Male	Chinese Female	Foreign Male	Foreign Female
Number (/96)	27	21	43	5
Percentage	28%	22%	45%	5%

Table 13: Gender distribution in the *Advanced Reader*.

Gender	Chinese Male	Chinese Female	Foreign Male	Foreign Female
Number (/74)	28	6	37	3
Percentage	38%	8%	50%	4%

The *Elementary Reader* contains 96 primary characters, including 48 Chinese and 48 foreigners. The *Advanced Reader* presents 74 primary characters, including 34 Chinese and 40 foreigners. The statistics in Tables 12 and 13 show both *Readers* are severely imbalanced in terms of gender distribution. In the *Elementary Reader*, 70 out of 96 primary characters (72%) are male. More noticeably, men constitute a disproportionately large percentage (88%) of primary characters in the *Advanced Reader*. Foreign women are largely invisible in cross-cultural encounters in the two *Readers*: only five female foreign characters are represented pictorially in the *Elementary Reader* and three in the advanced one. The average ratio of males to females is approximately 4:1 in the two *Readers*. This underrepresentation of female characters may be interpreted by the preconceived idea that women, especially foreign women, would be less socially engaged than men in the Olympic events.

Tables 14 and 15 summarise occupational identities of primary characters of both genders in the two *Readers*. Clearly, primary characters in the two *Readers* are assigned gendered occupational roles. The majority of Chinese female characters (16 out of 21 in the *Elementary Reader*; 5 out of 6 in the *Advanced Reader*) are engaged in service trades in low-skilled service positions, taking stereotypical female jobs such as waitress, receptionist and shop assistant. In sharp contrast, Chinese male characters are more involved in the administration work of the Olympic Games (such as BOCOG staff and volunteers) and enjoy higher socioeconomic status (such as school principal or bar owner). Both *Readers* seldom

Table 14: Occupational identities of primary characters in the *Elementary Reader*.

Chinese Characters			Foreign Characters		
Occupational Identity	Male: 27	Female: 21	Occupational Identity	Male: 43	Female: 5
Taxi driver	4	–	Journalist	2	–
Tour guide	6	1	Photographer	1	–
Physician	1	1	Professor	1	–
School principal	1	–	Teacher	3	4
Teacher	1	1	Student	3	–
Athlete	1	–	Athlete	1	–
Student	3	2	Undefined (i.e. generic foreign visitor)	32	1
Volunteer	2	–			
Hotel reservationist	–	2			
Hotel receptionist	–	1			
Room attendant	–	1			
Waitress/waiter	–	3			
Cashier	–	1			
Nurse	–	1			
Store assistant	–	3			
Store manager	–	1			
Bus conductor	–	2			
Undefined (i.e. generic Beijing resident)	8	1			

assign an important and active role to foreign female characters. Teacher and journalist are the only professional occupational identity options offered to foreign female characters in the textbooks. Foreign athletes, team leaders and officials participating in the Beijing Olympics are imagined as exclusively masculine. In general, female characters (both Chinese and foreign) are not only marginalised in numbers but also disadvantaged in occupational identity and socioeconomic class. This gender distribution rests on a notion of male superiority and female subservience, as well as a belief that the male is radically distinct from the female.

Table 15: Occupational identities of primary characters in the *Advanced Reader*.

Chinese Characters			Foreign Characters		
Occupational Identity	Male: 28	Female: 6	Occupational Identity	Male: 37	Female: 3
BOCOG staff	7	–	Athlete (one is disabled)	12	–
Bar owner	1	–	Team leader	3	–
Student/ Volunteer	20	1	Official	2	–
Laundry worker	–	1	Journalist	11	2
Waitress	–	4	Undefined (i.e., generic foreign visitor)	9	1

The marginalisation of female characters can be observed from the exclusion of female characters in the conversational topics of the two *Readers* (see Table 11). The *Elementary Reader*, for instance, rather than integrating Chinese female characters fully throughout the textbook, confines more than half of them (12 out of 21, i.e. 57%) within three units: Unit 2 "Serving at a Hotel," Unit 3 "Working in a Restaurant," and Unit 6 "Selling at a Store." A complete exclusion of female characters can be observed in Unit 1 "Being a Taxi Driver," Unit 9 "Meeting at a Competition Venue" and Unit 10 "Serving as a Tour Guide." The exclusion of women is even more striking in the *Advanced Reader*: only 6 out of 28 situational dialogues give voice to Chinese female characters and 3 to foreign female characters. Some situational dialogues depict female characters in the cartoons but do not assign communicative roles to them in the text. For example, in the *Elementary Reader* Unit 8, Dialog 2 is a short conversation between a local tour guide and a foreign tourist in an antique shop in Beijing. Both of the two main characters are male. In the cartoon illustrating the text, a female shop assistant is positioned in the right corner of the picture, standing with hands folded in front. Her voiceless role in the text and submissive posture clearly show her humbleness and inferior status.

Another good example of the exclusion of women can be found in the *Advanced Reader* in Unit 7. This unit comprises four dialogues describing scenes of social events as the end of the Olympic Games approaches, held respectively at a local Chinese restaurant, a bar at Beijing's Shichahai Street, the international zone of the Olympic village, and the News Plaza hotel. It is worthwhile noting that the characters who are represented in both text and cartoon as BOCOG staff, Olympic volunteers, local bar owner, foreign athletes, journalist, and visitors are all male. The only female character in this unit is present in Dialog 1 "Dining out at a Restaurant." This dialogue depicts the scene where a local restaurant waitress helps a group of foreign male athletes make their order. Even though the Chinese waitress plays a prominent communicative role in the verbal text, she is not represented pictorially in the cartoon that accompanies the text.

In sum, both of the two *Readers* are characterised by an imbalanced gender distribution. Specifically, female characters (both Chinese and foreign) are marginalised in numbers and professional identities. Furthermore, female images as members of the upper-middle class are largely, if not completely, absent in the two textbooks. Such underrepresentation serves to reproduce the existing social hierarchical order within China. The imbalanced gender distribution of main characters in various identity categories of the *Readers* reflects the intersection of multiple forms of discrimination and oppression against women. In the next section, I will explore in more detail how the two *Readers* validate certain identity repertoires and construct imagined communities for targeted learners.

4 Imagined communities

Textbooks contribute to creating what a society recognises as legitimate and truthful through imagination. Imagination is a social and discursive process, and those in power oftentimes do the imaging for the rest of their fellow citizens, offering them certain identity options and leaving other options "unimaginable" (Shardakova and Pavlenko 2004, p. 29). In this section, I will discuss three imagined communities respectively in relation to Chinese characters, foreign characters, and Beijing as the Olympic host city by examining various identity options and their intersections.

4.1 Chinese characters as targeted learners

Linguistically and visually, the two *Readers* construct a male-dominated community in which Chinese are seen as always accessible, polite, and happy to service foreigners. As discussed in the preceding section, Chinese male characters in the two textbooks are invariably superior to female characters both in numbers and socioeconomic status. In fact, both *Readers* offer stereotyped gender identities to targeted learners. In the *Elementary Reader* (see Table 14), Chinese female characters are mostly depicted as engaged in service trades, working as hotel reservationists, hotel receptionists, room attendants, waitresses, cashiers, nurses, bus conductors (bus conductors are stereotypically female jobs in the Chinese context), store assistants or store managers. In contrast, the typical occupations assigned to Chinese male characters are taxi drivers, athletes and school principals. The *Advanced Reader* (see Table 15) also tends to stereotype gender roles. Although most Chinese characters of both genders are Olympic volunteers, this textbook assigns the roles of BOCOG staff (government official) and bar owner (businessman) to Chinese males and the roles of laundry worker and waitress to Chinese females. In general, the distribution of gendered occupational roles in the two *Readers* reflects an unspoken ideology that Chinese males enjoy superior socio-economic status to that of Chinese females.

Homogeneity is another distinguishing feature of Chinese characters present in both *Readers*. In terms of occupations and social status, most strikingly, the textbooks present a complete eradication of the masculine imagery of the working class and the stereotyping of female service personnel. Moreover, the verbal texts of the two *Readers* provide no information on Chinese characters' ethnic backgrounds. Visually, the ethnicities of the Chinese characters portrayed in the two textbooks are not distinguishable in terms of dress and physical appearance. In the *Elementary Reader*, Chinese female characters working in various service trades are noticeably dressed in work uniforms, whereas Chinese male characters always wear shirts and ties. Chinese characters of both genders who appear in the *Advanced Reader* are all uniformly dressed: Olympic volunteers in green uniforms and BOCOG staff wearing business suits and ties. More strikingly, the cartoon characters in the two textbooks are westernised in that they have big eyes with double eyelids and big noses. In effect, both *Readers* present a socially and ethnically homogeneous Chinese society. This homogeneity can be explained by the integration policy China has applied to its socially, linguistically and culturally diverse population and by the political conception proposed before the Olympic Games of constructing China as a "harmonious" society. Both policies aim at strengthening a unified Chinese identity among its population, developing shared values, and building a sense of national pride in being citizens of the country. Considering this, the focus of the two *Readers* is therefore to present a unified harmonious nation state rather than reflect the social and ethnic diversity of China.

In both *Readers*, Chinese characters are portrayed as accessible, polite, helpful and trustworthy people who speak fluent English. On every occasion, they are able to avoid misunderstandings. Judging from the content, the two *Readers* are primarily concerned with various services and courtesies for foreign visitors, from giving foreign tourists directions to accompanying foreign Olympic officials on a visit to the exhibition about the preparatory work for the Beijing Olympic Games. Excessive selflessness of Chinese characters and dedication to foreigners can be seen in examples such as the following: in the *Elementary Reader*, Unit 4, Dialog 3 is about a cross-cultural encounter in which a senior Beijing resident offers his private toilet to a young White male tourist. Unit 7, Dialog 3 describes how a local passenger finds a seat for a sick young White male passenger in a crowded bus. In Unit 9, Dialog 3, a local college student meets a foreign student outside a venue ticket centre and offers him a ride. In Unit 10, Dialog 3, a local resident provides his foreign friend with a free-of-charge tour guide in a tourist site. In addition to their selflessness and courteousness, the Chinese characters are described as law-abiding and trustworthy people. In a restaurant conversation (*Elementary Reader*, Unit 3, Dialog 4), a local waitress declines a foreign customer's tip and kindly informs him "no tips in Beijing." In another dialog (*Elementary Reader*, Unit 10, Dialog 1), a local tour guide tells a foreign tourist that he adheres to the standard rate for the guide fee. The two *Readers* were designed so that they were not only about teaching English, but also aimed at promoting exemplary courtesies and ethical practices.

Being an important supplement to verbal texts, visual meaning-making resources play an important role in the realisation of the attitudinal orientation of the main characters. The cartoons in the two *Readers* are mostly inscribed with positive sentiments, which can be observed from the perpetual smiles on main characters' faces. The Olympic volunteers and BOCOG staff in particular, even when they are discussing difficult problems with foreign interlocutors, always look as if they are grinning with delight. In the *Advanced Reader*, Unit 5, Dialog 4, two Ethiopian journalists complain to a BOCOG staff member that their media commentator has been located too far away from the competition site and their cameras have been moved by other media staff. In addition, they request the BOCOG staff member to move their seats forward in the press conference room to make up for their disadvantageous position in the interview after competition. Although the BOCOG staff member verbally declines their requests in a polite but resolute manner, a mood of happiness is added to the multimodal text via visual affective inscriptions. The BOCOG staff member listens with a friendly and courteous attitude, which can be observed from the character's facial expression of smiling and squinting. Interestingly, while making a complaint, the Ethiopian journalists also look quite happy. In addition, they do not continue arguing their case but readily accept the refusal of their request. In this example cross-cultural misunderstandings and conflicts are ignored by the textbook producers. Indeed, misunderstanding and conflicts seldom occur in the imagined international community of English in the two readers, and thus skills to handle cross-cultural misunderstanding and conflicts are not provided in the textbooks. Smiling was considered especially important to, and was expected of, all volunteers. This message is revealed through a foreign character in a conversation at an Olympic

Stadium (*Advanced Reader,* Unit 3, Dialog 2). While this foreign character is going through a security checkpoint with the help of a local volunteer, she comments: "You volunteers are always friendly and helpful here in Beijing. I love your smiling faces." The generic politeness, friendliness, helpfulness, and professionalism of Chinese characters are co-initiated by the linguistic and visual meaning-making recourses of the two *Readers*. Overall, the two *Readers* function as an official guide to teach targeted Chinese learners "civilised" behaviours, common courtesies, professional morality, and even subservience in English.

Stipulated by BOCOG in the *Beijing Olympic Action Plan* (2002), Beijing was also committed to all-out efforts to "upgrade the moral standards for its citizens and thereby raise the level of the city's urban civilisation in preparation for the Olympics." The basic ethical standards to be promoted were "patriotism, law abiding behaviour, politeness, integrity, friendliness, diligence and industry, professionalism and dedication." The Beijing Olympic authority believed volunteers to be an important force to stimulate the enthusiasm of Beijing residents for foreign language learning, call for the public to participate in social welfare activities, and enhance the socio-cultural level to establish the image of a civilised city around the world. Following the motto that "the smile of a volunteer is the best name card of Beijing" (BOCOG, 2002), the Beijing Olympic authority urged 400,000 volunteers to engage in urban services and more than 70,000 volunteers were providing services for Olympic competitions to give the best image of Beijing with their smiles (Zhang, 2009, p. 22). Priority was also given to those working at the airports, train stations, customs offices, and hotels, or in the subways and buses, and for sectors providing food, recreation, culture, retail, medical services, banking, and taxi driving (BOCOG, 2002). Steps had been taken to help service industries to improve the attitude, expertise, discipline and performance of their staff. In addition, uniforms were introduced in these service industries. As part of the governmental efforts, Beijing strongly promoted such moral principles as social courtesy, helpfulness, care for public property, environmental protection, and law-abidingness among Beijing citizens. Before the 2008 Olympics, Beijing was blanketed with billboards, posters, and TV commercials advocating *Wenming* (civility) and advising citizens on behaviour that was deemed socially unacceptable. In the buses and subways, LCD monitors endlessly played promotional films geared towards creating "a harmonious society." The pedagogic goal of promoting civilised behaviours, common courtesies and professional morality in the two official English training textbooks embodies such governmental emphasis on "urban civility."

4.2 Foreign characters as represented visitors

Overall, the foreign characters in the two textbooks share much in common – both are predominantly White male, middle to upper class, well cared for by local residents and volunteers, and show a tireless interest in traditional Chinese culture. We first take a look at the gender distribution and occupational identities of foreign characters. In marked similarity to my analysis of targeted learners in Section 4.1, the foreign characters in the two *Readers* constitute a pronounced male-dominated imagined community. In both *Readers*, English-speaking characters are predominantly male, and foreign women are marginalized in terms of professional occupation. As analysed earlier in Tables 14 and 15, most foreign male interlocutors have occupational identities as journalists, photographers, professors, teachers, athlete team leaders and government officials. In sharp contrast, only one foreign woman appears as a teacher in the *Elementary Reader*, Unit 11, Dialog 3. Most foreign female characters are depicted as anonymous visitors/spectators without being given any occupational identity in the texts. In the *Advanced Reader*, foreign characters are, similarly, predominantly males, representing athletes, journalists, spectators, team leaders and government officials. Noticeably, none of the only three female characters are depicted as athletes, team leaders, or government officials who are directly involved in the Beijing Olympic Games. Commensurate with the findings from analysis of the *Elementary Reader*, foreign females are not only underrepresented in numbers but also devalued in terms of occupational identities. One possible effect of this underrepresentation and devaluation of foreign women is that targeted Chinese learners were likely to be under-prepared with useful linguistic recourses and communicative strategies to deal with professional female English-speaking interlocutors. Moreover, such underrepresentation may further reinforce the idea of male superiority in the minds of Chinese learners of English.

Table 16 presents a summary of the racial and citizenship identities of foreign characters in the two *Readers*. The racial identity of foreign characters is not indicated in the language, but in the skin colour and physical countenance depicted in the pictures. As shown in Table 16, interlocutors from non-White backgrounds are largely invisible in both *Readers*. The virtual absence of Asian-looking characters is particularly striking. In both *Readers* Asians do not take any communicative role in the multimodal texts. Even though the *Elementary Reader* has four English-speaking black interlocutors, three of them are in one unit, "Talking to a Patient," appearing as patients or a friend of a patient. This racial composition of imagined foreign interlocutors may contribute to prejudice against non-White people as legitimate speakers of English and

Table 16: Race and citizenship of foreign characters.

	Elementary Reader				Advanced Reader			
Race	Citizenship	Male 43	Female 5	Race	Citizenship	Male 37	Female 3
White	USA	6	–	White	USA	2	–
	Undefined	33	5		Argentina	1	–
					Australia	1	–
					Czech Republic	1	–
					Denmark	1	–
					UK	2	–
					Pakistan	1	–
					New Zealand	1	–
					Switzerland	2	–
					Sweden	2	1
					South Africa	1	–
					Turkey	2	2
					Undefined	17	–
Black	South Africa	1	–	Black	Ethiopia	2	–
	Undefined	3	–		South Africa	1	–
Asian	–	–	–	Asian	–	–	–

discourage Chinese learners from engaging with diverse English speakers. The *Advanced Reader* shows an attempt to raise the awareness of internal diversity among English-speaking foreign interlocutors. Table 16 shows that a much wider range of imagined characters with diverse citizenships are written into this *Reader*. However, foreign characters are still predominantly White males with light-coloured hair. Moreover, it is assumed that citizens of multilingual and multicultural countries such as USA, UK, Australia, and New Zealand are exclusively White. Visually, the cover pages of both *Readers* explicitly depict an imagined English-speaking community dominated by White people, mostly youngsters. Again, the assumption that associates English with White people has the potential to impair targeted learners' understanding of multi-ethnic communities of the target language and their intercultural competence in English.

In terms of variety of English, the two *Readers* show a special preference for American English. American English is assumed to be the default language of the imagined English-speaking community. The situational dialogues between Chinese and foreign interlocutors in both *Readers* were pre-recorded exclusively in "Standard American English" voices. Additionally, both *Readers* used American English spellings, pronunciations and idiomatic expressions. For example, in a restaurant conversation in Unit 3, Dialog 4, a White male foreign customer comments that one appetizer he had in a local restaurant tastes like "Buffalo wings" and then asks for a "doggy bag" to take away his leftovers. In language tips after the text, the targeted learners are given explanations on the meaning and etymology of the two expressions in American English. In addition, the "proper" way of tipping in North America is also briefly introduced in language tips: the tip is generally 20 percent of the bill. Text notes which attach importance to American ways of speaking English may serve to set up the American variety of English as the standard reference among targeted Chinese learners and, again, leave them underprepared for other varieties and cultures, including English as a lingua franca, which was the more likely function of English in the context of the Beijing Olympics.

A decade before the Beijing Olympics, Kirkpatrick (2000) observed the fact that the Chinese Ministry of Education and Chinese professionals argued strenuously for a native variety standard in ELT: for the government, British English represented the standard, although younger people were leaning towards an American standard. In my analysis of the official Olympic English popularisation campaign in Beijing in Chapter 4 and Chapter 5, the government still showed a strong preference for native speaker varieties. The strong sense of native variety standard had a great influence on ELT textbooks in China. Xu (2002) examined 40 focus texts of *College English*, the designated ELT textbooks for non-English majors in China. He found that the popular textbooks used across China since the 1980s exclusively contain texts by British or American authors or from British or American sources. The two *Readers* in this study, though not from British or American sources, also exhibit a strong preference for American English. In addition to five Chinese reviewers, an American scholar (John A. Gordan) was also enlisted in the review committee of the textbooks. The native speaker standard in Chinese ELT textbooks evidently affected Chinese learners' English learning practices. My interviewees' understanding of correct English use was reflected in their strong sense of British and American English as "Standard English." Du Jie, an English teacher at Wuhan New Oriental School, for instance, asserted that it was of primary importance to teach "Standard English" to Chinese learners. Zhao Chan, a postgraduate in a leading Chinese university, said with certainty that his sense of "Standard English" is British or American English. Their remarks were and still are highly representative among ELT practitioners and learners in China. For a long time, Native Speaker English (i.e., 'Standard' British/American English) has been considered as the most acceptable kind of English for academic purposes and official use in China, and many people have held rather negative views of the English of non-native English speakers (NNESs). However, there is great diversity among and within English varieties. The real English world is not constituted by only two 'standard varieties.' This exclusive focus on American English and the promotion of an American-centric view in the Olympic English textbooks obscures the reality of the world's linguistic and cultural diversity and is unhelpful for Chinese English learners in intercultural communication.

Going hand in hand with the selflessness, dedication and courteousness of the Chinese characters described above, foreign characters in the two *Readers* are always well cared for, highly satisfied, and show tireless interest in both traditional and modern aspects of Beijing. In the *Elementary Reader*, Unit 8, "Taking a walk downtown," all the foreign tourists show great interest in discovering Beijing's "traditional culture" (antique shops, ancient architecture, calligraphy, tea houses, and so forth) and express amazement at the city's modernity (e.g., Wangfujing shopping area, cafes, the Bar Street, Chinese hip hop, Chang'an Street, the National Theatre). In the *Advanced Reader* Unit 6 Dialogue 1, an American athlete is sightseeing at the Summer Palace in the company of a local volunteer. After seeing the Tower of Buddhist Incense, a landmark building in the Summer Palace, the American athlete is filled with wonder at the sight and says to the Chinese volunteer that his friends in the United States are "all crazy about China." In the texts, foreign characters openly express their high levels of satisfaction with the successful hosting of the Beijing Olympics. In the concluding unit of the *Advanced Reader*, a foreign journalist comments on his experience in Beijing: "I thought I'd get homesick, but it has been so pleasant here in Beijing that I'm none the happier knowing that I would be home this time tomorrow" (Unit 7, Dialog 4, page 221). Positive appraisals of Beijing and its people by foreign characters feature prominently throughout the *Readers*. All the examples above show how the textbook authors expected Westerners to be interested in Chinese culture and satisfied with their experience in Beijing.

Despite being the first English-language training material regarding Paralympic services in China (Official Website of the Beijing 2008 Olympic Games, 2008), the *Readers* give surprisingly little attention to foreign interlocutors with a disability. Among the 76 situational dialogues of the two *Readers*, only one contributes to the discussion of Paralympic services. The only disabled foreign character is a White male athlete in the *Advanced Reader,* Unit 3, Dialog 4, who is being taken on a tour to the competition venue with the help of a Chinese volunteer. Again, the text serves as a guide for a civilised behaviour: providing assistance to people with disabilities. In sum, the official textbooks project an American-centric, White male dominated, middle-class utopian community. White males speaking American English were imagined as the most desirable English-speaking foreign interlocutors.

4.3 Beijing as a harmonious Olympic city

The two *Readers* present Beijing as a mixture of tradition and modernity. On one hand, Beijing can offer foreign visitors an ancient and rich cultural heritage. On the other hand, the city can provide foreign visitors with modern infrastructure and efficient services. The most frequently mentioned locations in the *Readers* include both tourist sites with a long history (such as the Great Wall, Forbidden City, Summer Palace, Tiananmen Square, *hutongs*) and newly constructed venues with modern design (the Olympic Green, National Stadium, Olympic village, Media Village, National Theatre, Capital International Airport). In the interactions, foreign characters are told that they can either visit antique shops or enjoy live Chinese hip hop music at local cafes. In the *Advanced Reader*, Unit 1, Dialog 2, a foreign journalist says he is quite amazed at the "modern and glamorous" capital international airport compared to how it looked eight years ago. The modern side of Beijing is sometimes compared to American cities by foreign visitors, including New York (*Elementary Reader*, Unit 8, Dialog 1) and Washington, DC (*Elementary Reader*, Unit 8, Dialog 4). This comparison demonstrates the Chinese government's firm commitment to establish Beijing as a "world city" and build "a spectacular image of urban modernity through a massive urban transformation project" (Xinhua, 2008f). At the same time, however, the *Readers* express the government's concern that Beijing would lose its appeal for foreign visitors after the urban transformation project. In the *Elementary Reader*, a foreign tourist says he prefers "culturally refined" tea houses to Westernised cafes in Beijing (Unit 8, Dialog 3). Another foreign tourist states that he is not an admirer of the modern design of the National Theatre and prefers "Chinese ones" (Unit 8, Dialog 4). An Orientalist interpretation of "Chineseness" is generated here through the gaze of imagined foreign visitors.

"Building a harmonious society" was placed at the top of CPC's agenda in 2006 and is an important theme of the *Readers*. As discussed previously, in the imagined harmonious community of Beijing, local residents are portrayed as accessible, polite, helpful, and law-abiding, and foreign visitors are taken care of, satisfied and cheerful. It is also worth noting that the two *Readers* avoid any reference to failed cross-cultural communication. Chinese characters all speak fluent English and seldom encounter any misunderstanding in English with foreign characters in the imagined community of Beijing. In doing so, the targeted learners may lose their opportunity to learn the skill of negotiating misunderstanding, which is crucial for intercultural competence. Visually, the harmonious image of Beijing can be best demonstrated by the visual display of the cover page of the *Elementary Reader*. The cover page is a synthesised photograph that contains three separate images. The background image is the grand red wall of the Forbidden City, representing the political and cultural centre of China – Beijing. Standing out against the red background, an elderly Chinese citizen is helping an elderly White tourist to read a map of Beijing. Both of them are smiling with delight. In the foreground, a group of White youngsters are enthusiastically cheering with their mouths open and waving their hands. All the youngsters are looking at the front horizontally, and as such their eyelines directly meet those of the viewers. The visual display, together with the inscribed happiness, present to the viewers the scenes of a "harmonious" Beijing society in which local residents are helpful and foreign visitors are cheerful. Below the image of the White youngsters is the slogan of the Beijing Olympics – "One World, One Dream [同一个世界，同一个梦想 tongyige shijie, tongyige mengxiang]." The slogan had actually given rise to much controversy since its official announcement on 26 June 2005. According to the Official Website of the Beijing 2008 Olympic Games (2005b), the English slogan highlights the theme that "the whole of mankind lives in the same world and seeks the same dream and ideal" and reflects the Confucian philosophy of "harmony of man with nature" and "peace enjoys priority." In contrast, some critics argued "'One World One Dream' is a fallacy" (Liao, 2009), which understated the diversity of the world as well as existing differences and contradictions. Applying the Olympic slogan of "One World One Dream" on the cover page of the *Readers* may imply to targeted learners the idea of "one world one language": a monolingual international community with English as *the* uniting language.

The prominent social phenomenon of English fever among Chinese people in their preparation for the Beijing Olympics is also featured in the two *Readers*. In the *Advanced Reader*, Unit 5, Dialogue 4, two Ethiopian journalists say they have long heard about the 'English learning programme' for Beijing citizens, especially for the volunteers. In the same text, a BOCOG staff member claims that all the volunteers have received systematic language training before the Games. A picture entitled "a foreign language training class in Beijing" is attached to the text which features a group of Beijing community residents ranging from children to elderly citizens enthusiastically learning *English 100 for Beijing Citizens*, an ELT material which contains 100 commonly used English sentences and was widely distributed to English language beginners in Beijing. In the *Elementary Reader*, Unit 11, Dialog 3 (see the dialog on page 166), a local high school teacher explains the reasons for Chinese people learning English when asked why school students in Beijing are crazy to be learning English. These reasons are: (1) "It's a useful tool"; (2) "China needs bilingual citizens"; (3) "For college education"; (4) "It's a research language." The four arguments for the learning of English by

Chinese citizens manifest the government's decisions to promote English at all levels of education and the inclusion of English proficiency in the development of citizenship in the school curriculum in the 21st century (Ministry of Education of PRC, 2000). However, the assumption that English is a useful tool for education and research and is required for fostering a bilingual Chinese society is a precise exemplification of ideological hegemony. By neutralising English and granting the usefulness of English a status of common sense the government was actually exercising control by consent. As a result, individuals may accept this dominant ideology and misrecognise it as non-ideology, taking the usefulness of English for granted even in the absence of proof in their own life trajectories. Noticeably, some Chinese characters in the *Readers* exhibit intense desire for English and the West (US and UK). A good example can be found in the *Elementary Reader*, Dialog 4, Unit 11 (see the dialog on page 166). In this situational dialogue, a foreign teacher is surrounded by a group of Chinese high school students who hope to receive his advice on their future studies. All the Chinese students express their longing for going abroad (more precisely, to the UK and US) after college. The most desirable life vision suggested in the text for high school students is to go to Peking University first, and then further their study in "Oxford" or "Harvard" afterwards, and finally become a professor of English. It also projects the UK and US as the most desirable overseas study destination.

5 Summary

The two *Readers*, though different from each other in terms of targeted learners and pedagogical contents, both feature similar identity constructions. To begin with, female characters are marginalised in numbers and professional identities. Under the current patriarchal ideologies dominant in Chinese society, it might not be surprising to see that most female characters are positioned as inferior to male characters in professional occupations and social class. However, the biased portrayals of women in the two *Readers* are inconsistent with the fact that women are consistently found in prestigious occupations in higher career ladders in China and beyond. Gender bias in language textbooks may not only negatively affect the pedagogical value and goals of textbooks but also be a factor in constructing and sustaining gender inequality in Chinese society. Previous research has shown that the non-inclusion of women and girls in language teaching materials seriously impairs learners' understanding of the target language and its culture(s) (Rifkin, 1998).

Targeted Chinese learners are afforded the opportunity to imagine themselves having an engaged role in the Olympic host city, interacting in English with a set of native and other speakers who are predominantly White middle-class males. In cross-cultural encounters, Chinese characters are portrayed as accessible, polite, helpful and trustworthy people who speak fluent English and are able to avoid misunderstandings on every occasion. Foreign visitors are imagined as predominantly White males, middle-to-upper class, well-cared for by local residents and volunteers, and showing tireless interest in Chinese traditional culture. Moreover, the two *Readers* present a native speaker ideology and an essentialist link between English and the White race. In line with Cummins (1994), I argue that curriculum and textbooks that reflect mainly the experiences and values of the middle-class White male native-English speaking population effectively suppress the experiences and values of targeted Chinese students.

Beijing is discursively constructed as a harmonious society with a good mixture of both tradition and modernity, where Chinese are earnestly going about learning English as the international language while preserving cultural traditions. Under the Olympic theme of "One World One Dream," the international community is imagined as a monolingual space with English as *the* international language. In the imagined harmonious community of Beijing, Chinese and foreign characters seldom encounter any misunderstanding. The imagined harmonious community of Beijing in the two *Readers* is exactly a manifestation of the state's determination to "turn this sporting mega-event into the celebration of a Chinese renaissance and the harmonisation of world civilisations" (Xu, 2006, p. 90). Consequently, social contradictions and conflicts are completely avoided in the texts. By imagining Beijing as a harmonious community free of misunderstandings and conflicts and recognising this imagination as legitimate knowledge, the state was maintaining governance by practising ideological hegemony.

The two *Readers* offer misrepresented, stereotyped, and oversimplified identity options to the targeted learners, with potential implications not only for the learners' understanding of the role of English in the Games, but also for speakers of other languages – and particularly French, the other official language – whose identities and place within the Games might be erased as they are amalgamated into a homogenous whole. As language textbooks are a powerful instrument for turning ideologies into practices, learners may accept the embedded ideology in the official Olympic English textbooks as a non-ideology, and misrecognise it as a normal state of affairs (Bourdie and Thompson, 1991). Moreover, it is my contention that misrepresenting, stereotyping, and oversimplifying identity repertoires in language textbooks may leave learners without important linguistic means of self-representation and lead to cross-cultural misunderstandings, frustration, offence, and conflict, as well as to resistance from students in cases where their own linguistic and cultural values come into conflict with those imposed on them by the texts (see the case study of Wei Ru in Chapter 5).

Shohamy (2006, p. 133) suggests that language policy manifests itself not only through such overt items as policy documents and test materials but also through linguistic landscape (LL) – language objects that mark the public space. In the next chapter, I will enquire into how public signs as language objects were used as a symbol for constructing identities and turning language ideologies into practices.

Elementary Reader, Unit 11 Dialog 3
On a high-school campus

A: So many English speakers!
B: They study English every day.
A: Where do they practice it?
B: In class, in the lab.
A: I heard of the English Corner.
B: Yes. They go there very often.
A: How often?
B: Every other night.
A: They are crazy for it. How come?
B: Why, it's a useful tool.
A: For communication?
B: Yes. China needs bilingual citizens.
A: For college education, too?
B: That's right. It's a research language.
A: Any other foreign languages?
B: Japanese is also their favorite.
A: At the college level?
B: Oh, yeah. Russian and French, too.
A: Good for them.
B: You foreign friends are popular here.

Elementary Reader, Unit 11 Dialog 4
In a high-school classroom

A: Hope you are back soon.
B: I will, kid. Plan to go abroad?
A: Oh yeah. After college.
B: Where to?
A: Europe. Maybe the States.
B: How to choose a college?
A: It all depends.
B: I see. What do you plan to do?
A: I'll be a professor. Probably in English.
B: Great. PKU may be a choice.
A: Yes, Oxford afterwards.
B: Harvard may also be good.
A: Yes. In the meantime. I should study hard.
B: You are a volunteer, aren't you?
A: No. But I would like to work for the Games. Why ask?
B: Just curious. A waste of time?
A: Oh no! I need the experience.
B: For what?
A: For the Olympic Spirit. For my own future.
B: I am proud of you.

Note: PKU is the abbreviation for Peking University

Chapter 7
The linguistic landscape of the Olympic city

1 The language policy environment

The reconceptualisation of Beijing's identity in the spotlight of the 2008 Olympic Games led to a massive urban transformation project. A total of 280 billion yuan (approximately 40 billion USD) was invested in urban infrastructure to build a spectacular image of urban modernity (Xinhua, 2008f). Within this massive urban infrastructure construction, a priority had been given to public signs, which constituted part of the linguistic landscape (LL) of the Olympic host city. In this section, I will discuss governmental policy and planning for public signs in Beijing and the outcome of the Olympic English signage standardisation campaign.

1.1 Governmental planning for public signs

Beijing started using bilingual signs (in both Chinese and English) as a concrete measure to indicate its opening up in the late 1980s, especially in preparation for the 1990 Asian Games (Xinhua, 2005). After Beijing's successful bid for the 2008 Olympic Games, bilingual signage became increasingly visible at tourist attractions, major hotels, street crossings, transportation hubs, and other major public locations. As early as 2002, BOCOG (2002) laid down overall objectives for the transformation of public signs in *Beijing Olympic Action Plan*. Soon afterwards, specific tasks and working procedures were drawn up in the *Action Plan for the BSFLP* (Organising Committee of the BSFLP, 2003). The transformation and upgrading of public signs for the Games in Beijing was clearly centred on the standardisation of English signage translations.

Before the Games, Beijing had started a battle to eradicate "Chinglish" and replace it with "Standard English." Chinglish refers to speech or writing in English that shows the interference of Chinese language or the influence of Chinese culture. Liu Yang, the Deputy Director of the BSFLP Organising Committee, accused Chinglish of being defective English, ranging from careless spelling and bad grammar to cultural misinterpretation (Beijing Review, 2004). Some of the most popularly discussed Chinglish examples taken from the official website of BSFLP include: a directional sign reading "Export" (Exit), a sign saying "Guest Go No Further" (Staff Only/Authorised Personnel Only), a sign reading "Careful Landslip Attention Security" (Wet Floor) at Beijing Capital International Airport, and a street sign pointing the way to "Racist Park" (Chinese Ethnic Culture Park). In Chinese public and academic discourses, the "correctness" and "accuracy" in the learning and use of English are always measured against a native speaker standard (Kirkpatrick, 2000; Xu, 2002). The term "Chinglish" has been used with inferior and deficient implications in contrast to "Standard English," which is symbolically associated with authority, prestige, modernity and globalisation (Kirkpatrick, 2000; Xu, 2002). This dominant language ideology connects "Standard English" with the image of Beijing as an Olympic and global city, and relates "Chinglish" to the early days of the opening up and the unregulated market economy.

As early as 2005, the website of *China Daily* (2005), the largest English-language portal in China, launched a campaign entitled "Use Accurate English to Welcome the Olympics – Public Bilingual Sign Standardisation Drive" in major Chinese cities, such as Beijing, Shanghai, Xi'an and Guangzhou. This activity was supported by the Cultural and Education Section of the British Council and the Public Affairs Section of the Canadian Embassy (China Daily, 2005). A number of renowned Chinese universities, including the University of International Business and Economics, also supported the campaign. The organiser said the campaign aimed to "prepare for the 2008 Beijing Olympic Games by creating a better language learning environment, and more importantly, enhancing the nation's international image" (China Daily, 2005). Their joint efforts to promote "accurate English" which took the "native-speaker" as a point of reference soon turned into a governmental campaign. In 2006, the Foreign Affairs Office of the Beijing Municipal Government established an advisory council and an office dedicated to launching a citywide English signage standardisation campaign in collaboration with the BSFLP Organising Committee. The aim of this campaign was to ensure that all public signage in Beijing was "grammatically correct and free of 'Chinglish'" (Xinhua, 2007a). Two initiatives were undertaken to achieve this aim: one was the proactive formulation of English translation standards and the other was the reactive establishment of a Chinglish-reporting system.

1.2 Olympic English signage standardisation campaign

Language standardisation is an important aspect of top-down language corpus planning. From 2006 to 2008 the Beijing Municipal Government enlisted the help of the consulting group of the BSFLP and progressively launched a series of local standards for English translations of public signs. Liu Yang, who headed the BSFLP and the English signage standardisation campaign, insisted: "If English translation is needed it must be subject to the standards set forth in the regulations" (Associated Press, 2007). These standards were modelled on native speaker varieties.

The promulgation of local English translation standards exerted a wide-ranging influence on the linguistic landscape of Beijing. On 1 December 2006, the Beijing Municipal Local Standards on English Translations of Public Signs (Foreign Affairs Office of the Beijing Municipal Government, 2006) came into force, making Beijing the first city in China to implement local standards on English signage translations. These standards cover nine areas: road traffic, tourist attractions, museums, commercial establishments, cultural facilities, bus and metro systems, health and medicine, sports venues, and sanitation facilities. A total of 5,398 pieces of standard English translations and a set of translation principles had been worked out from 2006 to 2008 (Foreign Affairs Office of the Beijing Municipal Government, 2008b). According to the Foreign Affairs Office of the Beijing Municipal Government (2008b), the official standards had been put into practice in all kinds of road traffic facilities, over 60 scenic spots, 11 municipal parks, 22 museums, 927 cultural sites, 152 sports venues, 320 key commercial enterprises, 3,600 medical institutions, 641 bus lines, 16,000 buses, 37 subway trains, 66,000 taxis and 34,000 public toilets, which led to the update and replacement of 825,700 existing signs. The next move was to update English menus used by private businesses in Beijing's catering and hotel industry. In December 2007, the Beijing Municipal Government issued Beijing Municipal Standards on English Translations of Chinese Menus (2007), specifying 2,862 Standard English translations of Chinese dishes and general translation principles. The official standards were distributed to and implemented in more than 1,300 enterprises including restaurants around commercial districts and Olympic venues, top restaurants, and 119 contracted hotels in Beijing. The adoption of the Beijing Municipal Local Standards on English Translations of Beijing Organisations' Names and Administrative and Professional Titles (Foreign Affairs Office of the Beijing Municipal Government, 2008a) was another important measure to carry forward the English signage standardisation campaign. These standards regulate the English names of the municipal party committee and government, people's congresses, CPPCC committees, courts and prosecutors' offices, mass organisations and municipal enterprises, as well as the English titles of related personnel and professional and technical qualifications.

After the promulgation of these local standards, a long-term mechanism for strictly enforcing the standardisation system of English translations was developed. First, extensive publicity was given to the glossary regulations on English translations through the official website of the Beijing Municipal Government (www.beijing.gov.cn/), the official website of the BSFLP (www.bjenglish.com.cn/), and other mainstream media. In order to step up the efforts to promote "Standard English," the BSFLP Organising Committee set up a "Chinglish" sign reporting system on its website and carried out a citywide "Chinglish correction" campaign to mobilise local citizens and student volunteers to help remove Chinglish from English signs in Beijing (Xinhua, 2007a). Chinglish was added to the list of things Olympic organisers sought to ban, along with spitting, run-down housing and bad manners. All of these were seen as embarrassing and harmful to the official image Beijing strived to create through the Olympic Games. The Beijing Municipal Government asserted that the mechanism was "a driving force for the development of Beijing into a modern international metropolis" (Foreign Affairs Office of the Beijing Municipal Government, 2008b). Ideologically, the English signage standardisation campaign was guided by the assumptions that "Standard English" was beneficial to societal development and "Standard" American or British English was the proper reference point for all varieties of English. I will now move on to a literature review of linguistic landscape research and then explore how signage standardisation policies were actually implemented in the linguistic landscape of the Olympic city.

2 Linguistic landscape research

In recent years an increasing number of researchers have started to pay attention to language texts that are present in public space. Linguistic landscape (LL) is a concept used in sociolinguistics as scholars study the "visibility and salience of languages on public and commercial signs in a given territory or region" (Landry and Bourhis, 1997, p. 23). LL is a relatively new area of attention in language policy and language use research, as most research tends to focus primarily on overt mechanisms of language policy such as policy documents or on language user experience and not on language objects in the public space. Shohamy (2006) points out that the presence (or absence) of language in public space transmits "symbolic messages as to the legitimacy, relevance, priority and standards of languages and the people and groups they represent" (p. 111). Therefore, LL serves as a mechanism to "affect, manipulate and impose de facto language policy and practice in hidden and covert ways" (Shohamy, 2006, p. 111). Similarly, Cenoz and Gorter (2006, p. 67) argue that the relationship between LL and sociolinguistic context is "bidirectional." On the one hand, LL reflects the relative power and status of different languages in a specific sociolinguistic context. On the other hand, because the language(s) in which signs are written can influence people's perception of the status of those languages, LL can affect language practices and contribute to the construction of the sociolinguistic context. LL, then, is a battlefield between different languages as well as a field of identity construction and negotiation between different groups. The present study examines the patterns and functions of LL as a mechanism of language policy as well as a symbol for identity construction.

In the Olympic host city Beijing, urban dwellers and visitors alike were immersed in various forms of linguistic objects, the whole of which constitute the city's linguistic landscape "where society's public life takes place" (Ben-Rafael et al. 2006, p. 8). In this study, I focus on signs in the public places frequented by Olympic visitors in Beijing. Kress (1993) maintains that "all signs are equally subject to critical reading, for no sign is innocent" (p. 174). Van Leeuwen (1993) also cautions that no matter how "ideologically innocent" signs (and the social practices of which they are a part) may seem, they may in fact be powerful instruments in the (re)production of the social world in which they form part of the landscape. The public signs surrounding Beijing residents and Olympic visitors might be taken for granted as "given" settings and thus their embedded language ideologies readily accepted. Therefore, this chapter aims to reveal how the LL of Beijing served as a covert mechanism of language policy that turned language ideologies into language practices.

The first thing that needs clarification in LL research, as Gorter (2006) suggests, is to determine what belongs to the LL under study. There have been different views on what constitutes a "linguistic object", or in other words, the unit of analysis for LL research. Most researchers, following Landry and Bourhis (1997, p. 25), mainly consider language texts on relatively "fixed" signs such as "public road signs, advertising billboards, street names, place names, commercial shop signs, and public signs on government buildings", which have some degree of stability regarding their spatial position. There are other researchers who add "mobile" forms of signs to this list of objects. Such mobile signs could be "leaflets and flyers being distributed (and perhaps discarded) in the street, advertising on vans, buses and other vehicles that pass through the streets of the area under study, free tourist maps and other publications available on counters and desks of hotels and tourist information centres" (Torkington, 2009, p. 124), or even "personal visiting cards" (Ben-Rafael et al. 2006, p. 8) and "business cards" (Thurlow and Jaworski, 2010).

An important characteristic of LL, as identified by Ben-Rafael et al. (2006, p. 8) is that it is comprised of both "top down/official" signs issued by public authorities (for example governments, municipalities or public agencies) and "bottom up/non-official" signs issued by autonomous individuals, associations or firms acting within the limits authorised by official regulations. Backhaus (2006) notes that the two types of signs make different contributions to the LL of a given place. Applying this distinction may provide different pictures of a specific LL and thus reveal underlying ideological orientations and power relations behind language choice. Generally speaking, official signs are linguistic artefacts of a central or local government, which may reflect the overt language policies of a given state or region. In this sense they may be symbolic markers of status and power. Non-official signs, by contrast, may manifest local language practices and grassroots cultural identities. Together, they contribute to the symbolic construction of public space (Ben-Rafael et al. 2006, p. 10).

Studies of LL are mainly concerned with the visibility and salience of language codes on signs in a specific territory or region. These LL studies have hitherto largely been driven by quantitative research methods, usually by counting the occurrence of different languages contained on sampled signs in a specific geographic space, as Huebner (2006) and Backhaus (2006) did in their study of the LL of Bangkok and Tokyo respectively. In contrast, a few studies employ a qualitative approach to LL. For example, Piller (2007), utilising a sociolinguistic ethnography, discusses language choice in multilingual texts of a Swiss tourist portal at three levels: linguistic choice, content available in a given language, and relative positioning of available languages. Her study finds that language choice as a market-driven choice favours English as "the international default language" and "a 'cheap' resource" in the context of Swiss tourism. In another LL study, Puzey (2007) conducted a qualitative survey of the use of minority languages in road signage in public places in Norway, Scotland and Italy, and examined the formats of sampled signs with reference to legislation and reactions from the public and the media. This study shed light on the symbolic importance for identity of place names on signs. The current study takes a CDA-informed qualitative approach to the examination of the LL of Beijing during the Olympic Games for three main reasons. In the first place, a qualitative approach allows me to investigates the *why* and *how* of decision making, not just *what*, *where*, and *when*. In this way, it is more effective to reveal why a specific LL in Beijing was shaped in a certain way. In addition, in qualitatively driven LL research, sampled linguistic objects are studied holistically and contextually, rather than in a reductionistic and isolationist manner. Although quantitative analysis of language texts on signs can tell us how frequently a particular language appears in a given place, it often overlooks the sociolinguistic context and dominating ideologies that govern language practices. Last but not least, a qualitative approach has the advantage of allowing for diverse and multiple interpretations.

On the basis of these general considerations, in the following section I will examine public signs sampled in my multi-site fieldwork in Beijing and look at how the LL of Beijing served as a mechanism for creating language policy, reproducing language ideologies, and constructing identities.

3 Standardised official signs

A range of photographs of official signs were taken and collected at key Olympic venues, tourist sites, commercial areas, and transportation hubs from 1 to 20 August 2008. There were three types of standardised official signs that could be distinguished in Beijing's linguistic landscape: monolingual signs (Chinese), bilingual signs (Chinese and English), and multilingual signs (Chinese, English and French).

3.1 Monolingual signs

Monolingual signs in Beijing were predominantly in Simplified Chinese characters, which is the nationally official writing system used in Mainland China. There are two distinct sets of writing systems for the Chinese language: 繁体字 *fantizi* [Traditional Chinese characters] and 简体字 *jiantizi* [Simplified Chinese characters]. Traditional Chinese is a traditional version of scripts that had been written by Chinese people and continuously evolved for thousands of years. Its characters often appear to be more complex and contain more strokes. Nowadays, it is the main writing system used in Hong Kong, Macau, Taiwan, and many overseas Chinese communities. In the early days of the PRC, the general level of Chinese education was low. The net primary education enrolment rate was 20 percent and the gross junior secondary education enrolment rate was only 3 percent. There were only 117,000 college students and 80 percent of the Chinese population was illiterate (Information Office of the State Council, 2019). In the 1950s, the new Chinese government decided to restructure and simplify some of the most complex characters as part of a movement to raise the literacy rate of the nation. The Ministry of Culture and the Text Reform Committee of China published the official list of Standard Simplified Chinese characters in 1956, marking the national roll-out of the Simplified Chinese system. The simplification process was completed by 1960, and the new writing system has been in use in Mainland China ever since. Like all official publications and education resources, public signage is always in Simplified Chinese script.

After the signage upgrading movement, a large number of bilingual signs were used to replace monolingual signs in Beijing's major roads, stations and stops, tourist sites and key cultural sites. On the eve of the Beijing Olympics, official Chinese monolingual signs could be seen in public spaces that manifest state sovereignty and the legitimacy of the government, such as the Tiananmen Rostrum and the Monument to the People's Heroes. Most of these Chinese signs were made of durable materials for long-term use. Another type of Chinese monolingual sign was made for temporary display to domestic audiences only. On 6 August 2008 I spotted a series of Chinese publicity signboards at the Qianmen Street bus stop. One of them said "文明引导行动：文明进一步你我同进步 [Civility campaign: Let's progress together with the improvement of civilised behaviours]" (see Photograph 11). Another signboard was used to educate spectators in courteous behaviours (see Photograph 12). These Chinese publicity signs were set up under the supervision of the Office of the Central Steering Committee on Spiritual Civilisation Construction as part of the government's civility campaign to prepare for the Olympic Games. In 2006 the Beijing municipal government and BOCOG actively launched a three-year campaign to promote civility among its citizens with an aim at creating a more favourable social environment for the 2008 Olympic Games. The civility campaign focused on such tasks as the release of publicity materials, preparation for the selection of model persons, volunteer lectures on spectator courtesy, orderly queuing at transport stations and eradication of spitting and littering in public places.

Photograph 11: A publicity signboard promoting civilised practices at Qianmen bus stop.

Image: Chinese Young Pioneers wearing red scarves

Spectator Courtesy Contest for the 29th Olympic Games

Question 30: What are the etiquettes for spectators to make exit?

A: Take bottles and other rubbish with us while exiting.
B: Push our way through the crowd to have photos taken with athletes.
C: Force our way out before others.

See the answer on the back

Answer to Question 29: C

Qinglongqiao Street Office,
Haidian District, Beijing

Photograph 12: A publicity signboard promoting spectator courtesy at Qianmen bus stop.

3.2 Bilingual signs

In Beijing's LL before the Olympics, the number of official Chinese-English bilingual signs was second only to that of monolingual signs. As required by the *Action Plan for the BSFLP* (Organising Committee of the BSFLP, 2003), bilingual signs in both Chinese and English were standardised and set up in public places and facilities such as major tourist attractions, cultural venues, commercial facilities, Olympic venues, bus lines, highways, streets, stations, subways and airports.

3.2.1 Olympic volunteer service desk/station

Chinese-English bilingual signs were most salient in locations relating to Olympic volunteer services. Volunteers for the 2008 Beijing Olympic Games and Paralympic Games of 2008 were accredited personnel, recruited and managed by BOCOG for the Games of the XXIX Olympiad. These key individuals shouldered critical Games-time responsibilities, working at times and in positions assigned to them by BOCOG during the 2008 Beijing Olympic Games and the Paralympic Games of 2008 without compensation. Volunteers for the Olympic and Paralympic Games were mainly recruited in the Beijing area, with college students constituting the majority as well as a certain number made up of personnel from relevant departments, residents of various provinces, municipalities and autonomous regions, compatriots from Hong Kong, Macao and Taiwan, overseas Chinese and foreigners. It is said that one million social volunteers, 400,000 urban volunteers and 100,000 Games-time volunteers were recruited for the Beijing Olympiad and Paralympic Games. Games-time volunteers mainly served at various Olympic venues (including competition venues, training venues and non-competition venues). Their service roles included protocol, translation, security, medical care, liaison, among others. Urban volunteers provided information consultation, language translation, and emergency services in urban volunteer service stations installed in public places where domestic and international tourists often visited (see Photographs 13 & 14). Social volunteers provided services to the community more generally, such as maintaining traffic order at intersections and caring for the elderly (see Photograph 15).

Photograph 13: Olympic volunteer service desk at Beijing Capital International Airport.

3 Standardised official signs — 177

Photograph 14: Beijing Olympic Games urban volunteer service station at Black Bamboo Park.

Photograph 15: Volunteer service desk at a Beijing Subway Station.

3.2.2 Bus and metro systems

Bilingual signs in Chinese and English became ubiquitous in Beijing's bus and metro systems (see Photographs 16 & 17). Route maps, direction signs and warning signs in buses and subways were all upgraded to bilingual signs. In 2006, BOCOG set up 38 Olympic special bus lines to provide free travel modes for volunteers and journalists around the 16 Olympic stadiums. Chinese and English bilingual timetables were available for passengers taking these special lines (see Photograph 18). Additionally, announcements in buses and on subways were also broadcast in both Chinese and English.

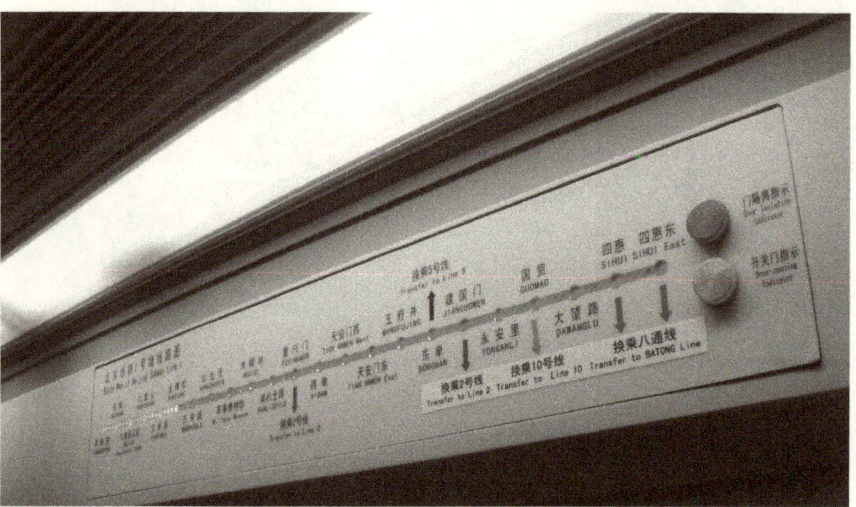

Photograph 16: Bilingual route map of Beijing subway line 1.

3 Standardised official signs — 179

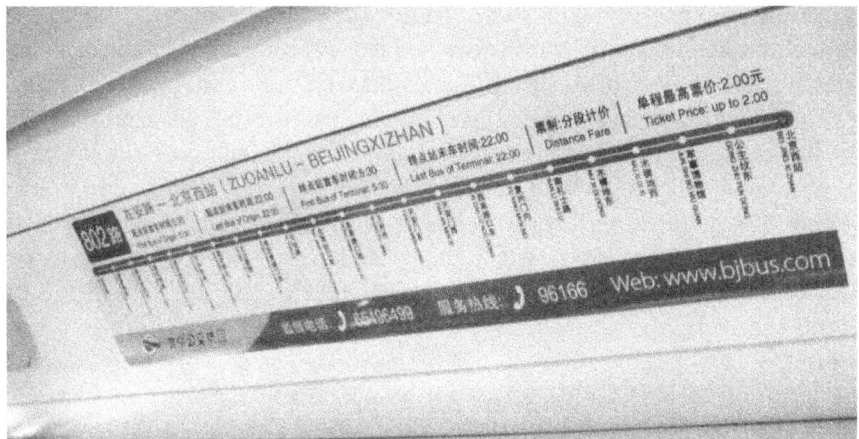

Photograph 17: Bilingual route map in bus No. 802.

Photograph 18: The front and back of the sign for the Olympic special bus line 2.

3.2.3 Road traffic

Standardisation of English translations for place names was one of the most important parts of the English signage standardisation campaign. Based on *English Translation of Public Signs General Specifications*, place names were translated by combining Chinese pinyin and English terms (see Photograph 19). Chinese pinyin was required to be capitalised. English words had to adopt mixed case with the initial letter in uppercase and the remaining letters lowercase. When rendering the names of different types of thoroughfares, the English word 'Avenue (Ave)' was only used for the translations of '长安街 (CHANG'AN Ave)' and '平安大街 (PING'AN Ave)'. All the other '街 (*jie*)' and '大街 (*dajie*)' were translated into 'Street (St)', for example, 隆福寺街 LONGFUSI St. The components '小街 (*xiaojie*)', '条 (*tiao*)', '巷 (*xiang*)', and '夹道 (*jiadao*)' were generally translated as 'Alley', for example, 东直门北小街 (DONGZHIMEN North Alley), 东四十条 (DONGSISHITIAO Alley). The English translation of '路 (*lu*)' was usually 'Road (Rd)', such as 北辰路 BEICHEN Rd. Finally, '高速公路 (*gaosu gonglu*)' was translated as 'Expressway (Expwy)' whereas '公路 (*gonglu*)' was 'Highway'.

Photograph 19: Traffic signs near the National Stadium.

3.2.4 Tourist attractions

Situated in the heart of Beijing, the Forbidden City, also known as the Palace Museum, was the Chinese imperial palace during the middle and late Ming and the Qing Dynasties. In 1987 it was listed as a UNESCO World Heritage site. On 8 August 2008 I visited the Forbidden City to investigate the language service provisions there. Inside the Forbidden City, the top tourist attraction in Beijing and the most visited museum in the world, English was the only language other than Chinese used on various bilingual signs – from notice boards outsides the ticket office, via warning signs at the security check point, to touch screen e-guide facilities in the Palace Museum (see Photograph 20).

Photograph 20: A bilingual sign at the Palace Museum.

3.3 Multilingual signs

The *Beijing Olympic Action Plan* (BOCOG, 2002) required multilingual signs to be available in certain special premises and stadiums. In fact, foreign languages other than English and French were barely visible in the LL of the Olympic host city. As an official language of IOC, French along with English appeared on a few official multilingual signs temporarily set up in special premises and stadiums closely related to the Games. Because the presence of French was mainly related to the Olympics, most of these multilingual signs were removed from Beijing's LL in the post-Games era. Clearly, the language choice of the Beijing Municipal Government favoured English in the context of the Beijing Olympics. In her study on language choice in Swiss tourism marketing, Piller (2007) argues that language choice is investment choice. The ubiquity of English in Beijing's LL is partly a consequence of the fact that it is an 'economical' resource compared to other foreign languages. English was more readily available than any other language other than Chinese after Beijing's English popularisation campaign. In contrast, linguistic signs in other languages require a much higher investment in translation and production, while serving much smaller target groups. Sections 4.4 and 4.5 will talk more on the visibility of foreign languages other than English in Beijing's LL in the Olympic context.

4 Language choice, ideology, and identity

A linguistic landscape entails countless language choices, and as Piller (2007) points out, no language choice is neutral or arbitrary, but rather is fundamentally linked to specific contexts, ideologies and practices. Similarly, both Spolsky and Cooper (1991) and Landry and Bourhis (1997) suggest that language choices in the LL may serve as important informational markers on the one hand, as well as symbolic markers of the relative power and status of the linguistic communities inhabiting the place on the other. Following Piller (2007), I will investigate language choices on sampled signage at three levels (linguistic choice, content, and position) and then address which languages were given visibility in Beijing's LL and what were their specific functions and symbolism.

4.1 Chinese and Beijing as the capital of the harmonious nation

My fieldwork in various key Olympic venues, tourist sites, commercial areas and transportation hubs across Beijing shows that, unsurprisingly, Simplified Chinese was the most visible and salient language in the LL of the city. The national language was not only presented on monolingual signs but also in the foreground position of bilingual and multilingual signs. Simplified Chinese always came first on bi/multilingual signs, and its font size was usually larger than that of other languages. Though a great number of bilingual and multilingual signs were set up or updated at Beijing's major roads, stations and stops, tourist sites and key cultural sites, there were a lot more official and non-official monolingual signs all over the city. The linguistic landscape of Tiananmen Square provides a good example.

On 6 August 2008, two days before the opening ceremony of the Beijing Olympics, I visited Tiananmen Square, where an Olympic flower show was being staged. Parterres in the show combined auspicious Chinese cultural elements and Olympic symbols to build a cordial festive atmosphere. Tiananmen Square was one of the key cultural sites where bilingual signs were highly visible. However, the fenced exhibition space for the flower show presented a salient monolingual space. Textual information relating to the flower show was mostly presented in Simplified Chinese characters, except for a few directional bilingual signs which were considered necessary to guide foreign visitors and media professionals around the place.

One of the most eye-catching signs was a 16.9-meter-high official emblem of the 2008 Summer Olympics, "Chinese Seal, Dancing Beijing" (see Photograph 21), standing in the centre of a flower bed. The emblem draws on various elements of Chinese culture, depicting a traditional red Chinese seal above the phrase "Beijing 2008" and the Olympic rings. According to the Beijing Olympic Organising Committee (2003), the seal is engraved with a calligraphic character 京 (*Jing*, meaning "capital," from the name of the host city 北京) in the form of a dancing figure. The curving strokes suggest a wriggling Chinese dragon, a traditional symbol of power,

Photograph 21: The official emblem of the 2008 Summer Olympics stands between two huge placards in the flower show. Tiananmen Square, 8 August 2008.

strength, and good luck in China. The figure resembles a runner crossing the finish line. The open arms of the figure symbolise the invitation of China to the world to share its culture. On both sides of the emblem were two giant red placards inscribed with slogans (see Photograph 21): "五湖四海喜庆奥运盛会 *Wuhu sihai xiqing aoyun shenghui* [Warmly welcome friends from all over the world to the Beijing Olympic Games]" and "改革开放共谱和谐篇章 *Gaige gaifang gongpu hexie pianzhang* [Write a new chapter of harmonious development in the reform and opening-up]." The theme of "和谐" *hexie* [harmony] highlighted the political and economic agendas of the Beijing Olympics. The two giant red monolingual placards in the flower show responded to the other two placards hanging on the western and eastern walls of Tiananmen gate (conventionally translated as "Gate of Heavenly Peace"), reading "中华人民共和国万岁 *Zhonghua renmin gongheguo wansu* [Long live the People's Republic of China]" and "世界人民大团结万岁 *Shijie renmin datuanjie wansu* [Long live the great union of the peoples of the world]" in Simplified Chinese characters. The two monolingual slogans and the portrait of Mao Zedong sited between them together symbolise the legitimacy of the Communist Party of China and, once again, the philosophy of "harmony" as the quintessence of Chinese culture. Given the monolingual language choice evident, the messages both in the flower show and on the Tiananmen rostrum were clearly directed at a national audience. The monolingual language choice was based on the notion of nation-state. In nation-states, the ideology of "one nation one language," which associates a national identity with a particular language, usually the language of the dominant group, is a common strategy for social and cultural governance (Piller, 2007; Shohamy, 2006).

In the carefully planned LL of Tiananmen Square, Chinese (in its standard spoken and written form: *Putonghua* and Simplified Chinese characters) was used as a prominent identity marker of Beijing as the capital of a united harmonious Chinese nation. China, the world's most populous country, has 1.33 billion people on the mainland, and recognises 56 ethnically and sociolinguistically diverse "nationalities" (National Bureau of Statistics of China, 2010). Han people are the largest ethnic group, constituting 91.51 percent of the total population of the PRC (Mainland China) (National Bureau of Statistics of China, 2010) and 95.69 percent of Beijing's registered population (Beijing Municipal Bureau of Statistics, 2009). Residing in 60 percent of the land, 52 ethnic minority groups have their own native languages (the exceptions being the Hui, Manchu and She minorities[19]), sometimes more than one, amounting to a total of over 100 languages

---

19 In fact, the Manchu and the She do have their own traditional ethnic tongues; however almost all members only speak varieties of Chinese today.

from five language families (Tsung, 2009, pp. 11–12). Despite the fact that China is a multilingual and multi-ethnic country, Han language, the language of the largest Chinese ethnic group, is easily equated with "the Chinese language" in public discourses. Due to thousands of years of immigration and assimilation of various regional ethnicities and tribes within China, Han people are characterised by considerable internal genetic, linguistic, cultural, and social diversity (Wen et al, 2004). Therefore, what is customarily referred to as "Chinese/the Chinese language" is a language family consisting of various spoken varieties of Han Chinese language, mostly mutually unintelligible to varying degrees. Despite the existence of many unintelligible spoken varieties, one factor in Han ethnic unity are Chinese characters (汉字 *Hanzi*), which possess a unified standard form. This unity is credited to the Qin dynasty, which unified the various forms of writing that existed in China at that time. For thousands of years regardless of dynastic changes, *Hanzi* was used as the unified writing system between speakers of all Chinese varieties, and as a written lingua franca between Han Chinese and other ethnic groups in China. In contemporary China, 简体汉字 *Jianti hanzi* [Simplified Chinese characters] are the uncontested written language for inter-ethnic communication, and the script used in government, law, and formal education in Beijing and the rest of the country, even though it is technically the script of only one ethnic group, the dominant Han people. In this way, a unified Chinese language in its standardised form (Putonghua and Simplified Chinese characters) is regarded as the foundation of the Chinese national identity.

The use of Simplified Chinese characters together with the theme of "harmony" highlighted in the texts on the sampled signs conveyed the government's desire to promote the nation's "harmonious development" through holding the Olympics. The Confucian philosophy of "harmony" advocates "和而不同 *he er butong*" ([meaning literally "harmony with differences"], emphasising the importance of both diversity and balance (Feng, 2005). The philosophy of "harmony" gave birth to most traditional Chinese cosmological beliefs and encouraged values such as tolerance, compatibility, conformity, peace, unity, integrity, and stability. In 2006, at the Central Committee meeting, the Communist Party of China put forward the "和谐社会 *hexie shehui* [harmonious Society]" doctrine as a response to the numerous socio-economic problems faced by the nation in the structural transformation period. Building China as a harmonious socialist society was seen as an important strategy for carrying out a scientific concept of development. Before the Beijing Olympics, "harmony" had become the major theme in Chinese political discourses as the Chinese central government rediscovered "harmony" as a useful tool to regulate social contradictions and assure stability (Feng, 2005). It was in such a socio-political environment that the Chinese government stepped up its efforts to promote the standard use of Chinese (in its spoken and written form) and gave it the highest visibility in the LL of Beijing as an Olympic city. What is more, the Chinese government recognised that promoting Standard Chinese was an important strategy for China to attain soft power, and the Olympics presented an ideal opportunity. The *Beijing Olympic Action Plan* (BOCOG, 2002) states that the global attention that the Olympics would attract to China in general and to Beijing in particular could be used as an opportunity to "teach and promote the Chinese language to the world, and to demonstrate that Chinese is in fact a language used worldwide." The ambition to promote "the Chinese language" to the world and thus enhance the country's soft power resources also underlay the pre-eminence of Chinese in the LL of Beijing.

4.2 English and Beijing as a global city

It is evidenced in a growing body of empirical studies that English has been rapidly infiltrating the public spaces of non-Anglophone modern metropolises and regions in Asia (Backhaus, 2006, 2007; Huebner, 2006; MacGregor, 2003) and Europe (Griffin, 2004; Hult, 2003; Piller, 2007; Schlick, 2003; Torkington, 2009). My study of the LL of Beijing confirms the high visibility of English in such spaces. In addition to Simplified Chinese, English, of course, was given considerable prominence in the LL of Beijing. Almost as omnipresent as Chinese, English could be seen on traffic signs, at bus and subway stations, on store fronts, in shop windows, inside and outside Olympic venues, tourist sites and public buildings, on billboards and other street advertisements, on brochures and maps, and in leaflets and menus. The high concentration of English signs often marked a tourist site or a public location frequented by an imagined English-speaking community. In my fieldwork at major transportation hubs like Beijing Railway Station, Beijing West Railway Station, and Beijing Capital International Airport as well as subway stations across the city, English was the only language other than Simplified Chinese that could be seen on guiding signs, commercial billboards, Olympic billboards, tourist maps, signboards and signposts, and electronic stop reporting systems. Clearly, English topped the linguistic hierarchy when the host city committed to provide "barrier-free" language services and transform into a 'global city'. If the identity of Beijing as capital of the harmonious Chinese nation is linked with Chinese as the uniting language, then the identity of Beijing as a global city was symbolically linked with English as the international 'default' language that promises the widest reach.

English translations of public signs were a high priority of the governmental English signage standardisation campaign. Ostensibly, this was to help foreigners make better use of public facilities. But a close examination of Beijing's bilingual public signs suggests that many English signs carry more symbolic than informative functions. In my fieldwork at Tiananmen subway station, for instance, I found two bilingual public signs: one prohibition signboard hanging on the wall of the passageway (see Photograph 22) and one instructive signboard placed in front of an escalator (see Photograph 23). The prohibition signboard contains four drawings together with four phrases in both Chinese and English: "禁止吸烟 *Jinzhi xiyan* [No Smoking]," "请勿坐卧停留 *Qingwu zuowo tingliu* [No Loitering]," "禁止摆卖 *Jinzhi baimai* [No Vendors]," and "禁止乱扔废弃物 *Jinzhi luanreng feiqiwu* [No Littering]." Interestingly, there were police officers and volunteers on guard at a security checkpoint which was not far from the prohibition signboard. According to my on-site observation, it is very unlikely that any English-speaking foreign vendors would appear in Beijing's public locations, especially under such close surveillance before and during the Beijing Olympic Games. As a matter of fact, English-speaking streets vendors were unlikely to be a frequent enough problem in Beijing to warrant a prohibition sign dedicated to them. The presence of English on this prohibition signboard is

Photograph 22: Prohibition sign. Tiananmen subway station, August 6, 2008.

Photograph 23: Instructive sign. Tiananmen subway station, August 6, 2008.

thus more because of its symbolic meaning of international cosmopolitanism than for its informational and instructional content.

The symbolic function of the English sign is even more obvious in an instructive signboard placed in front of an escalator at Tiananmen subway station (see Photograph 23). Compared to the Chinese text, the English translation is minimised both in content and font size. The eight regulations in the notice to passengers foregrounded on the upper half of the signboard do not have an English translation. Inscribed at the peripheral position, the only English translations include "Take Care of Your Children," "No Cargo," "Stand on Right," "Watch Your Foot" and "Stand on Right; Pass on Left." The salience of Chinese on this signboard suggests the relative importance of Chinese in informing members of the public and regulating their behaviours with respect to escalator use. It can be argued that English texts on these two signboards had little to no practical informational significance but predominantly served an indexical function as identity markers for Beijing as an emerging 'global city.'

4.3 English for sale and global elitism

Studying language policy through LL can also be undertaken through an examination of advertising (Shohamy, 2006, p. 133). As the hypercentral language of globalisation, English is ubiquitous in the commercial discourses of the non-English speaking world (Piller, 2012). When English is used instead of (or alongside) the national language in advertising and commercial discourses, it is often used to index modern, cosmopolitan, professional and successful identities (Piller, 2012). Photograph 24 is a photo of a display window for Olympic-themed Nike sports shoes that I captured in Beijing Oriental Plaza, one of the largest commercial centres in Asia. Headquartered in the United States, Nike is the world's leading sporting goods manufacturer. By the end of 2008, China was Nike's largest single sourcing country. Most Nike products purchased by Chinese consumers were made in China. Using English in the advertisement in the Chinese market can successfully transfer the positive association of the language onto the Nike products.

In the LL of Beijing, English was not only present as medium, but also as content. By "present as content" I mean non-official signs which were mainly presented in Simplified Chinese but had the aim of promoting the "consumption" of English: billboards advertising English training institutions. The Chinese texts on these advertising billboards directly address a national audience. In many cases, images of White people were an inseparable part of advertisements promoting the

Photograph 24: A display window in the Oriental Plaza.

sale of English training products. As the commodity value of English had been ever increasing in the Chinese context and English training institutions had been springing up all over Beijing in the years prior to the Olympics, these billboards increasingly became part of the LL of the city. English First (EF), one of the Beijing Olympic official language services suppliers, was the one that, through my fieldwork observations, appeared to most vigorously promote its services through outdoor advertising. In the busy passageway of the Wangfujing subway station, for instance, I found a row of neon signs promoting the Beijing Olympic Games. Beside them, an advertising billboard for EF was at the centre of attention (see Photograph 25). In the picture, a pretty young Chinese woman is tied to a professional-looking White man with a rope, presenting, in a striking manner, the selling point of the advertisement: "24 小时'私人英语教练' [24-hour 'private English instructor']."

This EF advertisement promotes highly racialised, gendered and sexualised discourses. The choice of language code and the woman's image clearly position young Chinese women as targeted potential consumers. The juxtaposition between the White man and the Chinese woman in this advertisement

Photograph 25: Advertising billboard of *English First*. Wangfujing subway station, August 4, 2008.

constructs two discourses that have been discussed in Takahashi's (2006) study on Japanese Women Learning English: handsome Western men dressed in suits and ties as "desirable and effective English teachers" on the one hand and young Asian women as "desirous consumers of Western masculinity and of English as an international language" on the other (p. 125). The tied-up arms symbolise EF's personalised one-on-one English lessons, suggesting that everyone can possess English and an "intimate" experience with an ideal native English teacher. The physical "intimacy" between the White man as an ideal "native teacher" and the young woman as a desirous "client" is intensified by the sexually charged advertising slogan, implying "private" and "intimate" times with White men. In terms of body position, the White man is standing slightly in front, leading the Chinese woman with his tied arm. The dark suit and blue tie image of the man symbolises the quality and professionalism of EF "native teachers." Additionally, the raised arm and fist is a gesture of fight and triumph. Though led by the Western man, a smile of triumph lights up the young woman's face, showing her complete control of and great satisfaction with the "private English teacher." The EF commercial advertisement suggests to potential customers that their value-added English teaching service offers every Chinese learner an identity-transforming opportunity, and possibly interracial romance. On the top right corner, the Olympic logo was used to indicate EF's official status as the language service supplier for the Beijing Olympics, which provided official assurance for its personalised English lessons.

This kind of sexually charged advertisement by English language schools is not a singular instance. In Takahashi's (2006) study of Gaba, one of the most rapidly expanding *eikaiwa* (English conversation) schools in Japan, she dissected a similar advertisement in which a Japanese woman was handcuffed to a White man. According to Takahashi (2006), advertisements for Gaba's *mantsuman*[20] (individual) lessons are designed to appeal to Japanese women's desire for "private" and "intimate" times with White men in a fashionable space. Different from the Chinese woman in EF's advertisement who is led by the White "native teacher," the Japanese woman in Gaba's advertisement is positioned as the holder of power, by her "knowing smile" and her "pull on the handcuffs" (Takahashi, 2006, p. 126). For Japanese women, English is presented as the means of obtaining what they passionately desire – the West and Western men. English language learning in Japan has become conflated with romantic desire for Western men (Piller and Takahashi, 2010). Their Japanese example as well as my analysis above demonstrate that advertisements for language schools are areas where English is gendered, sexualised and racialised to sell English language learning and teaching. Bringing the Olympic brand into full play, EF promoted its featured personalised English lessons as gendered and romanticised products.

In the previous section, I demonstrated how English was promoted as the language of the imagined international metropolis through two instructive signs and served predominantly as an identity marker for Beijing as a global city. In contrast, this EF advertisement promotes a native speaker ideology in which English is not an international language but the property of White native speakers. The ideology of "native speaker superiority" has been taken for granted as natural and common sense in foreign private language schools in China such as EF. This ideology legitimises native speakers of English as ideal English teachers and as the ideal model for non-native speakers in English language learning. In recent decades, an increasing number of researchers (e.g., Brutt-Griffler and Samimy, 1999; Canagarajah, 1999; Cook, 1999; Kaplan, 1999; Kirkpatrick, 1997; Mckay, 2003; Pennycook, 1998; Phillipson, 1992; Piller, 2001; Rampton, 1990) have demonstrated that the "native speaker" is not an empirical fact but rather a social construct. In many cases, the nature of "nativeness" has more to do with the ideology and identity of a dominant group than with linguistic competence.

---

[20] This is a direct borrowing of the English expression "man-to-man."

For example, Piller (2001) insists that the "native speaker" ideology should be discarded because linguistically it is a useless, idealised concept, and socially the "birthright mentality" attached to it is debilitating and unfair (p. 14). Even though a "native speaker" does exist, Piller (2001) argues that their early acquisition of a language does not guarantee them status as the sole arbiters of correct language practices in various contexts. Phillipson (1992) claims that non-native speakers possess certain qualifications which native speakers may not have, such as "the experience of acquiring English as a second (foreign) language and insights into the linguistic and cultural needs of their learners" (p. 195). Rampton (1990) has outlined five features of expertise regarding native speakers and demonstrated that "it is special education or training that makes one an expert in one field or another" (p. 97). A native speaker is not necessarily qualified and has not necessarily acquired the "expertise" required in the language classroom. In other words, training and experience play a greater role in defining a teacher's success in a language classroom.

4.4 French and Beijing as Olympic city

According to the Olympic Charter (International Olympic Committee, 2007, p. 53), both French and English are the official languages of the IOC. In addition to those two languages, the language of the host country also serves as an official language of the Olympic Movement during the Games. This means that all announcements, services and facilities relating to the 2008 Olympic Games should be available in the three languages. In Beijing's LL, the presence of French was much stronger in the official/top-down signage issued by the public authorities than the unofficial/bottom-up signage issued by autonomous social actors. In particular, in the Beijing Olympic context French mostly appeared on only a few official/top down multilingual signs set up in certain special premises and stadiums closely related to the Games. These multilingual signs consisted primarily of signboards for Olympic special buses (see Photograph 26), directional signs outside Olympic venues (see Photograph 27), and signs identifying workstations at the entrance to Olympic venues (see Photograph 28). The presence of French on guiding signs is closely linked with Beijing's identity as the Olympic host city.

Moreover, most of these French signs were temporarily set up for the purposes of the Games, which means that these signs were much less "fixed" and hence were subject to removal after the Olympics. In terms of salience, although the size of the font used for French was the same as that of English on multilingual signs, French always appeared last after Chinese and English,

4 Language choice, ideology, and identity — 193

Photograph 26: Stop sign for the Olympic special bus at Tiananmen Square.

Photograph 27: Direction board. Entrance to the Olympic venue in Peking University.

Photograph 28: Spectator security checkpoint in Shunyi Olympic Rowing-Canoeing Park.

suggesting a lower rank in order of importance. French was virtually absent on non-official signs produced by local individual, civil or corporate actors. The under-representation and temporality of French in Beijing's LL is evidence that the municipal government did not accord French a position of equal importance to English in Beijing's urban planning. It is also evidence that French, its official Olympic status notwithstanding, had much less popularity and symbolic capital than English in local language practices and ideologies.

4.5 Other languages and the invisible city

As discussed in previous sections, the officially planned LL of Beijing gave the highest visibility to three languages: Chinese (for Beijing as a the capital of a harmonious society), English (for Beijing as a global city) and French (for Beijing as an Olympic city). Compared with these three languages, other languages were attached less importance and had limited visibility. On 7 August 2008, one day before the opening ceremony of the Beijing Olympic Games, Qianmen Street re-opened after a year of renovations. The renovated historical commercial street drew a mass of tourists on the re-opening day. Standardised bilingual signs in Chinese and English were set up along the street. On the southern end of the street, several student volunteers were providing information to tourists at an urban volunteer service station. A number of copies of the *Beijing Olympic Accommodation Service Guide* were lying on the reception desk (see Photograph 29). This guide was issued on 24 April 2008 and available in eight languages: Chinese, English, Japanese, Korean, Russian, German, Spanish, and Arabic (Beijing Evening Newspaper, 2008). However, because none of the volunteers at this service station could speak any of the six foreign languages except English, the publications turned out to be a mere formality. The prominence of English in Beijing's LL remained unchallenged.

Photograph 29: *Beijing Olympic Accommodation Service Guide.* Qianmen Street, August 8, 2008.

Multilingual facilities and services were available in premier tourist sites in Beijing. On 8 August 2008, I visited the Forbidden City to investigate the language service situation there. I noticed that a multilingual audio guide service was available at the 午门 *Wu men* [Meridian Gate] and 神武门 *Shenwu men* [the Gate of Divine Prowess]. The audio guide is an electronic device that can automatically respond and offer on-the-spot instructions in 20 languages (including Putonghua and Cantonese) as tourists go along a tour route. At the entrance, a large signboard at the ticket office displayed the languages available for this audio guide service (see Photograph 30). Icons of national flags were used together with language names in their respective scripts to indicate the audio guides available. The national flags represented the ownership of a particular language (Piller, 2012). Clearly, what underlay this practice is the ideology of "one nation, one language," which links a national identity with a particular language. People who hold this ideology believe that "monolingualism or the use of one single common language is important for social harmony and national unity" (Piller, 2015). Furthermore, "nativeness" in language is connected with a certain nation-state or region by virtue of birth. On the signboard, English, following two Chinese

Photograph 30: Signboard for multilingual automatic guide service. Entrance to the Forbidden City, August 8, 2008.

varieties – Putonghua and Cantonese – precedes all the other languages in sequence and comes on top of other languages, suggesting differences of importance and status. The Union Jack, the national flag of the United Kingdom, was used as a symbolic marker for the English language. This signboard is not a singular instance in Beijing's LL. On the official website of Beijing Tourism Administration (www.english.visitbeijing.com.cn), the British flag was also used as the symbolic marker for English. The assumption that UK, as the birth land of English, holds the ownership of the language is self-evident. This ideology privileges British English (and/or American English in some other cases) above all other varieties, implying it to be intrinsically authoritative and better for some or all purposes. In a study on English in Swiss tourism marketing, Piller (2007) observed a similar practice. She argues that the practice of associating language with the nation where it is spoken renders small nations or non-national language use invisible. This also helps explain why Chinese ethnic minority communities and communities of "minor" foreign languages had no or limited presence in Beijing's LL.

In fact, as many other societies, Beijing has a multi-ethnic and multilingual population, and many of the long-term foreign residents and the Olympic visitors came from diverse linguistic backgrounds. In ethnic minority communities in Beijing, multilingual practices are common. Ethnic minority community languages were basically invisible in Beijing's LL, which reflects the centre-periphery relations between Chinese and ethnic minority languages. In the Chinese context, it was assumed that international communication mainly took place with people from the economically and technologically developed English-speaking countries, particularly the US and UK. In fact, more than half of the foreign residents and tourists in Beijing are from a non-English background, and are mainly drawn from two neighbouring Asian countries: South Korea and Japan. However, the planning of Beijing's LL in the Olympic context showed a strong preference for English over Korean and Japanese, the languages of neighbours, of two major groups of foreign residents and tourists, and in the case of Koreans also an ethnic minority. It is highly debatable to claim that English is extensively used as lingua franca among various foreign groups or between local Chinese and foreign residents. Despite the internal diversity of foreign resident and tourist populations in Beijing during the Olympics, foreign languages other than English and French were found to be practically absent on official signs at key public and cultural spaces. The dominance of Chinese and English and the near invisibility of other languages reflect unequal power relations between different languages in the Chinese context.

5 Summary

LL provides a new perspective on language policy and language use research. Given LL's role as a mechanism of language policy, the consequence of using LL in public space is that it reaffirms the languages and groups that are in power while marginalising other languages and groups that are not (Shohamy, 2006, p. 124). Beijing is an ethnically and linguistically heterogeneous city, however not all languages and groups were equally presented in the Olympic context. The LL of Beijing was an arena for power struggles among diverse languages. The outcome of these struggles is a mixture of three language ideologies and identities: Chinese to symbolise Beijing as the capital of a harmonious society, English for Beijing as a global city and French for Beijing as an Olympic city. As examples in this chapter demonstrate, these language choices further reinforce existing power inequalities between languages and groups. The ongoing Olympic English signage standardisation campaign has been driven by the "Standard English" ideology. The relevant departments and professionals involved in this campaign had a strong preference for native speaker varieties (especially British English and

American English) over the English varieties of non-native speakers in the Outer and Expanding Circles. The Chinese government's strong sense of a native variety standard led to a citywide crackdown on "Chinglish" as an "inferior" and "deficient" variety of English. Rules and regulations were formulated to standardise English translations of public signs, menus, and professional titles. The official attitudes about "Standard English" that defined what was perceived as the "correct" way to speak English could also be inferred from the practice of associating a particular language with a national flag. In this practice, a close connection was made between the ownership of English and UK (and less frequently US) as the place of origin. The commodity value of English in the Beijing Olympic context resulted in a high visibility of English as "content" in advertising. Advertisements for English language schools featured, as also discussed in Takahashi's study (2006), gendered, sexualised and racialised discourses in which White male "native speakers" were imagined as "ideal English teachers." All of these language practices and ideologies evidenced in the LL of Beijing contributed to reproducing a narrow understanding of what English is and to whom English belongs, and hindered a full understanding of the cultural and linguistic diversity in the Chinese and global communities.

Chinese foreign language education policies since the 1980s have favoured English and taken a neutral instrumental view of English education. This English craze reached a historical climax on the eve of the 2008 Beijing Olympic Games. With China's rising global political and economic status in the second decade of this century, an ideological transformation from 'English monolingualism' to national language capacity-oriented multilingualism is taking place in Chinese foreign language education. This transformation means that Beijing 2022 will build on the LPP legacies of the landmark Beijing 2008 Olympic Games and make great efforts towards multilingual services.

Chapter 8
China's Olympic language services – legacy, transformation and prospect

The Modern Olympic Games are linguistically complex events. The 2008 Beijing Olympic Games gave great impetus to the development of China's language services industry and provides a reference model of language services for future international and comprehensive sports games. At the same time, the preparations for the Olympic Games also prompted China's policy makers and academia to reflect on its national foreign language policy. A transformation in the mode of provision of language services is quietly happening as we enter an age of accelerated development of artificial intelligence (AI) and telecommunication technology.

1 The language services legacy of the 2008 Olympic Games

The 2008 Beijing Olympic Games drew broader participation and bigger audiences than any previous Games. Jacques Rogge, President of the International Olympic Committee (IOC), acclaimed the Beijing Olympics as "truly exceptional Games" at the closing ceremony (Xinhua, 2008f). The International Olympic Committee (2009) commented that hosting the 2008 Olympic Games provided a number of tangible and intangible legacies for the Olympic Movement and China, covering areas such as infrastructure, environment, health and education. What the IOC failed to mention is that the Beijing Olympic Games were a landmark event in the development of the language services industry and provided valuable experience for hosting large-scale international events in non-Anglophone countries.

1.1 Olympic language services suppliers

As a new language service model, the establishment of language service providers in the 2008 Beijing Olympics has promoted the standardisation and normalisation of language services for the Olympic Games.

1.1.1 Olympic language training service suppliers
The 2008 Beijing Olympics marked the first time in Olympic history that 'language training services supplier' was officially considered to be an independent

sponsorship category. This category has been maintained in the subsequent Olympic Games hosted in non-Anglophone countries, and EF has become the default English training agency for the athletes, coaches, judges and officials of the host country. Since 1988, EF has provided language training services at the Olympic Games seven times (see Table 17). Between 2008 and 2020, only two Olympic Games hosted in English speaking countries did not nominate EF as their language service provider, namely the 2010 Vancouver Winter Olympic Games and the 2012 London Summer Olympic Games.[21]

Table 17: Past language services to the Olympics and Special Olympics.

Language Service Category
Official Language School of the Seoul 1988 Summer Olympics.
Official Language Training Services Supplier of the Beijing 2008 Summer Olympics.
Official Supplier of Language Programmes of the Sochi 2014 Winter Olympics.
Official Language Training Supplier of the Rio 2016 Summer Olympics.
Official Education Services Sponsor of PyeongChang 2018 Winter Olympics.
Official Supplier and Exclusive Training Provider to the Special Olympics World Games Abu Dhabi 2019.
Official Language Training Services Partner of Tokyo 2020 Summer Olympics.

It is thus obvious that English has remained the dominant language at the Olympic Games and will likely continue to be so for the near future, thus English training will still be one of the important contents of Olympic language service in non-Anglophone host countries. The worldwide diffusion of English has led to the variation of English. With regard to English training, Olympic language training service suppliers need to be aware that the existence of English varieties with different localized features has become the main trend of modern English. The often-cited statistics by Graddol (1997, 1999) and Crystal (1997) have shown that the non-native English speakers have outnumbered native English speakers and consequently the communication opportunities of non-native speakers are increasing. The latest statistics tell us that these days around 80% of spoken English is spoken between non-native English speakers. If English is, numerically speaking, the language of "others", then the center of gravity of the language is almost certain to shift in the direction of the "others". Accordingly, the purpose

---

21 This does not include the Winter and Summer Special Olympics World Games.

of English teaching should be to help users of World Englshes (Kachru, 1992), including speakers of both native and non-native varieites, communicate smoothly with each other. Therefore, the native-speaker norm is not only irrelevant but aslo a barrier to English-mediated intercultural communication at the Olympic Games. In fact, the Olympic Games is highly multilingual. Language services for past Olympic Games have proved that English monolingualism is unable to meet the language needs of linguistically and culturally diverse Olympic participants. In linguistically complex situations, Olympic organisers need to abandon English monolingual ideologies and embed multilingualism in the language policy and planning of Modern Olympic Games. In the future, Olympic language training service suppliers should take the IOC's language policy and the actual language needs of all Olympic organisers and participants into consideration, re-evaluate and re-plan its foreign language training services, and contribute to the development of multilingual communicative capacity for the host country.

1.1.2 The Beijing Olympic Multilingual Service Centre, BFSU

Founded in 1941, Beijing Foreign Studies University (BFSU) is China's first institution specialising in foreign language studies. The university taught 44 foreign languages in 2008, outnumbering those taught at any other university in China. BFSU's foreign language education level, to some extent, represents China's national foreign language capacity. The university used the 2008 Olympics as an excellent platform to get many of its students engaged in interpretation practice, and to create a volunteer culture on campus. During Games time, BFSU dispatched more than 3,000 interpreters who, both as volunteers and paid professionals, got involved in a wide range of language services and training programmes for the 2008 Beijing Olympic Games (Wang and Zhang, 2008). Wang Lidi (2008), Dean of the Graduate School of Translation and Interpretation (GSTI) at BFSU, claims that Beijing 2008 presented a global platform for BFSU-GSTI to display their achievements in foreign language teaching, especially in relation to interpreting.

The biggest tangible Olympic legacy to BFSU is the Beijing Olympic Multilingual Service Centre (MSC). The Centre was set up for the Olympics, but its mission goes beyond that. Like many facilities that were set up especially for the Olympics, the Centre ceased to operate after the event. But in 2010 it was reopened by BFSU with three full time staff members and 260 student volunteers who provide interpretation services in 8 languages including English, French, German, Russian, Arabic, Spanish, Japanese and Korean (Zhang, 2014). At present, the MSC has become a permanent institution at BFSU that provides multilingual services for foreign visitors or residents in local communities. The 2008 Beijing Olympics also endowed BFSU with numerous intangible legacies. They laid the foundations for a volunteer culture at the university. The Olympics also facilitated multilingual education at BFSU, as students became more enthusiastic to learn a second or third foreign language other than English.

1.2 The Beijing speaks foreign language programme

The Beijing Speaks Foreign Languages Programme (BSFLP) was launched in 2002. Since its implementation, important phased objectives and tasks have been included in Beijing Municipal Government's "折子 Zhezi [must-do]" projects over the years. In 2006, it was listed in the cultural Olympic heritage list by the IOC (Official Website of the State Council of PRC, 2007). After Beijing 2008, the Programme continued in operation with a renewed action plan. The Foreign Affairs Office of the Beijing Municipal Government set up an international language environment department to take charge of the BSFLP. The centralised leadership system ensures the development of the programme in a standardised, institutionalised and sustainable way (Official Website of the Beijing 2008 Olympic Games, 2012). At the operational level, the Municipal Government has mobilised various social forces to encourage the widest participation of its citizens in the Programme, including thousands of volunteers, 180 colleges and foreign language training institutions, an advisory committee of 36 Chinese and foreign experts for the BSFLP, a leading group of 35 experts responsible for the standardisation of English signs in public places, and more than 340 social units. At the same time, more than 40 central and local media outlets constantly follow the activities of the programme.

1.3 Volunteerism

The 2008 Olympic Games encouraged volunteerism and also left a pool of high-level professionals in China. In 2008, BOCOG employees in areas as diverse as venue design and construction, sports, marketing, hospitality, medical services, media operations, transport and many others delivered the biggest-ever world sports event. According to the statistics of the IOC (2009), 1,125,799 people applied to be volunteers for the 2008 Olympic Games, which was an Olympic record. At Games time, 100,000 volunteers provided a range of services at Olympic and Paralympic venues, and 400,000 city volunteers offered information, language interpretation and emergency services at designated service stations. After 2008, Beijing aimed to build on the Games volunteer system and looked to achieve a 20% public participation rate in three to five years, with a registered number of volunteers totalling at least 2 million and annual voluntary service hours totalling over 50 per person (International Olympic Committee, 2009). All the different volunteer streams from the Games are merged into a regular volunteer service team. The Olympic volunteer services provided prior to and during the Games are continued and transferred into regular services for the city, including those offered by Games-time volunteers, city volunteers, pre-Games volunteers and volunteers participating in the "Smiling Beijing" themed activities. The 500 city volunteer service stations have been maintained and over 1,000 municipal welfare service programmes and 1,000 grassroots welfare service programmes remain in operation. A special fund for volunteerism has been established to provide necessary financial support for large-scale volunteer services.

2 Transformation in China's foreign language ideology

2.1 The *ti-yong* tension in the Beijing Olympic context

In the lead up to the 2008 Olympic Games, the Olympic English popularisation campaign directed by the Chinese government and BOCOG pushed 'English fever' to a record high. The ideology that English learning could be imported for *ti* (internal essence) without harming the *yong* (external utility) of the Chinese culture began to draw criticism and challenges from the media and educators. Many newspaper articles have expressed a growing public concern over the hegemony of English in China. For example, Nan Zhou (2007) urged the Chinese government to promote the Chinese language instead of English with the platform of the Olympics and stay vigilant regarding English dominance in China's foreign language education policy. Lin Zhibo (2005) questioned the usefulness of English for all Chinese citizens and urged policy makers to abandon English-only policies in personnel training and selection. Zhang Qihua (2005) criticised the rising 'English fever' since the reform and opening-up for weakening the position of the Chinese language in the education system and causing a regression of Chinese proficiency and knowledge among the younger generations. Li Jiaquan (2005) claimed that the hegemony of English in Chinese education and employment posed a threat to Chinese language and culture. He suggested that the government should cultivate more qualified translators and increase investment in intelligent machine translation so as to resolve the contradictions between English learning and Chinese learning. In China's academic circles, many scholars also reflected on the relationship between English learning and Chinese learning. Wang Hui (2006) pointed out that in the face of the diffusion of English in globalisation, one critical issue facing China's language planning is the inequality between Chinese and English. This inequality was first manifested in the imbalanced development between English education and education of Chinese as well as LCTLs in China. Wang stressed that English hegemony posed a serious threat to the purity and development of the Chinese language. The spread of English has also made many Chinese people identify highly with the values of Anglo-American countries and despise Chinese language and culture. In addition, the huge discrepancy in prestige between English and Chinese in international domains and cyberspace also contributed to the inequality between the two languages. Li Yuming (2005) called for more attention to be paid to the protection and development of China's national language and native languages while developing foreign language education for international communication.

2.2 Resistance to 'English fever' in the post-Olympic era

For more than 30 years, three generations of Chinese people have been involved in 'English fever.' However, the year 2013 marked the beginning of a fundamental shift in the ways that China views the English language. In late 2013, the Chinese MOE (2013) released a draft overall plan for reforming enrolment and examination systems at all levels. The plan specified that the English test would not be included in the *Gaokao*, the unified National College Entrance Examination. Instead, English tests would be held several times a year to allow students to choose when and how often they sit the examination so as to alleviate study pressure and change China's once-in-a-lifetime examination system. Furthermore, there would be no more English classes for grade one and grade two students in primary schools. In accordance with the overall plan, all Chinese provinces were required to formulate specific implementing measures in 2014 and launch pilot reform projects before 2017. Recently, several Chinese provinces and municipalities have announced policy initiatives to reduce the weighting of English in local senior high school and college entrance examinations (中考 *Zhongkao* and 高考 *Gaokao*) in answer to the government's call. For example, the Beijing Municipal Education Commission (2013) proposed to reduce the total score of the English examination from 150 to 100 points in *Gaokao* and from 120 to 100 in *Zhongkao* beginning in 2016. At the same time, it suggests allowing students to take the English examination twice a year rather than giving them an once-in-a-lifetime chance. In the autumn semester of 2018, the *Curriculum plan of senior high schools and curriculum standards of Chinese and other subjects (2017 Edition)* formulated by the MOE (2018) began to be implemented nationwide. In order to optimise the senior high school curriculum structure, the Curriculum Plan requires adding German, French and Spanish to the original foreign language subjects (English, Japanese and Russian). Schools can choose the first foreign language on their own, and the MOE encourages schools to create conditions to offer a second foreign language. This also means that students can choose from six foreign language subjects in *Gaokao*. The English examination reform has sparked heated debate across the country. This nationwide discussion on the reform in the post-Olympic era reflects the multi-level contradictions between the individual development needs of foreign language learners and foreign language teaching practice, as well as between national development needs and national language police and planning. An ideological transformation from 'English monolingualism' or 'English-monolingual ways of seeing multilingualism' (Piller, 2016b) to national language capacity-oriented multilingualism is taking place in Chinese foreign language education.

2.3 National language capacity

The concept of "national (language) capacity" was first used by the American scholars Richard D. Brecht and A. Ronald Walton (1994) to refer to "the ability of the country to respond to demands for language competencies in particular languages for whatever reason, including the ability to create instruction in languages not currently or generally offered." In the United States, the term is mainly related to competence in LOTE, especially less commonly taught languages (LCTLs). The authors suggest that past approaches to providing this capacity have been of only limited success in the United States and that a national less commonly taught language strategic planning process should be initiated, aimed at creating a new architecture for managing the delivery of instruction in these languages. The development of globalisation and informatisation has made national language capacity an important part of national strength. It is hard power as well as soft power, playing a very important role in social progress and cultural inheritance, in promoting economic development and technological innovation, and in protecting a country's national security and international development. Nowadays, more and more countries attach ever-greater importance to the protection, development and management of their language resources, especially their language education.

With the progress in national economic development and the implementation of various major strategies, many linguists in China have raised the issue of language capacity to the level of national strategy, and 'national language capacity' has become a research hotspot in the last decade. Li Yuming (2011), the Chinese linguist who introduced the concept to China, defined it as 'the language capacity the nation needs to deal with various domestic and foreign affairs.' More specifically, national language capacity includes the citizens' individual language capacities and the overall social language capacity, as well as the language capacity needed by the state in dealing with various domestic and foreign affairs such as politics, economy, diplomacy, military affairs, science and technology, and various dimensions of culture (Yang, 2015). From the perspective of 'language as resource,' Zhao Shiju (2016) explained that 'national language capacity' is "the sum total of a nation's ability to grasp linguistic resources, provide language services, deal with linguistic issues, develop the language, and related tasks." Based on the literature review of studies on national language capacity both at home and abroad, Wen Qiufang (2019) redefines the concept as "the competencies of the government in using language to deal with domestic and international affairs involving national interests." According to her reconceptualisation of 'national language capacity,' the main bodies dealing with language affairs are government institutions, rather than individuals or non-governmental groups. In addition, these language affairs must involve national interests and be handled by means of language, not by military or other non-verbal means.

Although there are different definitions of "national language capacity," these Chinese sociolinguists all agree that foreign languages have become one of the indispensable resources in the process of national development, a component of national core competitiveness and an important embodiment of national soft power. Many Chinese scholars (Dai, 2011; Li, 2010; Shen, 2015; Wen, Su and Jian, 2011; Zhao, 2015) call for a strategic transformation in foreign language planning and the development of China's foreign language capacity. However, China is poor in terms of foreign language resources. Even though a huge number of Chinese people are engaged in foreign language learning, the overwhelming majority of them are English learners. According to the statistics of the National Dynamic Database of Foreign Language Talents (Wen, 2019), in the period from 2010 to 2015 there were 44 non-English foreign language courses offered in colleges and universities in China, and the total number of students enrolled during those six years was only 80,000. By 2016, the numbers of foreign language courses had increased to 65, covering 24 official languages of EU countries and 10 official languages of ASEAN countries. In 2020, BFSU offered 101 foreign languages, which cover the official languages of all countries that have established diplomatic relations with China. However, the country still lacks the language competence needed for dealing with international affairs involving national interests. Of the more than 6,000 languages currently in use in today's world, China understands only 101 foreign languages at the very most and has a reasonable competence in only 20 (Zhao, 2016). Although the Chinese government has issued many language policies to strengthen the education of LCTLs in the past decade and the types of foreign language courses in China's higher education have developed rapidly, there is still a significant gap in foreign language capacities between China and many developed countries with culturally and linguistically diverse immigrant populations. In 2013, American colleges and universities were able to offer 263 foreign language courses, including 248 LCTLs,[22] and course enrolments in LOTE tallied more than 1.5 million (Goldberg, Looney and Lusin, 2015). As for China's foreign language planning, Li Yuming (2011) holds that four kinds of foreign languages are in urgent demand. The first type consists of languages commonly used in international affairs such as English and French. The second group embraces languages involving national interests, such as the languages of neighbouring countries, resource-rich regions, countries with relations of close cooperation, and rival countries and regions. The third category comprises "languages for emergency response," which are languages needed in emergency situations, such as anti-terrorism, anti-narcotics, peacekeeping and disaster relief. The fourth type are those needed in conducting scientific research, which can be called "academic language." A country that goes to the world must attach importance to the study of the world. Li (2011) calls on Chinese linguists and policy makers to pay attention to the study of official languages of all countries and regions in the world, and to the study of Asian and African languages, especially the study of cross-border languages in China. As noted by Spolsky (2004), "English as a global language is now a factor that needs to be taken into account in its language policy by any nation state (p. 91)". Even though English still has a major role to play in communication between and across countries and cultures, and English dominance in China's foreign language planning will not waver or change in the short term, China has taken an important step toward multilingualism, at least in theory.

3 China's language services in the post-Olympic era

3.1 China's language services industry at a glance

The language services industry emerged with the reform and opening-up in the 1980s and the development of information technology in the 1990s. In the early days, the content of language services was mainly translation and interpretation.

---

[22] The Modern Language Association of America defines the "less commonly taught languages (LCTLs)" as all languages which are not included in the top fifteen languages taught in United States institutions of higher education.

The Translators Association of China (TAC)[23] was founded in 1982 and is the only national association for the translation and interpreting community in China. Under the lead of TAC and BOCOG, translators and interpreters provided language services in 44 languages at the 2008 Beijing Olympics. In September 2008, TAC and BOCOG jointly held a conference honouring translators and translation institutions in service of the Beijing Olympic Games as a way to celebrate International Translation Day 2008. Over 1,700 individuals and 13 institutions that had rendered translation service during the Beijing Olympic Games and Paralympics were commended (Translators Association of China, 2020). In the 21st century, economic globalisation and China's "Belt and Road initiative" have promoted the rapid development of the language services market. The Chinese government advocates that language services play an important role in helping China improve its soft power and achieve the vision of the "Belt and Road initiative."

With the world becoming increasingly interconnected, the global language services market has seen rapid growth. China's language services industry has entered the fast lane of development after the 2008 Beijing Olympic Games. According to the *2019 China Language Services Industry Development Report* (Translators Association of China, 2019), the global language services market has doubled in size over the last ten years, reaching 50 billion US dollars for the first time. At present, there are 369,935 companies in China that included language and language-related services in their scope of business, among which 9,734 listed language services as their major business and are referred to as language services providers (LSPs). The total revenue of LSPs by the end of 2019 is estimated at 37.22 billion yuan (roughly USD 5.36 billion). These LSPs differ tremendously in terms of registered capital, ranging from less than 100 thousand yuan to over 100 million yuan. In general, LSPs remain quite small, with 82.06% of businesses having less than one million yuan in registered capital. The majority of the LSPs are private businesses, 55.62% of which are located in the eastern part of the country, where the market is flourishing and demand is high, particularly in Beijing (2,231), Shanghai (2,072) and Guangzhou (1,111).

China's LSPs provide diversified services to facilitate multilingual and cross-cultural exchanges. While translation and interpreting services are their major sources of revenue, some are also involved in language consultancy, tools and applications, education and training, and other language-related services. They serve a wide range of sectors and industries such as law and contracts, chemicals and energy, machinery building, and construction and mining, probably because demand in these industries is higher as a result of increased Sino-foreign cooperation

---

23 http://tac-online.org.cn/en/

in those fields (Luo, Meng and Lei, 2018). China's language services industry now provides a variety of translation services. Among them, information technology, education and training, and government publicity have become the top three areas in which translation orders were undertaken by language service providers, accounting for 63%, 52%, and 45.3% respectively (Translators Association of China, 2019).

With the promotion of active cooperation with countries along the "Belt and Road," the demand and supply factors related to translation services in China's language service market present a diversified development trend. Russian, English, Arabic, German, and French are the top five languages in terms of demand for translation services. Besides these more prestigious languages, LCTLs including Thai, Japanese, Vietnamese, Belarusian and Polish also account for a relatively high proportion of that demand. On the supply side (the LSPs), the language service industry is dominated by commonly used foreign languages, while recent years have witnessed an increasing provision of translation services in LCTLs. It is noteworthy that there is considerable discrepancy between language service providers' urgent requirements for trained language professionals and the talent emerging from higher institutions. At present, China's language service providers face a shortage of trained professionals for many languages; in that respect, the top ten most urgently needed languages are Italian, Arabic, Portuguese, Spanish, Thai, Russian, Turkish, Vietnamese, Belarusian and Filipino, which are primarily languages of countries along the "Belt and Road." In the 2019 China Language Services Industry Development Report (Translators Association of China, 2019), 67.3% of LSPs were in dire need of LCTL translators, and 85.7% said that it was difficult for them to recruit LCTL professionals. The lack of translators of LCTLs and the high cost of talent recruitment are the greatest challenges facing China's LSPs. However, the same report also notes that the top ten languages which most urgently need to be offered more widely in universities are Albanian, Azerbaijani, Estonian, Belarusian, Bulgarian, Polish, Bosnian, Persian, Tetun and German (Translators Association of China, 2019). There is clearly still a big gap between the LCTL teaching capacity in colleges and universities and the actual needs of the language services market in China. In recent years, under the encouragement of national policies, foreign language colleges and universities in China have shown a high enthusiasm for the development of programmes in LCTLs, and the number of LCTL programmes is growing rapidly. However, the provision and distribution of LCTL programmes in colleges and universities has not been organically connected with the construction of 'national foreign language capability' at the theoretical and practical levels, and the problem of irrational development and lack of overall planning has been exposed. Therefore, the urgent task for the development of Chinese

LCTL talents is to carry out foreign language education planning based on demand analysis, so as to clarify the country's short-term and long-term needs with respect to LCTL professionals.

3.2 The standardisation of language services

Since the 2008 Beijing Olympics, progress has been made in the standardisation of language services in China. As the only national association for the language service sector, TAC has done a lot to promote standardisation for the industry by organising efforts to develop guidelines for language services (Luo, Meng and Lei, 2018). It has lobbied for the enactment of a law on translation and led efforts in drafting three standards which later became national standards, namely: *Specifications for Translation Service Part 1: Translation*; *Target Text Quality Requirements for Translation Services*; *Specifications for Translation Services Part 2: Interpretation*. It has also piloted the writing of 10 specifications, including: *Specifications for Quotation for Translation Services*; *Specifications for Quotation for Interpretation Services*; *Basic Terminologies for Localization Services*; *Specifications for Quotation for Localization Services;* and *Specifications for Selecting Localization Service Providers*. In addition, TAC has sponsored or participated in the writing of other specifications, such as *General Rules for Translating Chinese Proper Nouns*; *Guidelines for the Use of English in Public Service Areas – Part 1: General Rules*. TAC also organised a team of experts who wrote a pamphlet entitled *A Beginner's Manual for Localization*, which aims to introduce localisation services to language service users. Standardisation in China is basically an industry-initiated process led by TAC as a way to self-regulate the sector. However, accreditation of businesses based on the above standards is not yet available. As a result, a small number of LSPs have applied for international accreditation or accreditation under a framework applying to related industries, whereas about 83.5% of LSPs are operating without any accreditation.

3.3 The technological innovation of language services

Innovations in computer-aided translation (CAT), machine translation (MT) and Internet-based language service platforms are reshaping the economic structure and growth models of China's language service industry (Luo, Meng and Lei, 2018). The survey (see Figure 10) results in Luo Huifang, et al. (2018) show that CAT is the most widely used technology by China's LSPs (70.6%), among which SDL Trados has the largest number of users (91.1%), followed by memoQ (56.8%). Machine translation, though used by only 17.2% of LSPs, is expected to have a significant impact on the language services industry in the foreseeable future. As investment pours into AI from the top e-commerce and technological companies in China (notably Baidu, Alibaba and Tencent), machine translation may see a boost with each breakthrough in the research and development of the deep neural network. In a country the size of China, machine translation is generally considered to be an ideal approach to help cope with the huge demand for translation and interpretation. As a matter of fact, some major players in the industry have either developed their own machine translation applications or have adopted such technology in their daily operations. Constant progress is also being made in voice recognition, human-machine dialogue and writing technologies. China's language services industry has also seen the development of Internet-based language service platforms, where resources are pooled and transactions are made easy. Of the LSPs surveyed, 6.8% indicated that they were developing their own translation tools, mostly online language business platforms and project management applications. In another survey (Translators Association of China, 2019), 80% of interviewed LSPs held that "the use of translation technology can reduce translation costs," 67% said that "the use of translation technology can improve translation quality," and 58% agreed that "the use of translation technology can improve translation skills."

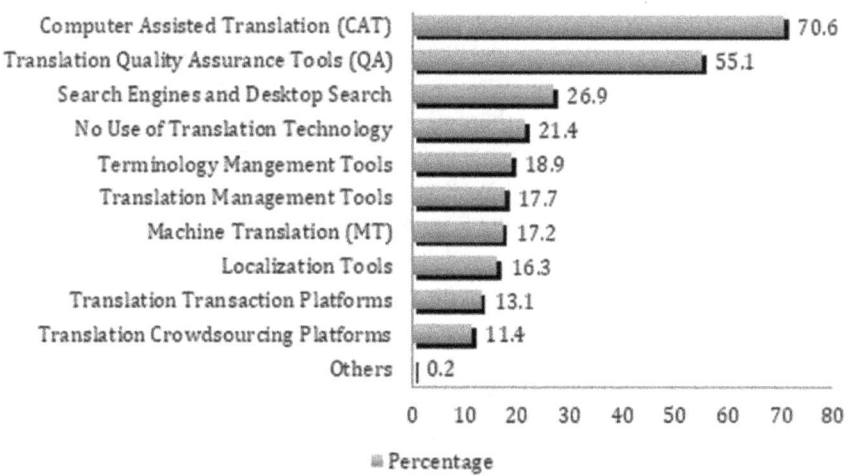

Figure 10: Application of translation technologies.

Adoption of information technology in language services is the overriding trend as traditional models of the language service industry call for innovation and transformation. China's LSPs find the need to redefine their development strategies through immediate business model upgrading and redesign. They are aware that traditional patterns of thinking, organisational structure, organisational behaviour, and business models may very soon become things of the past as they move into the new era of information technology. Thanks to the few major players which in some cases have already had very strong in-house research and development capability, China's language services industry is on a fast track in technological innovation. These technological innovations will play an increasingly important role in serving future international sports events, including the 2022 Winter Olympic Games.

3.4 Education and training of language professionals

Rapid development of the language services market has provided significant impetus to the education and training of translators and interpreters. In 2007, the professional degree Masters in Translation and Interpretation (MTI) was approved by the Academic Degrees Committee of the State Council. By the end of 2018, a comprehensive translation and interpretation (T&I) education system had been established, covering BA, MA and PhD. There are 272 BA programmes in translation and interpretation involving nine languages: English, French, Japanese, Russian, German, Korean, Spanish, Arabic and Thai (Zhong, 2019). The number of MTI programmes had increased from 15 universities in 2007 to 249, covering eleven foreign languages, with a total enrolment of nearly 60,000 (Zhong, 2019). There are more than 40 doctoral programmes in translatology, with over 1,000 PhD graduates (Zhong, 2019). The training of translation professionals has entered the stage of large-scale development. At the same time, a series of guidelines, such as *Teaching Requirements for Undergraduate Programmes in Translation and Interpretation* and *Basic Requirements for MTI Programmes*, have put translation and interpretation education on the path of standardised development.

In addition to T&I programmes in several more prestigious languages, the provision of LCTLs also provide an important talent pool for China's language services industry. In recent years, with the improvement of China's comprehensive national strength and the all-round development of the "Belt and Road initiative," the training of LCTL professionals has also been accorded great importance by the Chinese government, ushering in a new era of rapid development. In China's foreign language education, the six working languages of the United Nations (Chinese, English, French, Russian, Arabic and Spanish) together with German and Japanese are defined as "commonly used languages." Accordingly, all the other languages are called "less commonly used languages" or "less commonly taught languages" (Su, 2017). Since the approval by the MOE in 2001, Peking University, Beijing Foreign Studies University and other universities have begun to build undergraduate training bases for LCTLs. In 2010, Chinese Ministry of Education (2010b) issued the first national education plan in the 21st century, the *Outline of China's Medium and Long Term Education Reform and Development Plan (2010–2020)*, as a programmatic document guiding China's educational reform and development in the next decade. The Plan underscored that the country should cultivate a large number of talents and have an international vision, familiarity with international rules, and the ability to participate in international affairs and international competition so as to meet the requirements of national economic development and opening up. With the encouragement and support of relevant national policies, the number and scale of foreign language programmes in colleges and universities has increased significantly. As of June 2019, there were 1,040 foreign language colleges and universities in China. Among the various provinces of China, Jiangsu and Hubei rank first in the number of foreign language colleges and universities, with 64 each, followed by Shandong (59), Guangdong (58), Beijing (54), Hebei (53) and Zhejiang (52) (Translators Association of China, 2020). According to statistics issued in March 2016, there were 66 LCTL majors and 391 programmes in 167 colleges and universities with more than 32,000 undergraduate students across the country (Ding, 2017).

4 Looking to the 2022 Beijing Winter Olympic Games

At the 128th IOC session in Kuala Lumpur, Malaysia, held 31 July 2015, the IOC awarded the 2022 Winter Olympic Games to Beijing, stating that the city hosted an "exceptional" Games in 2008 and promised to do even better this time. Beijing won 44 nods in the IOC voting, against 40 for the Kazakh city of Almaty, with one abstention, becoming the first ever city to host both summer and winter Olympics. Beijing 2022 aims to create abundant new legacies from the Games, while enhancing the legacies from the Beijing 2008 Summer Olympic Games.

4.1 Changing socio-economic environment

4.1.1 China's growing global power

The past decade has seen a boom in China's economic power. Since 2010, China has occupied the position of the world's second largest economy, with Japan surrendering its 42-year-old ranking. The stable growth of China's economy has made the country a major engine of global economic recovery. The country's contribution to world economic growth has increased continuously, reaching around 35% in 2017 according to the IMF (Liu, 2017). China aims to double its 2010 GDP and per capita income by 2020 as an important component of becoming a "moderately prosperous society" in all respects (China Economic Net, 2014). Experts have predicted that after sweeping past Germany, France, UK and Japan, China will catch up with US by as early as 2030.

This rising economic power has given China a more proactive role in global governance. China launched the highly ambitious "Belt and Road Initiative" in late 2013, aiming to build a trade and infrastructure network connecting Asia with the Middle East, Europe, Africa and beyond. The initiative, proposed by Chinese President Xi Jinping, is intended to reinvigorate the ancient trade routes that once linked east and west. The "Belt and Road Initiative" is gathering momentum. More than 100 countries and international organisations have already participated in the initiative. In the first three quarters of 2019, China's new investment in 56 countries along the "Belt and Road" amounted to US $11.46 billion, accounting for 12.7% of China's overall outbound investment during the period, up 4 percentage points year on year (Ministry of Commerce of the PRC, 2019). China's trade with countries along the routes has also risen significantly. In 2017, the country's trade volume with Russia, Poland, and Kazakhstan expanded by 27.7%, 24.8% percent, and 41.1% respectively (Liu, 2017).

China's "Belt and Road Initiative" affords immense opportunities for deeper integration in education in the regions and countries along the routes. On the one hand, the "Belt and Road" countries are gradually becoming a new hot spot for Chinese students studying abroad in addition to the traditional major destination countries such as UK, US, Australia and Canada. On the other hand, China has become the second largest recipient country of international students in the world and the countries along the routes are important sources of international students in China. In 2018, 492,185 foreign students from 196 countries and regions studied in 1,004 institutions of higher learning in 31 Chinese provinces and provincial level regions and cities,[24] and nearly half of those were from the "Belt and Road" countries (Ministry of Education of the PRC, 2019a). The top ten source countries of international students in China are: South Korea, Thailand, Pakistan, India, the United States, Russia, Indonesia, Laos, Japan and Kazakhstan (Ministry of Education of the PRC, 2019a).

---

24 The above statistics do not include the students from Hong Kong, Macao and Taiwan.

Between the two Olympic Games hosted and yet to be hosted in Beijing, China is transforming from a modernising country seeking international recognition, especially recognition from the West, to the largest and most powerful developing country striving for a greater voice in global policymaking and governance. Since 2008, China has hosted a series of major international events and activities such as the 2009 Harbin Winter Universiade, 2010 Shanghai World Expo, 2010 Guangzhou Asian Games, 2011 Shenzhen Universiade, 2014 Nanjing Summer Youth Olympic Games, 2019 Beijing International Horticultural Exhibition and 2019 Wuhan Military World Games. As China takes an increasingly proactive role in global governance, its foreign language ideology is gradually moving away from an "English monolingualism" (Piller, 2016b) to national language capacity-oriented multilingualism.

4.1.2 Olympic Agenda 2020

While the development strategy of China has been changing, the Olympic Movement has been changing as well. With the complication of their super large scale, the frequent occurrence of doping and corruption scandals, and the overwhelming commercial imperative, the management and organisation of the Olympic Games have become increasingly difficult. Some critics even claim that the Olympic Games are becoming an obstacle to the realisation of the Olympic ideal. Due to the expensive and inefficient candidature procedure, the IOC found itself facing a shortage of candidates willing to host the Olympic Games, and it has become apparent that reform is necessary. The IOC has reacted to this situation by introducing *the Olympic Agenda 2020*, a reform process making the Olympic Games more attractive for potential hosts. This *Olympic Agenda 2020* (International Olympic Committee, 2014) was unanimously agreed at the 127th IOC Session in Monaco on 8 and 9 December 2014. The reforms followed a year of discussion and consultation with all stakeholders of the Olympic Movement, as well as external experts and the public. The 40 detailed recommendations are like individual pieces of a jigsaw puzzle, which when put together give us a clear picture of what the future of the Olympic Movement will look like. Some of the key areas addressed by Olympic Agenda 2020 are:

1) Changes to the candidature procedure, with a new philosophy to invite potential candidate cities to present a project that fits their sporting, economic, social and environmental long-term planning needs.
2) Reducing costs for bidding, by decreasing the number of presentations that are allowed and providing a significant financial contribution from the IOC.
3) Move from a sport-based to an event-based programme.

4) Strengthen the 6th Fundamental Principle of Olympism by including non-discrimination on the basis of sexual orientation in the Olympic Charter.
5) Launch of an Olympic Channel to provide a platform for sports and athletes beyond the Olympic Games period, 365 days a year.
6) Adapting and further strengthening the principles of good governance and ethics to changing demands.
7) Athletes remain at the centre of all 40 of the proposals, with the protection of clean athletes being at the heart of the IOC's philosophy.

Work has already started on the implementation of *Olympic Agenda 2020*. The IOC has begun working on the Olympic Channel. The new Invitation Phase has already been launched for the 2024 bidding process, which allows cities to present an Olympic project that best matches their long-term sports, economic, social and environmental plans.

As the first host city to fully benefit from *Olympic Agenda 2020*, the Beijing 2022 Olympic and Paralympic Winter Games organisers have made great strides in incorporating the new way of working spelled out by the IOC (Xinhua, 2018). Since the inception of the bid for the 2022 Games, Beijing has planned an inspired vision of a 'Joyful Rendezvous upon Pure Ice and Snow,' highlighting the three bidding concepts of hosting a Winter Games that are "athlete-centred, sustainable and economical." These three concepts are in line with *Olympic Agenda 2020*. In 2018, the IOC announced an ambitious set of 118 reforms, focusing on six recommendations of Olympic Agenda 2020 related to the organisation of the Games, and aims to ensure that the Games are affordable, beneficial and sustainable. Beijing 2022 has focused singularly on complying with these reforms by putting on a Games that is "green, inclusive, open and clean" to honour China's commitment to host a "fantastic, extraordinary and excellent" Games. IOC president Thomas Bach expressed his confidence that "Beijing 2022 can set a new bench mark for a sustainable Olympic Games, on one hand benefiting from the legacy of the Beijing 2008 and on the other developing a new winter sports destination in a sustainable way" (Xinhua, 2018).

4.2 *Action plan on language services*

Language services are an important part of the preparations for the Beijing Winter Olympic Games, which carries the important task of communication and contact among various participating groups. On 2017, the Beijing Organising Committee for the 2022 Winter Olympic Games (BOCWOG), the Ministry of Education and the National Language Commission (2017) jointly launched the *Action Plan on*

Language Services for Beijing 2022. The main contents of the *Action Plan* are as follows:[25]

4.2.1 Main objectives

Beijing 2022 promises adherence to the principle of hosting a green, shared, open and uncorrupted Games. BOCWOG will give full play to the advantages of the language resources of the National Language Commission, and organise and coordinate the relevant departments, universities, research institutions, enterprises and social forces to work together and jointly host the Olympic Games, so as to create a good language environment for the successful holding of the 2022 Winter Olympics, provide high-quality language services, demonstrate the charm of Chinese language and culture, and make sure the 2022 Beijing Winter Games are fantastic, extraordinary and excellent.

4.2.2 Principles of action

The Ministry of Education, the National Language Commission and the BOCWOG should:

1) Play an overall coordinating and organisational role, strengthen the linkages with relevant departments, integrate the participation of all parties, and promote the implementation of the *Action Plan*.
2) According to the language service needs of this Winter Olympic Games, integrate multiple language resources, and give full play to universities, research institutions, enterprises and relevant social forces. Participating parties should work in cooperation and with a due division of labour, and form an interactive development relationship via co-construction and sharing.

    Make full use of the latest achievements in the development of language and information technology; promote the close combination of language services and information technology through a project implementation mechanism to achieve "High-tech Olympics."

    Undertake a timely follow up of the needs of preparations for the next five years in the run up to the Winter Olympic Games, make timely adjustments and improvements to the contents of the Action Plan projects, and test their application through major international events and activities so as to promote the project's achievements to an advanced level.

---

25 The following contents of the Action Plan on Language Services for Beijing 2022 are my translation.

4.2.3 Key projects

In accordance with the needs of the preparation for the Winter Olympic Games, relevant projects will be promoted in advance for the construction of basic resources, the establishment of standards, and the improvement of the urban language environment.

1) Develop language technology integration and services

Carry out relevant terminology development work and build a cross-language terminology service platform. On the basis of this platform, develop multilingual service systems and intelligent APPs; integrate technical achievements such as speech recognition and synthesis, machine translation, and human-computer dialogue; and build a human-computer intelligent exchange platform to provide real-time, convenient and all-round multilingual services for the Winter Olympics.

2) Provide language translation and training services

According to the needs of the Winter Olympic Games for language services and language translation, a team of language experts will be set up to check the translation of important conference materials and documents, and recommend experts for evaluating the open bidding of the Winter Olympic Games language translation service providers.

Organise experts to formulate multilingual training standards according to the needs of the Winter Olympic Games and relevant standards. Prepare language training materials, provide language and cultural training for Chinese and foreign volunteers, and provide language training services for domestic technicians, translators, staff of BOCWOG, the 2022 Winter Olympic volunteers, and so forth.

3) Improve the Olympic language environment

Organise the inspection of the use of languages and scripts in Beijing and Zhangjiakou, and release the inspection results to the public, so as to ensure that the use of languages and scripts in the Beijing Winter Olympic Games conforms to the relevant national language policies and standards.

Check the English signs at the various Winter Olympic venues and put forward suggestions for revision.

Compile the *Manual of Terminology of Sports Events for the 2022 Beijing Winter Olympic Games and Paralympic Games*, and promote the standardisation of the terminology of sports events for the Winter Olympic Games. Set up "Beijing public language and culture lecture hall", and compile the handbook *Welcome the Winter Olympics: Language and Culture*.

4) Carry out foreign language volunteer training

According to the language service needs for the preparation and holding of the Winter Olympic Games, formulate a foreign language volunteer training plan aimed at improving organisational ability and professional levels, and coordinate foreign language colleges and universities to provide foreign language training services for volunteers before and during the Winter Olympic Games.

5) Carry out the Winter Olympic language and culture exhibition experience project
With the theme of "language and sports culture," cultural exhibitions at the venues of the Beijing Winter Olympic Games should showcase the cultural advantages of Beijing, introduce the languages and cultures involved in the Winter Olympic Games, and carry out various forms of language and culture exhibition and experience projects.

4.3 Action plan on Olympic volunteer services

Volunteers are important contributors to ensure the success of the Olympics and Paralympics. On 10 May 2019, BOCWOG released the *Action Plan on Volunteer Services*, marking the Beijing 2022 1000-Day Countdown. At the Countdown ceremony Zhang Jiandong, Executive Vice President of Beijing 2022, said that Beijing, the only city to hold both Summer and Winter Olympic Games, would pool wisdom from volunteers all around the world in order to deliver a "fantastic, extraordinary and excellent Games" (Xinhua, 2019). Beijing 2022 kicked off the global recruitment programme for Games-time volunteers on 5 December 2019. As of 5 January 2020, the number of volunteers applying for the Beijing Winter Olympic Games has exceeded 630,000 (Xinhua, 2020).

According to the Plan, five volunteer services projects would be launched, including Pre-Games Volunteers Project, City Volunteers Project, Test Events Volunteers Project, Volunteer Service Legacy Conversion Project, and Games-time Volunteers Project. Multiple plans including communication, recruitment and training would also be put into operation for the sake of wider public participation.

BOCWOG (2019) plans to recruit 27,000 Games-time volunteers for the Winter Olympic Games and 12,000 Games-time volunteers for the winter Paralympic Games. The Games-time volunteers are expected to be sourced mainly from domestic college and high school students, overseas Chinese, international volunteers, and the volunteers selected at the provincial level plus Hong Kong, Macao, and Taiwan. BOCWOG also encourages athletes specialised in winter sports to apply for positions of professional volunteers.

4.4 Olympic language services suppliers

The language services legacy of the 2008 Beijing Olympic Games has been well inherited in the 2022 Winter Olympic Games, offering templates for how to establish bodies with relevant responsibilities, in addition to a wide range of resources and capacities that were created for those first Games and are now mature and multidimensional.

4.4.1 Official language training services exclusive supplier

In readiness for the return of the Olympic Games to China, EF was nominated as the Official Language Training Services Exclusive Supplier of Beijing 2022 on 20 August 2019 (EF Education First, 2019b). EF's long history in China and rich experience in providing language services at previous Olympic Games gave EF incomparable advantages over other language training institutions. Yan Cheng, Director General of Beijing 2022's Human Resources Department, stated that Beijing 2022 and EF will jointly develop training plans, and organise a range of tailored and practical programmes for the paid staff of BOCWOG, National Technical Officials, and volunteers, to help them adopt a global view and enhance their language abilities (EF Education First, 2019). EF China CEO Jacob Toren said the company would deliver a language training programme in line with 'Olympic Agenda 2020,' focusing on legacy and sustainability.

4.4.2 Official automated translation software exclusive supplier

On 16 September 2019, AI company iFLYTEK was announced as the exclusive supplier of automated translation software for the 2022 Beijing Winter Olympics and Paralympics (Cheng, 2019). Founded in 1999, iFLYTEK specialises in artificial intelligence, speech recognition, natural language processing and autonomous learning. In recent years they have begun expanding their business into consumer electronics, including a portable translator providing real-time translation in 60 languages. The company will provide technological support on voice recognition, voice compound and machine translation at the Games, for example, multilingual presentation of events results, multilingual translation of major events, multilingual broadcasting, and machine translation communication between staff and athletes. BOGWOG believe that such products and services will create a sound communication environment for the Games and also help reduce repetitive work to improve efficiency. Liu Qingfeng, chairman of iFLYTEL, said the firm aims to leverage advanced technologies to help spread Chinese voices and stories to more people across the world. It is the first time that "the automated translation software supplier" has been officially set up as an independent sponsorship category in the Olympic history. Thus, the form of language services at major international events has gradually moved from human translation to AI technology-based machine translation so as to meet the demand for timely, convenient and low-cost multilingual services.

4.4.3 Beijing Olympic Multilingual Service Centre, BFSU

The "Beijing Olympic Multilingual Service Centre" was China's first governmental language service organisation, aiming to provide "barrier-free" language services in 44 languages at the 2008 Beijing Olympic Games. After the Games, the centre was renamed as "Beijing Multilingual Service Centre", a permanent body at BFSU. In this new guise the centre, relying on student volunteers from BFSU, has undertaken multilingual services for numerous conferences and events, including the APEC conference and Guangzhou Asian Games. Since April 2010, MSC has successively established a connection with hotlines for police and first aid. At present, the centre has set up landlines in eight standing languages including English, French, German, Russian, Arabic, Japanese and Korean to provide language services for the public emergency hotlines in the capital city through three-way communication, in which English translation services are in operation 24-hour a day. In response to the Chinese government's call to build 'national language capacity' (Zhao, 2015), BFSU committed itself to producing more multilingual graduates and expanding language categories. By 2020, BFSU has opened 101 foreign language majors, covering all the official languages of 175 countries with diplomatic relations with China (Beijing Foreign Studies University, 2019). It can be anticipated that MSC will provide more comprehensive multilingual services for the foreign athletes, coaches, judges and officials participating in the Beijing Winter Olympic Games.

4.5 Technology-supported multilingual services

Technology-supported language services will be one of the highlights of the 2022 Beijing Winter Olympic Games (Department of Language Information Management of Ministry of Education of the PRC, 2018). According to the *Action Plan on Language Services for Beijing 2022*, Beijing Advanced Innovation Centre for Language Resources (ACLP) at Beijing Language and Culture University (BLCU), with the support of the State Language Commission, has set up three Beijing Winter Olympics Language Intelligence Service projects.

4.5.1 "Olympic Winter Games Term Portal" project

On 11 December 2019, the "Olympic Winter Games Term Portal Version 2" (owgt.blcu.edu.cn) was officially handed over to BOCWOG, following the delivery of Version 1 on 13 December 2018 (ACLR, 2019). The Olympic Winter Games Term Portal Project is managed by Prof. Liu Heping at BLCU, and an expert panel has been set up with senior Olympics interpreter Daniel Glon as the Chief Expert. The expert panel consists of 11 members including senior terminology experts, translation experts, and language service experts for the Olympics from countries of China, the United States, Korea, Japan, Russia, Canada, among others. So far, under the guidance of BOCWOG, MOE and the State Language Commission, and with the efforts of the experts, remarkable achievements have been made on Version 2. The portal includes about 125,000 terms in total, among which there are 9,539 terms for core events, 27,022 Chinese terms, 30,015 English terms, 19,166 French terms, 12,388 Japanese terms, 16,111 Russian terms, 11,135 Korean terms, and 9,539 German terms. Hundreds of specialised vocabularies and thousands of commonly used Chinese-English public signs extracted from the Olympic Winter Games Language Service Style Book were added to this version. In addition, common vocabularies and terms will be added in real time according to the requirements of test events. It is expected that by the end of 2021 the "Olympic Winter Games Term Portal Version 3" will have been built with parallel Chinese, English, French, Japanese, Korean and Russian terms. As groundwork for Olympic language services, the Olympic Winter Games Term Portal has collected a large number of standard expressions related to the Olympics, which will provide accurate and timely query services for the hosts, participants and spectators.

4.5.2 "Machine translation for the Beijing Winter Olympics" project

The "Machine Translation for the Beijing Winter Olympics" project is headed by Associate Professor Liu Yang of the Department of Computer Science and Technology of Tsinghua University. The project aims to build a machine translation textual database and develop a Chinese-English machine translation system based on neural networks technology for the 2022 Beijing Winter Olympic Games. By April 2019, nearly 1.3 million pairs of high-quality domain text corpus and nearly 200,000 pairs of speech corpus had been collected (Gao, 2019). The synchronous two-way translation model proposed by the project team is believed to greatly improve translation performance. The current translation system has taken the lead in the evaluation of the international open dataset and the Winter Olympics dataset. The research results of the project will be applied to the relevant fields of the Games; for example, the text translation system can be embedded in the official website of the Beijing Winter Olympic Games.

4.5.3 "Knowledge map based intelligent Q-A system for the Beijing Winter Olympics" project

In response to the challenges of the fragmentation of information knowledge, and deficiencies in intellectuality and personalisation in information service systems, a Chinese intelligent Q-A system for the Beijing Winter Olympic Games was designed based on a big data knowledge map. On 26 September 2019, the intelligent Q-A system was officially released (Deng, 2019). The project constructed a large-scale knowledge map covering five types of Winter Olympic core entities, designed various types of knowledge display services, and developed a "smart Q & A platform" with voice and text input modes. The system, which provides real-time and convenient Q & A services for the Winter Olympic Games, is a comprehensive and three-dimensional means for popularising Winter Olympic knowledge and promoting Winter Olympic culture.

4.6 English signage standardisation

According to the Beijing Public Security Bureau, on a typical day there are likely to be more than 200,000 foreigners in Beijing, including permanent residents, visitors and tourists (China Daily, 2019). As the 2022 Winter Olympic Games approaches, the Beijing Municipal Government has decided to further correct English translations of public signs to help foreigners make better use of public facilities and establish the capital as a more open and friendly place. On 20 June 2017, the Standardisation Administration, the MOE and the State Language Commission jointly held a press conference in Beijing to issue *Guidelines for the use of English in public service areas (GB/T 35302)* (Department of Language Information Management of Ministry of Education of the PRC, 2017a), a series of national standards for regulating English translation and writing in public service areas in China. These guidelines specify the principles, methods and requirements of English translation in 13 public service areas, including transportation, tourism, culture, entertainment, sports, education, health, medicine, post, telecommunications, catering, accommodation, commerce and finance, and provide standard translations for common public service information in these areas. They came into effect on 1 December 2017. Shortly afterwards, *Guidelines for the use of Japanese in public service areas (GB/T 30240)* (Department of Language Information Management of Ministry of Education of the PRC, 2017b) and *Guidelines for the use of Russian in public service areas (GB/T 35303)* (Department of Language Information Management of Ministry of Education of the PRC, 2017c) were issued at the end of 2017 and came into effect on 1 July 2018. The compilation of *Guidelines for the use of Korean in public service areas* has also been completed and awaits release (Department of Language Information Management of Ministry of Education of the PRC, in preparation). At present, GB/T35302, GB/T30240 and GB/T35303 constitute a series of national standards on the norms of foreign language translation in the field of public services. On the basis of these guidelines, the Beijing Municipal Government will organise language experts from home and abroad to revise the *Beijing Municipal Local Standards on English Translations of Public Signs*, which took effect in 2007, and issue a series of local standards on public signs in foreign languages before the 2022 Winter Olympic Games.

In 2018, the capital created an annual white paper with 1,005 standard translations for public signs and added 6,061 new translations to create a favourable environment for foreigners (China Daily, 2019). Since the launch of the campaign on correction of erroneous public sign translations in March 2018, more than 2,600 erroneous translations were identified in 28 popular tourist areas in the city (China Daily, 2019). In the future, the city will encourage more institutions including international schools, hospitals and international talent communities to participate in corrections to continuously improve the standard of international public service.

Technological innovations have been applied in the on-going public signage standardisation campaign in preparation for the 2022 Winter Olympic Games. An online platform "Online Correction of Erroneous Public Sign Translations" (www.interview.qianlong.com/zt/bjpubsign) has been established to collect, analyse and rectify the capital's translations to improve efficiency. An electronic database has been built to collect and retrieve Standard English translations for public signs. In addition to the English translation database, databases for signage translation in French, Spanish, Russian, Korean, Italian and other LCTLs will also be built before 2022. The Beijing Municipal Government also encourages innovation in the forms of foreign language signage. New forms of public signs such as electronic screens, mobile navigation applications, and intelligent touch screens will be used to maximise the information capacity on public signs per unit area (Beijing Daily, 2019).

5 Summary

Language skills and services are vital not only in ensuring a quality experience for athletes, visitors, and the Olympic family during the events, but in creating a legacy for communities and citizens in the years after the Games. The Beijing 2008 Olympic Games has promoted the rapid development of China's language service industry and accumulated valuable language service experience for China in hosting mega sporting events. After 2010, the language ideology of China's mainstream society has changed to the view of language as resource, which has promoted the implementation of national language capacity-oriented multilingual policies. In the recent decade, the Chinese government has strengthened the planning and training of LCTL professionals and the disciplinary development of language service, and attached increasing importance to the development of language intelligence and language technology. Today, the era of mobile Internet, cloud computing, big data and artificial intelligence is quietly coming. The continuous innovation of computer-aided translation, machine translation and online language service platform is reshaping the structure of China's language service industry. In this context, language services for the Beijing 2022 Winter Olympic Games will make full use of the latest achievements in the development of language services and information technology to achieve the "High-tech Olympics" (Ministry of Education of the PRC, 2017). In the future, language-related intelligence technology will play an increasingly important role in Olympic language services and other social domains.

Chapter 9
Conclusion

It has been two decades since Beijing's successful bid for the 29th Summer Olympic Games in 2001. Beijing is a city on the move. Its dynamic growth reflects that of China as a whole. With the continuous improvement of comprehensive strength, international status and influence, China is seeking a greater role in global governance system. Meanwhile, the focus of China's foreign language policy has shifted from 'English monolinguilism' to 'national language capacity-oriented multilingualism.' In the medium and long-term educational reform and development guidelines (Ministry of Education of the PRC, 2010), the Chinese government attached increasing emphasis on the cultivation of LCTL talents in line with national needs. This transformation in national language policy is based on an ideological change from the 'language-as-problem' orientation to the 'language-as-resource' orientation. The former view holds that language diversity creates troubles for society, while linguistic homogeneity is seen to facilitate economic growth and national unity. In sharp contrast, the latter view considers all languages to be valuable social and cultural recourses and calls on institutions to preserve, develop and utilise language recourses. On 18 February 2019, China's MOE and UNESCO jointly issued the 岳麓宣言 *Yuelue xuanyan* [*Yuelu Proclamation*], a document on protection and promotion of the world's linguistic diversity (Ministry of Education of the PRC, 2019b). Being UNESCO's first permanent document themed on linguistic diversity protection, the proclamation called on the international community to reach consensus and take measures to protect and promote linguistic diversity. Linguistic diversity is not a novelty of our age, but rather has been "the normal human experience all along" (Piller, 2016a, p. 30). In fact, the diversity of the world's languages is decreasing. However, our perception of linguistic diversity has increased because more and more people experience linguistic diversity on a daily basis in the 21st century (Piller, 2016a). Promoting intercultural communication under the premise of protecting linguistic diversity and social justice is a major research issue facing us today, and an appropriate subject for future research.

Coinciding with the lead-up to the Beijing 2022 Winter Olympic Games, our world is gradually entering the age of artificial intelligence, and we need to learn how AI is likely to impact our lives and how we will coexist with AI. Recent years have witnessed the exponential development of neural machine translation technology, and multilingual intelligent human-machine interaction has been a hot spot in the field of speech recognition. In the future, machine translation will provide the possibility for intercultural communication in native languages. AI has changed and will continue to change the way people with different linguistic backgrounds interact. Given the significance and pace of these developments, policymakers need to position themselves on the front line and guide the future direction of language policy and planning. The Beijing 2022 Winter Olympic Games will symbolise and spur on the city's commitment to technological advancement in language services. The governments of Beijing and China recognise that a far-reaching, creative and comprehensive response to the language challenges posed by the changing environment is an essential requirement for the development of a modern society in the 21st century.

International organisations are important actors of global governance, and they provide a platform for nation-states to participate in global governance. Language choices of international organisations have a bearing on the rights of member states and can be regarded as the representation of the international prestige and influence of states. In the sociolinguist ecological system of the international community, European languages, predominantly English, serve as the official or working languages of most international organisations. Although Chinese is the language with the largest number of speakers in the world and one of the six official languages of the United Nations, its usage in international organisations is very limited. Other non-European languages are in the same position. With Tokyo 2020 and Beijing 2022 coming up, the Olympics are now in an entirely Asian cycle. In a way, having three Olympic Games in a row in Asia tells us the IOC must recognise the multilingual backgrounds of its members and strengthen the voice of its non-Western members. Asian countries may offer a new model of language management and language services for the Olympics as the largest global celebration. Beijing's experiences as the first city to host both the Summer and Winter Olympics have profound implications for future research on LPP of international organisations and language services for linguistically complex events. The linguistic challenges that the host countries confront in preparing for and hosting the Olympic Games are probably the most complex ones in human history. The methods of bridging the gaps between official language policies and actual language practices in the Games will give great impetus for the development of language management and language services at the supernational level, and eventually contribute to maintain linguistic diversity and facilitate cross-cultural communication in this globalising world.

In Chapter 3, I said this book aims to present a holistic picture of LPP for the Modern Olympic Games in non-Anglophone countries, based on evidence from China. In order to achieve that, I not only gave a thick description of language policies formulated (Chapter 4) and language services provided (Chapter 5) for the Games, but also critically analysed how dominant language ideologies impacted on language practices from the perspectives of individual learning experiences (Chapter 5), language textbooks (Chapter 6), and linguistic landscape (Chapter 7). This longitudinal study also enabled me to observe the transformation of China's foreign language ideologies and corresponding language policies in China's changing socio-economic environment (Chapter 8). In addition, I also tried to combine China's "language service" research with western LPP research to promote cross-cultural academic communication. In language planning and management research, it is important to study how language ideologies (Joseph and Taylor, 1990; Piller, 2015; Schieffelin, Woolard and Kroskrity, 1998) or language planning goals (Kaplan and Baldauf, 2003) motivate decision making in language planning and impact on people's language practice. Being an international sporting event with broad participation, the Olympic Games involve multi-level actors in the LPP process. It is also important to look into how actors at macro level (IOC, BOCOG, national and local governments), meso level (institutions, media, education systems, communities) and micro level (athletes, coaches, judges, journalists, teachers, volunteers, service staff, Beijing citizens) make various efforts to influence language status, education and use for the Olympics. It is noteworthy that LPP research has long been interested in matters of language policy and planning at the macro level, that is, the level of the state, and thus from a top-down perspective. But, as Spolsky (2004, p. 56) points out, '[l]anguage policy studies that focus only on the individual nation state and its centralized language planning are likely to miss many significant features'. This criticism – together with others – has given rise to approaches that focus more on the micro level, investigating actual language use and speakers' attitudes. By doing so, LPP researchers attempt to bridge the gap between the macro level LPP and the micro level LPP by examining the interaction between the two, and try to ascertain to what extent, and in what way, the macro level influences the micro level and how micro-level process contribute to the creation and maintenance of macro-level objectives and processes (e.g., Baldauf, 2006; Canagarajah, 2005). Therefore, future research on LPP for international sporting events, or more broadly LPP at the supranational level, should pay greater attention to the agency of actors at the micro level LPP and to its interaction with the macro level LPP.

Maintaining linguistic diversity while ensuring the efficiency of language communication is probably one of the biggest challenges facing the world in the 21st century. Finally, I hope this book can appeal to sociolinguists and applied linguists for further research on complex and evolving issues of language management, language ideologies, language practices and language services involving the Modern Olympic Games.

Bibliography

21st Century. (2008, January 14). 2008 book exhibition: Olympics-related foreign language publications are popular. http://www.www.21stcentury.com.cn/story/39048.html (accessed 20 April 2010)
ACLR. (2019, December 11). ACLR's project of Olympic Winter Games Term Portal (Version 2) officially delivers to BOCOG. http://yuyanziyuan.blcu.edu.cn/en/info/1065/2059.htm (accessed 6 February 2020)
Adamson, Bob, Kingsley Bolton, Agnes Lam & Q. S. Tong. (2002). English in China: A preliminary bibliography. *World Englishes*, 21(2), 349–355.
Adamson, Bob. (2002). Barbarian as a foreign language: English in China's Schools. *World Englishes*, 21(2), 231–243.
Adamson, Bob. (2004). *China's English: A History of English in Chinese Education. Hong Kong*: Hong Kong University Press.
Agarwala, Ramgopal. (2002). *The Rise of China: Threat or Opportunity*? New Delhi: Bookwell.
Ager, Dennis. (2005) Prestige and image planning. In Eli Hinkel (ed.) Handbook of Research in Second Language Teaching and Learning (chapter 57). Mahwah, NJ: Erlbaum.
Aifly Education Technology Company. (2007a, June 18). Aifly has officially become Beijing 2008 Olympic Games language training services supplier. http://www.ai-fly.com/en/ (accessed 8 August 2008)
Aifly Education Technology Company. (2007b, June 26). An Olympic volunteer English learning storm. http://blog.sina.com.cn/s/blog_4ce6748401000a0m.html (accessed 18 September 2009)
Aifly Education Technology Company. (2008, August 22). Aifly trains 1.5 million people for the Beijing Olympics. http://www.prnasia.com/pr/08/08/08530011-1.html (accessed 18 September 2009)
Apple, Michael. W. (1990). *Ideology and Curriculum* (2nd edn.). New York; London: Routledge.
Apple, Michael. W. (1992). *The Text and Cultural Politics*. Educational Researcher, 21(7), 4–19.
Apple, Michael. W. (1996). Power, meaning and identity: Critical sociology of education in the United States. *British Journal of Sociology of Education*, 17(2), 125–144.
Associated Press. (2007, April 11). Bad English added to list of things Beijing Olympic officials want to ban. http://journeyeast.org/Beijing_2008_Summer_Olympics.htm (accessed 1 October 2009)
Associated Press. (2010, August 16). China overtakes Japan as world's second-largest economy. http://www.guardian.co.uk/business/2010/aug/16/china-overtakes-japan-second-largest-economy (accessed 14 December 2010)
Backhaus, Peter. (2006). Multilingualism in Tokyo: A Look into the Linguistic Landscape. *International Journal of Multilingualism*, 3, 52–66.
Backhaus, Peter. (2007). *Linguistic Landscapes: Comparative Study of Urban Multilingualism in Tokyo*. Clevedon; Buffalo: Multilingual Matters Ltd.
Baldauf Jr., Richard. B., (2006). Rearticulating the case for micro language planning in a language ecology context. *Current Issues in Language Planning*, 7(2&3), 147–170.
Bandura, Albert. (1986). *Social Foundations of Thought and Action: A Social Cognitive Theory*. Englewood Cliffs, N.J.: Prentice-Hall.
Basil, Michael. D. (1996). Identification as a mediator of celebrity effects. *Journal of Broadcasting & Electronic Media*, 40(4), 478–496.

Beijing Daily. (2019, November 26). Foreign language signs will be fully covered in public places in Beijing before the 2022 Winter Olympics. https://baijiahao.baidu.com/s?id=1651232340895722172&wfr=spider&for=pc (accessed 3 February 2020)

Beijing Evening Newspaper. (2008, July 7). Beijing issued accommodation service guide for Olympic spectators in eight languages. http://caofeidian.china.com.cn/sport/zhuanti/2008ay/2008-07/07/content_15967152.htm (accessed 25 June 2010)

Beijing Foreign Studies University. (2019, September 23). Introduction of university. https://www.bfsu.edu.cn/overview (accessed 5 February 2020)

Beijing Municipal Bureau of Statistics. (2007). *Beijing Statistical Yearbook 2007*. Beijing: China Statistics Press.

Beijing Municipal Bureau of Statistics. (2008). Number of tourists to Beijing. http://www.ebeijing.gov.cn/feature_2/Statistics/Tourism/t1059449.htm (accessed 16 June 2010)

Beijing Municipal Bureau of Statistics. (2009). *Beijing Statistical Yearbook 2009*. Beijing: China Statistics Press.

Beijing Municipal Bureau of Statistics. (2019, May 21). Gross domestic product (1978–2017). http://tjj.beijing.gov.cn/tjsj/cysj/201905/t20190521_153987.html (accessed 11 February 2020)

Beijing Municipal Education Commission. (2004). Beijing's work plan of the education ministry's experimental scheme of compulsory Education curriculum. http://www.bjedu.gov.cn/publish/mainmain/1442/2010/20100916104026888864980/20100916104026888864980.html (accessed 3 November 2010)

Beijing Municipal Education Commission. (2013, October 21). Announcement of Beijing Municipal Education Commission' public consultation on "the 2014–2016 framework for the reform of middle school entrance examination (Draft)" and "the 2014–2016 framework for the reform of college entrance examination (Draft)". http://jw.beijing.gov.cn/tzgg/201602/t20160202_1448713.html (accessed 24 January 2020)

Beijing Municipal Tourism Bureau. (2008, September 10). Woshi 2008 nian 8 yuefen jiedai rujing guoye lvyouzhe yu lvyou fandian jiedai renshu qingkuang [Number of inbound tourists to Beijing in August 2008. http://www.bjta.gov.cn/lyzl/tjzl/lstjzl/2008lstjzl/2008rjlyzqk/200652.htm (accessed 20 April 2010)

Beijing Review. (2004, September 10). Being Understood. http://www.china.org.cn/english/China/106704.htm (accessed 13 June 2010)

Ben-Rafael, Eliezer, Elana Shohamy, Muhanmmad husan Amara & Nira Trumper-Hecht. (2006). Linguistic landscape as symbolic construction of the public space: the case of Israel. International Journal of Multilingualism, 3, 7–30.

Blackledge, Adrian, & Aneta Pavlenko. (2004). *Negotiation of Identities in Multilingual Contexts*. Clevedon; Buffalo: Multilingual Matters.

Blain, Neil, Raymond Boyle & Hugh O'Donnell. (1993). *Sport and National Identity in the European Media*. Leicester; New York: Leicester University Press.

Block, David. (2003). *The Social Turn in Second Language Acquisition*. Washington, D.C.: Georgetown University Press.

Block, David. (2007). The rise of identity in SLA research, post Firth and Wagner (1997). *The Modern Language Journal*, 91(5), 863–876.

Blommaert, Jan. (2006). Language policy and national identity. In Thomas Ricento (Ed.), *An Introduction to Language Policy: Theory and Method* (pp. 238–254). Oxford: Blackwell.

Blommaert, Jan. and Ad Backus. (2013). Superdiverse repertoires and the individual. In I. de Saint-Georges and J. Weber (eds.), *Multilingualism and multimodality: Current challenges for educational studies* (11–32). Rotterdam: Sense Publishers.
BOCOG & Beijing Municipal Education Commission. (2007a). *A Conversational English Reader (Elementary)* (1st edn.). Beijing: Beijing Normal University Press.
BOCOG & Beijing Municipal Education Commission. (2007b). *A Conversational English* Reader (Advanced) (1st edn.). Beijing: Beijing Normal University Press.
BOCOG. (2002, March 28). *Beijing Olympic Action Plan.* http://en.beijing2008.cn/59/80/column211718059.shtml (accessed 3 November 2008)
BOCWOG. (2019, December 5). Announcement on global recruitment of volunteers for the 2022 Beijing Winter Olympics and Paralympics. https://www.beijing2022.cn/a/20191205/013659.htm (accessed 1 February 2020)
Bolton, Kingsley. (2002). Chinese Englishes: from Canton jargon to global English. *World Englishes*, 21(2), 181–199.
Bourdieu, Pierre, & Jean-Claude Passeron. (1977). *Reproduction in Education, Society and Culture*. London; Beverly Hills: Sage Publications.
Bourdieu, Pierre, & John B. Thompson. (1991). *Language and Symbolic Power*. Cambridge, Mass.: Harvard University Press.
Bourdieu, Pierre. (1986). The forms of capital. In John Richardson (Ed.), *Handbook of Theory and Research for the Sociology of Education* (pp. 241–258). New York: Greenwood.
Bradley, David. (2006). China: language situation. In Keith Brown (Ed.), *Encyclopedia of Language & Linguistics* (2nd edn) (pp. 319–323): Elsevier.
Braudy, Leo. (1986). *The Frenzy of Renown: Fame and Its History*. New York: Oxford University Press.
Brecht, Richard D., & A. Ronald Walton. (1994). National strategic planning in the less commonly taught languages. *The Annals of the American Academy of Political and Social Science*, 532(1), 190–212.
Brophy, Jere. (1999). Research on motivation in education: Past, present and future. In Timothy C. Urdan (Ed.), *Advances in Motivation and Achievement: The Role of Context* (pp. 1–44). Stamford, CT: JAL.
Brown, Graham. (2000). Emerging issues in Olympic sponsorship: Implications for host cities. *Sport Management Review*, 3(1), 71–92.
Brownell, Susan. (2005). Challenged America: China and America – women and sport, past, present and future. *International Journal of the History of Sport*, 22(6), 1173–1193.
Brownell, Susan. (2007). Will the Olympics change China, or will China change the Olympics? http://olympicstudies.uab.es/lectures/web/pdf/puig.pdf (accessed 14 November 2010)
Brutt-Griffler, Janina, & Keiko K. Samimy. (1999). Revisiting the colonial in the postcolonial: Critical praxis for nonnative-speaking teachers in TESOL program. *TESOL Quarterly*, 33(3), 413–431.
BTV. (2008). Bilingual policeman: Liu Wenli. Olympic Figures Talk Show. http://6.cn/watch/5524605.html (accessed 13 June 2009)
Burns, Robert B. (2000). *Introduction to Research Methods* (4th edn.). Frenchs Forest: Pearson Education.
Burton, Robert B. (2003). Olympic Games host city marketing: An exploration of expectations and outcomes. *Sport Marketing Quarterly*, 12, 37.
Cambridge ESOL. (2010). Beijing English Test System. http://www.cambridgeesol.cn/esol/exams/ShowArticle.asp?ArticleID=80 (accessed 18 November 2010)

Canagarajah, A. Suresh. (1999). *Resisting Linguistic Imperialism in English Teaching*. Oxford: Oxford University Press.
Canagarajah, A. Suresh. (2005). *Reclaiming the Local in Language Policy and Practice*. Mahwah, N.J.: L. Erlbaum Associates.
Cao, Jie. (2008, August 8). "Linguist" Police Officer – Liu Wenli. http://english.cri.cn/6066/2008/08/08/1721s391140.htm (accessed 15 May 2011)
Cenoz, Jasone, & Durk Gorter. (2006). Linguistic landscape and minority languages. *International Journal of Multilingualism*, 3, 67–80.
Chang, Junyue. (2006). Globalization and English in Chinese higher education. *World Englishes*, 25(3–4), 513–525.
Chen, Yumin. (2010). The semiotic construal of attitudinal curriculum goals: Evidence from EFL textbooks in China. *Linguistics and Education*, 21(1), 60–74.
Cheng, Yu. (2019, September 16). AI company iFlytek signs exclusive deal to provide translation software at 2022 Games. http://www.chinadaily.com.cn/a/201909/16/WS5d7f3ecba310cf3e3556bb4e.html (accessed 5 February 2020)
China Daily. (2005, May 26). Standard English for the 2008 Olympic Games. http://www.chinadaily.com.cn/english/doc/2005-05/26/content_445962.htm (accessed 25 June 2010)
China Daily. (2019, November 27). Beijing vows to do better at correcting city sign translations. http://www.chinadaily.com.cn/a/201911/27/WS5dddd6a3a310cf3e3557a47f.html (accessed 16 January 2020)
China Economic Net. (2014, April 25). China aims to join 'high-income club' by 2020. http://en.ce.cn/subject/exclusive/201404/25/t20140425_2721591.shtml (accessed 3 February 2020)
China Education and Research Network. (2001a). English Becoming Beijing Preschooler's Compulsory Lesson. http://www.edu.cn/200111_1473/20060323/t20060323_18930.shtml (accessed 15 June 2008)
China Education and Research Network. (2001b). English version Textbooks Enter University Classrooms. http://www.edu.cn/200108_1470/20060323/t20060323_14671.shtml (accessed 15 June 2008)
Chinese International Communication Research Centre. (2006). The 2008 Beijing Olympic Games and China's national image construction research. http://www.qzwb.com/gb/content/2006-12/28/content_2338028.htm (accessed 16 November 2010)
Chubarov, Llya, & Daneil Brooker. (2013). Multiple pathways to global city formation: A functional approach and review of recent evidence in China. *Cities*, 35, 181–189.
Collis, Jane. (2007). Opportunities for linguists at the 2012 Olympic and Paralympic. *The ATA Chronicle*, 36(8), 20–24.
Cook, Vivian. (1999). Going beyond the native speaker in language teaching. *TESOL Quarterly*, 33(2), 185–209.
CRIENGLISH. (2007, November 14). Li Yang, father of Crazy English. http://english.cri.cn/4406/2007/11/14/47@294362.htm (accessed 20 August 2009)
Crystal, David. (1997). *English as a Global Language*. Cambridge; New York: Cambridge University Press.
Cummins, Jim. (1994). Knowledge, power, and identity in teaching English as a second language. In Fred Genesee (Ed.), *Educating Second Language Children: The Whole Child, The Whole Curriculum, The Whole Community* (pp. 33–60). Cambridge; New York: University of Cambridge.

Dai, Mengchun. (2011). Guojia Yuyan Nengli, Yuyan Guihua He Guojia Anquan [National language capabilities, language planning and national security]. *Applied Linguistics*(4), 123–131.

De Varennes, F. (2012). Language policy at the supranational level. In Bernard Spolsky (Ed.), *Language Policy* (pp. 149–173). Cambridge: Cambridge University Press.

Deng, Hui. (2019, September 26). The release of "the knowledge map-based intelligent Q-A systerm for the Beijing Olympic Games". http://news.gmw.cn/2019-09/26/content_33191904.htm (accessed 5 February 2020)

Deng, Sujuan. (2009, December). Cherishing Beijing's Olympic legacy and enhancing the city's development. *Beijing This Month* (Beijing Speaks Foreign Language Program Special Issue), 8–13.

Department of Language Information Management of Ministry of Education of the PRC. (2016, September 24). Guidelines for the use of Russian, Japanese and Korean in public service areas have been approved by the experts. http://www.moe.gov.cn/s78/A19/moe_814/201609/t20160927_282349.html (accessed 3 February 2020)

Department of Language Information Management of Ministry of Education of the PRC. (2017a). *Guidelines for the use of English in public service areas* (Vol. GB/T 30240.2-2017). Beijing: China Standards Press.

Department of Language Information Management of Ministry of Education of the PRC. (2017b). *Guidelines for the use of Japanese in public service areas* (Vol. GB/T 35303–2017). Beijing: China Standards Press.

Department of Language Information Management of Ministry of Education of the PRC. (2017c). *Guidelines for the use of Russian in public service areas* (Vol. GB/T 35302–2017). Beijing: China Standards Press.

Department of Language Information Management of Ministry of Education of the PRC. (2018, November 12). The survey of BOCWOG and Department of Language Information Management on language services for Beijing Winter Olympic Games. http://www.moe.gov.cn/s78/A19/moe_814/201811/t20181112_354345.html (accessed 5 February 2020)

Department of Language Information Management of Ministry of Education of the PRC. (In preparation). *Guidelines for the use of Korea in public service areas*. Beijing: China Standards Press.

Ding, Chao. (2017). Observation and analysis of the current situation of the less commonly taught foreign languages education in China. *Foreign Language Education in China*, 10(4), 3–8, 86.

Djité, Paulin G. (1994). *From Language Policy to Language Planning*. Canberra: National Languages and Literacy Institute of Australia.

Djité, Paulin G. (2009). Language policy at major sporting events. *Current Issues in Language Planning*, 10(2), 221–233.

Dong, Jinxia. (2005). Women, nationalism and the Beijing Olympics: Preparing for glory. *The International Journal of the History of Sport*, 22(4), 530–544.

Dornyei, Zoltán, & Ema Ushioda. (Eds.). (2009). *Motivation, language identity and the L2 Self*. Bristol, Buffalo and Toronto: Multilingual Matters.

Dörnyei, Zoltán. (2005). *The psychology of the language learner: Individual differences in second language acquisition*. London, New Jersey: Lawrence Erlbaum.

Duchêne, Axexandre. (2009). Marketing, management and performance: multilingualism as a commodity in a tourism call center. *Language Policy*, 8(1), 27–50.

Dyreson, Mark. (2003). Globalizing the nation-making process: Modern sport in world history. *International Journal of the History of Sport*, 20(1), 91–106.

Eccles, Jacquelynne S., & Allan Wigfield. (2002). Motivational beliefs, values and goals. *Annual Review of Psychology*, 53, 109–132.

EF Education First. (2019a). 2019 EF English Proficiency Index. https://www.ef.com.tr/epi/ (accessed 28 December 2019)

EF Education First. (2019b, August 21). Beijing 2022 Signs EF Education First as Official Language Training Services Exclusive Supplier. https://en.prnasia.com/releases/apac/beijing-2022-signs-ef-education-first-as-official-language-training-services-exclusive-supplier-255204.shtml (accessed 15 January 2020)

en.olympic.cn. (2006, August 10, 2006). Bid for 2008 Olympic Games. http://english.cri.cn/3126/2006/08/10/269@125226.htm (accessed 20 August 2019)

English First. (2007, March 26). English First supports Beijing 2008 Olympic Games and helps China talk to the world. http://www.ef.com/master/about_ef/press/news_26_03_07.asp (accessed 31 March 2011)

English First. (2008a). EF English First Olympic English. http://www.ef.com.cn/englishfirst/englishstudy/olympics.aspx?lng=en (accessed 18 September 2009)

English First. (2008b). *Introduction to EF English First, Demos & Videos*. China: EF English First.

English First. (2009a, October 23). EF Education First will be the official provider of language courses for the "Olá, Turista" (Hello, Tourist) project. http://www.ef-australia.com.au/corporate/news/us/world-cup/. (accessed 20 April 2011)

English First. (2009b, July 17). EF selected as language training services supplier for the 16th Asian Games Guangzhou 2010. http://www.sz-ef.com/news.asp?ID=21&classId=1. (accessed 19 November 2010)

English First. (2010a). About EF. http://www.ef.com.cn/englishfirst/about/aboutef.aspx. (accessed 16 November 2010)

English First. (2010b). EF China Homepage. http://www.ef.com.cn/englishfirst/default.aspx?lng=en. (accessed 16 November 2010)

English First. (2010c). English Training for Companies. http://www.ef.com.cn/englishfirst/courses/corporate-courses.aspx. (accessed 16 November 2010)

English First. (2011a). EF – The Official Language Training Services Supplier of the Beijing 2008 Olympic Games. http://www.ef.com/master/about_ef/company/olympics.asp. (accessed 14 May 2011)

English First. (2011b, May 6). EF is Sochi 2014 Official Supplier. http://www.ef.com.cn/englishfirst/about/summary.aspx?id=1&index=0. (accessed 14 May 2011)

English First. (2011c). How does EF English First's EnglishTown System work? http://www.ef.com.cn/englishfirst/courses/adults/learnetown.aspx?lng=en. (accessed 31 March 2011)

Errington, Joseph. (2001). Colonial linguistics. *Annual Review of Anthropology*, 30(1), 19–21.

Essex, Stephen, & Brain Chalkley. (1998). Olympic Games: Catalyst of urban change. *Leisure Studies*, 17(3), 187–206.

Fairclough, Norman, & Ruth Wodak. (1997). Critical discourse analysis. In T. A. van Dijk (Ed.), *Introduction to Discourse Analysis* (pp. 258–284). London: Sage Publications.

Fairclough, Norman, Jane Mulderrig & Ruth Wodak. (2011). Critical discourse analysis. In T. A. van Dijk (Ed.), *Discourse Studies: A Multidisciplinary Introduction* (pp. 357–378). Thousand Oaks, California: SAGE Publications Ltd.

Fairclough, Norman. (1989). *Language and Power*. London; New York: Longman.

Fairclough, Norman. (1992). *Discourse and Social Change*. Cambridge, UK; Cambridge, MA: Polity Press.

Fan, Hong, Wu Ping & Xiong Huan. (2005). Beijing ambitions: An analysis of the Chinese elite sports system and its Olympic strategy for the 2008 Olympic Games. *International Journal of the History of Sport*, 22(4), 510–529.

Fan, Hong. (2010). The building-up and promotion of a country image: A multi-dimensional approach. *Global Media Journal*, 6, 1–19.

Farrow Ronan. & Mia Farrow, (2007, March 28). "The 'Genocide Olympics'", *Wall Street Journal*, p. A17.

Feng, Zhijun. (2005, March 23). The philosophy of 'harmony'. People's Daily (Overseas edn.) http://english.peopledaily.com.cn/200503/23/eng20050323_177974.html (accessed 28 February 2009)

Foreign Affairs Office of the Beijing Municipal Government. (2006, December 1). Beijing Municipal Local Standards on English Translations of Public Signs. http://www.bjenglish.net.cn/specialreports/english/standard/ (accessed 30 May 2010)

Foreign Affairs Office of the Beijing Municipal Government. (2007a, August 30). The announcement on enhancing the organization work of the BETS in Beijing "window" service industries. http://www.bjenglish.net.cn/specialreports/examination/Q_A/2007-08/30430.shtml (accessed 11 November 2010)

Foreign Affairs Office of the Beijing Municipal Government. (2007b). Beijing Municipal Standards on English Translations of Chinese Menus. http://www.bjenglish.net.cn/specialreports/english/standard/2008-09/12580.shtml (accessed 30 May 2010)

Foreign Affairs Office of the Beijing Municipal Government. (2007c). On incorporating the BETS into Beijing professional English proficiency testing system. http://www.bjenglish.net.cn/specialreports/examination/Q_A/2007-08/30428.shtml (accessed 3 November 2008)

Foreign Affairs Office of the Beijing Municipal Government. (2008a, August 1). Beijing Municipal Local Standards on English Translations of Beijing Organizations' Names and Administrative and Professional Titles. http://www.bjenglish.net.cn/specialreports/english/standard/2009-01/13586.shtml (accessed 30 May 2010)

Foreign Affairs Office of the Beijing Municipal Government. (2008b, July 17). The report on English signage standardisation campaign (No 11). http://www.bjenglish.net.cn/specialreports/english/trends/2008-08/07572.shtml (accessed 30 May 2010)

Foreign Policy, A. T. Kearney & Chicago Council on Global Affairs. (2008). The 2008 Global Cities Index. *Foreign Policy* (November/December), 68–76.

Fraser, Benson P. & William J. Brown. (2002). Media, celebrities, and social influence: Identification with Elvis Presley. *Mass Communication & Society*, 5(2), 183–206.

Freeden, Michael. (2003). *Ideology: A Very Short Introduction*. Oxford; New York: Oxford University Press.

French Cultural Centre, Beijing. (2013, April 8). Fayu, Aolinpike De Yuyan [French, the language of Olympics]. http://bj.xdf.cn/publish/portal24/tab15295/info735791.htm (Accessed on 1 November 2020)

Friedman, Thomas L. (2006). *The World is Flat: A Brief History of the Twenty-first Century* (1st updated and expanded ed.). New York: Farrar, Straus and Giroux.

Friedmann, John & Goetz Wolf. (1982). World city formation: an agenda for research and action. *International Journal of Urban and Regional Research*, 6, 309–344.

Friedmann, John. (1986). The world city hypothesis. *Development and Change*, 17, 69–83.

Fu, Bonan. (2001). Beijing vigorously promotes the construction of urban infrastructure and comprehensively improves the level of urban modern management. *China Urban Economy* (Z1), 58–59+79.

Gao, Erjie. (2019, April 9). The Winter Olympics project progress meeting held at ACLA. http://yuyanziyuan.blcu.edu.cn/info/1065/1208.htm (accessed 5 February 2020)

Gao, Yihong. (2009). Sociocultural contexts and English in China: Retaining and reforming the cultural habitus. In Joseph Lo Bianco, Jane Orton & Gao Yihong (Eds.), *China and English: Globalisation and the Dilemmas of Identity* (pp. 56–78). Bristol, England; Buffalo, NY: Multilingual Matters.

Gardner, Robert C. (1985). *Social Psychology and Second Language Learning: The Role of Attitudes and Motivation*. London: Edward Arnold.

Giroux, Henry A. (1988). *Teachers as Intellectuals: toward a Critical Pedagogy of Learning*. Granby, Mass: Bergin & Garvey.

Giroux, Henry A. (1989). *Schooling for Democracy: Critical Pedagogy in the Modern Age*. London: Routledge.

Goldberg, David, Dennis Looney & Natalia Lusin. (2015). *Enrollments in Language Other Than English in United States Institutions of Higher Education*, Fall 2013. New York: The Modern Language Association of America.

Gorter, Durk. (2006). Introduction: the study of the linguistic landscape as a new approach to multilingualism. *International Journal of Multilingualism*, 3(1), 1–6.

Graddol, David. (1997). The future of Engish?: A guide to forecasting the popularity of the English language in the 21st century. London: British Council.

Graddol, David. (1999). The decline of the native speaker. In D. Graddol & U. Meinhof (Eds.), English in a changing world (Vol. 13, pp. 57–68). Guildford: AILA Review.

Griffin, Jeffrey L. (2004). The presence of written English on the streets of Rome. *English Today*, 20(02), 3–8.

Gui, Tao, Dai Ying. (2008, August 9). Rogge: Beijing Aoyunhui Kaimushi Geiyu Fayu Tuchu Diwei [Rogge: the opening ceremony of the Beijing Olympic Games gives French a "prominent position"]. https://china.huanqiu.com/article/9CaKrnJkMCT (accessed 1 November 2020)

Guo, Xiaoyong. (2010). Zhongguo Yuyan Fuwu Hangye Fazhan Zhuangkuang, Wenti Ji Duice: Zai 2010 Zhongguo Guoji Yuyan Fuwu Hangye Dahui Shang De Zhuzhi Fayan [Development situation, problems and Countermeasures of Chinese language service industry: keynote speech at 2010 China International Language Services Industry Conference]. *Chinese Translators Journal* (6), 34–37.

Hall, Peter. (1966). *The World Cities*. London: Weidenfeld and Nicolson.

Hanson, John. (1997). The mother of all tongues: Review of David Crystal's English as a global language. *Times Higher Education Supplement*, 1288, 22.

He, Na. (2010, August 5). Rush to learn English fuels quality issues. China Daily http://www.chinadaily.com.cn/china/2010-08/05/content_11098499.htm (accessed 28 April 2011)

Heller, Monica & Alexandre Duchêne. (2016). Treating language as an economic resource: disourse, data and debate. In Nikolas Coupland (Ed.), *Sociolinguistics: Theoretical Debates*. Cambridge: Cambridge University Press.

Heller, Monica & Boutete J. (2006). Vers de nouvelles formes de pouvoir langagier? *Langue(s) et identite dans la nouvelle economic Langage et societe*, 118, 5–16.

Heller, Monica. (2005). *Language, skill and authenticity in the globalized new economy*. Noves Sl: Revista De Sociolingüística.

Heller, Monica. (2010a). *The commodification of language. Annual Review of Anthropology*, 39, 101–114.

Heller, Monica. (2010b). Language as resource in the globalized new economy. In N. Coupland (Ed.), *The Handbook of Language and Globalization* (pp. 349–365). Blackwell: Malden.

Henning, Ryan. (2014, February 6). The role of language services in the 2014 Sochi Winter Olympics. https://translationexcellence.com/role-language-services-2014-sochi-winter-olympics/ (accessed 20 March 2020)

Hogan, Jackie. (2003). Staging the nation: Gendered and ethnicized discourses of national identity in Olympic opening ceremonies. *Journal of Sport & Social Issues*, 27(2), 100–123.

Holborwo, Marine. (2018). Language, commodification and labour: the relevance of Marx. *Language Sciences*, 70, 58–67.

Houlihan, Barrie. (1997). Sport, national identity and public policy. *Nations and Nationalism*, 3(1), 113–137.

Hu, Angang. (2007). *Zhongguo Jueqi Zhilu* [Roadmap of China's Rising]. Beijing: Peking University Press.

Hu, Guangwei. (2003). English language teaching in China: Regional differences and contributing factors. *Journal of Multilingual & Multicultural Development*, 24(4), 290–318.

Hu, Guangwei. (2005). English language education in China: Policies, progress, and problems. *Language Policy*, 4(1), 5–24.

Hu, Guangwei. (2008). The misleading academic discourse on Chinese–English bilingual education in China. *Review of Educational Research*, 78(2), 195–231.

Hu, Qunfang. (2007, October 10). Three companies competing for control of Beijing Olympic language training market. http://nd.oeeee.com/F/html/2007-10/10/content_273722.htm (accessed 14 November 2010)

Hu, Yuanyuan. (2007). China's foreign language policy on primary English education: What's behind it? *Language Policy*, 6(3–4), 359–376.

Hu, Yuanyuan. (2008). China's English language policy for primary schools. *World Englishes*, 27(3–4), 516–534.

Huang, Yanjun. (2009, May 24). Harbin Eyu Jiaoyu Bu Yinggai "Duanceng" [Russian language fast losing ground in Harbin]. Harbin Daily, pp. 1–2. http://news.sina.com.cn/c/2009-05-24/053315676376s.shtml?from=wap (accessed 1 October 2010)

Huc-Hepher, S., Kelly, D. & Phipps, A. (2008). *Languages and international events. Are we ready to talk to the world in 2012?* University of Southampton, Southanpton Routes into Languages.

Huebner, T. (2006). Bangkok's Linguistic Landscapes: Environmental Print, Codemixing and Language Change. *International Journal of Multilingualism*, 3(1), 31–51.

Hult, Francis M. (2003). English on the streets of Sweden: An ecolinguistic view of two cities and a language policy. *Working Papers in Educational Linguistics*, 19(1), 43.

Huntington, Samuel P. (1996). *The Clash of Civilizations and the Remaking of World Order*. New York: Simon & Schuster.

Hussain, Owais A., Faraz Zaidi & Celine Rozenblat. (2018). Analyzing diversity, strength and centrality of cities using networks of multinational firms. *Networks and Spatial Economics*, 19, 791–817.

Ikhioya, Okhakume Sunday. (2001). Olympic Games as instruments in fostering national identities. *Journal of the International Council for Health, Physical Education, Recreation, Sport & Dance*, 37(1), 14–17.

Independent news. (2009, August 29). Crazy English: How China's language teachers became big celebrities. http://www.independent.co.uk/news/world/asia/crazy-english-how-chinas-language-teachers-became-big-celebrities-1777545.html (accessed 1 October 2009)

Information Office of the State Council. (2019, September 22). White Paper: Seeking Happiness for People: 70 Years of Progress on Human Rights in China. http://www.xinhuanet.com/politics/2019-09/22/c_1125025006.htm (accessed 1 December 2019)

International Olympic Committee. (2001). *Report of the IOC Evaluation Commission for the Games of the XXIX Olympiad in 2008*. Lausanne, Switzerland: International Olympic Committee.
International Olympic Committee. (2007). *Olympic Charter*. Lausanne, Switzerland: International Olympic Committee.
International Olympic Committee. (2009). *Beijing 2008 Facts & Figures*. Lausanne, Switzerland: The International Olympic Committee.
International Olympic Committee. 1949. *Olympic Charter*. https://stillmedab.olympic.org/media/Document%20Library/OlympicOrg/Olympic-Studies-Centre/List-of-Resources/Official-Publications/Olympic-Charters/EN-1949-Olympic-Charter-Olympic-Rules.pdf (accessed 12 November 2020)
International Olympic Committee. (2019). *Olympic Solidarity Annual Report 2019*. https://olympicsolidarity.touchlines.com/annualreport2019/en/static/_content/olympic_solidarity_annual_report_2019.pdf (accessed 12 November 2020)
International Olympic Committee. (2020). *Olympic Charter*. https://stillmedab.olympic.org/media/Document%20Library/OlympicOrg/General/EN-Olympic-Charter.pdf (accessed 12 November 2020)
International Olympic Committee. (2014). *Olympic Agenda 2020: 20 + 20 Recommendations*. Switzerland: International Olympic Committee.
International Olympic Committee. (2020a). ATHENS 1896. https://www.olympic.org/athens-1896 (accessed 29 February 2020)
International Olympic Committee. (2020b). ATHENS 2004. https://www.olympic.org/athens-2004 (accessed 29 February 2020)
Jaffe, Eugene. D., & Nebanzahl, Israel. D. (1993). Global promotion of country image: Do the Olympics count? In Nicolas Papadopoulos & Louise Heslop (Eds.), *Product-Country Images: Impact and Role in International Marketing* (pp. 433–452). New York: International Business Press.
Ji, Lin. (2009, December). Preface. *Beijing This Month* (Beijing Speaks Foreign Language Program Special Issue), 3–5.
Jia, Xi. (2007, July 24). Five thousand bus conductors can announce stops in English. http://jtcx.beijing.cn/bus/gjdt/n214036689.shtml (accessed 31 January 2011)
Joseph, John Earl & Talbot J. Taylor. (1990). *Ideologies of Language*. London: Routledge.
Kachru, Braj B. (1985). Standards, codification and sociolinguistic realism: The English language in the Outer Circle. In R. Quirk, H. G. Widdowson, Y. Cantáu & British Council. (Eds.), *English in the World: Teaching and Learning the Language and Literatures: Papers of An International Conference Entitled 'Progress in English Studies' Held in London, 17–21 September 1984 to Celebrate the Fiftieth Anniversary of the British Council and Its Contribution to the Field of English Studies Over Fifty Years* (pp. xi,275p). Cambridge: Cambridge University Press for the British Council.
Kachru, Braj B. (1986). *The Alchemy of English: The Spread, Functions, and Models of Non-Native Englishes* (1st edn.). Oxford; New York: Pergamon Institute of English.
Kachru, Braj B. (1992). *The Other Tongue: English across Cultures* (2nd edn.). Urbana: University of Illinois Press.
Kaplan, Robert B. (1999). The ELT: Ho (NEST) or not ho (NEST)? *NNEST Newsletter*, 1(1), 5–6.
Kaplan, Robert B. & Richard B. Baldauf. (2003). *Language and Language-in-Education Planning in the Pacific Basin*. Dordrecht; Boston: Kluwer Academic Publishers.
Kearney, A. T. (2019). 2019 Global Cities Report. https://www.atkearney.com/global-cities/2019. (accessed 28 December 2019)

Kennedy, Paul. M. (1987). *The rise and fall of the great powers: economic change and military conflict from 1500 to 2000* (1st edn.). New York: Random House.
Kirkpatrick, Andy. (1997). Future directions for English, English language teaching and research. EA Journal, 15(1), 28–35.
Kirkpatrick, Andy. (2000). English as an Asian language: Implication for the English language curriculum. In Adam Brown (Ed.), *English in South East Asia*. Singapore: National Institute of Education.
Knight, Nick. (2006). Reflecting on the paradox of globalisation: China's search for cultural identity and coherence. *China: An International Journal*, 4(1), 1–31.
Kong, Fanmin. (2006). Cohesiveness of Chinese people as seen in the involvement of overseas Chinese in Beijing Olympic Games. *China Academic Journal Electronic Publishing House*, 4(3), 84–86.
Krashen, Stephen. (2003). Dealing with English fever. *Paper presented at the Twelfth International Symposium on English Teaching*, Taipei.
Kress, Gunther. (1993). Against arbitrariness: the social production of the sign as a foundational issue in critical discourse analysis. *Discourse Society*, 4(2), 169–191.
Kroskrity, Paul. V. (2005). Language ideologies. In Alessandro Duranti (Ed.), *A Companion to Linguistic Anthropology* (pp. 496–516). Oxford: Blackwell.
Kubota, Ryuko. (2002). The impact of globalization on language teaching in Japan. In David Block & Deborah Cameron (Eds.), *Globalization and Language Teaching* (pp. 13–28). London and New York: Routledge.
Lam, Agnes. (2002). English in education in China: Policy changes and learners' experiences. *World Englishes*, 21(2), 245–256.
Lam, Agnes. (2005). *Language Education in China: Policy and Experience from 1949*. Hong Kong; London: Hong Kong University Press; Eurospan distributor.
Landry, Rodrigue & Richard Y. Bourhis. (1997). Linguistic landscape and ethnolinguistic vitality: An empirical study. *Journal of Language and Social Psychology*, 16(1), 23–49.
Li, Demin. (2001, July 16, 2001). Eight Years-Recalling Beijing's 1993 Olympic Bid. http://en.people.cn/english/200107/16/eng20010716_75095.html (accessed 20 August 2018)
Li, Jiaquan. (2005, March 10). Dominant English and declining Chinese: Whose failure is this? *Guizhou CPPCC Newspaper*.
Li, Lanqing. (1997). Zai guojia jiaowei waiyu jiaoxue zuotanhui shang de jianghua [The talk at a conference on foreign language teaching organized by the state education commission]. *Journal of Jiangsu Foreign Language Teaching and Research*, 2.
Li, Xianle. (2010). Yuyan Ziyuan He Yuyan Wenti Shijiao Xia De Yuyan Fuwu Yanjiu [A Study of Language Services from the Perspective of Language Resources and Language Problems]. *Journal of Yunnan Normal University* (Humanities and Social Sciences Edition)(5), 16–21.
Li, Xun. (2008, August 27). Liu Wenli, the policeman capable of 14 foreign languages. Wuhan Evening Newspaper. http://cjmp.cnhan.com/whwb/html/2008-08/27/content_405609.htm (accessed 28 August 2008)
Li, Yuming. (2005). *Language Planning in China*. Changchun: Northeast Normal University Press.
Li, Yuming. (2010). Some thoughts on foreign language planning in China [Zhongguo Waiyu Guihua De Ruogan Sikao]. *Journal of Foreign Languages*, 33(1), 2–8.
Li, Yuming. (2011). Reflections on promoting state language competence. *Nankai Linguistics*, (1), 1–8.

Li, Yuming. (2013, February 25). GuoJia De Yuyan Nengli Wenti [The issue of national language capacity]. *China Science Daily*. http://news.blcu.edu.cn/info/1025/12922.htm (accessed 1 October 2019)
Li, Yuming. (2015). Language Planning in China. Berlin: De Gruyter Mouton/The Commercial Press.
Li, Yuming. (2016). Yuyan Fuwu Yu Yuyan Chanye [Language services and the language services industry]. *East Journal of Translation*(4), 4–8.
Liao, Yi. (2009, August 8). 'One World One Dream' shi ge miuwu ['One World One Dream' is a fallacy]. *Lianhe Zaobao* [Lianhe Newspaper].
Lin, Angel & Peter W. Martin. (2005). *Decolonisation, Globalisation: Language-in-Education Policy and Practice*. Clevedon; Buffalo: Multilingual Matters.
Lin, Zhibo. (2005, Febuary 21). Is English really that important? Lishui Daily Newspaper.
Lindlof, Thomas R., & Bryan C. Taylor. (2002). *Qualitative Communication Research Methods* (2nd edn.). Thousand Oaks, Calif.: Sage Publications.
Liu, Baoku. (2017, December 18). China's contribution to global economic growth. http://www.scio.gov.cn/32618/Document/1613753/1613753.htm (accessed 1 October 2019)
Liu, Daosheng. (1987). Xin Shiqi De Yuyan Wenzi Gongzuo [Language and script Work in the new era]. In Secretary of the National Conference on language and script (Ed.), *Xin Shiqi De Yuyan Wenzi Gongzuo: Quanguo Yuyan Wenzi Gongzuo Weniian Huibian* [Language and script work in the new era: Documents of national conference on language and script] (pp. 16–34). Beijing: Language Press.
Liu, Haixia. (2008, January 15). 2007 education research: the survey on consumption in foreign language training industry. Sohu Learning Online http://learning.sohu.com/20080115/n254677364.shtml. (accessed 5 November 2008)
Lo Bianco, Joseph. (1994). Language policy and planning and the Olympic Games: a paper presented to Committee for the Economic Development of Australia. *Paper presented at the Seminar "Coping with the commitment – the Sydney 2000 Olympic Games"*, Deakin, ACT, National Languages and Literacy Institute of Australia.
Lo Bianco, Joseph. (2007). *Games Talk: Language Planning for Sydney 2000: A Legacy to the Olympic Movement*. Melbourne; London: CILT (National Centre for Languages).
Lu, Wenjun. (2009, September 5). Beijing Olympics draws 4.7 billion global viewers, sets new world record. http://china.huanqiu.com/roll/2008-09/218465.html (accessed 28 March 2009)
Luo, Huifan, Yongye Meng & Yanlin Lei. (2018). China's language services as an emerging industry. *International Journal of Translation*, 64(3), 370–381.
Ma, Ivy (2008). Yuyan "Duanzao" Gongchang [Language training factory]. http://www.forbeschina.com/cmslive/articledetail.jsp?contentid=10002 (accessed 1 December 2009)
MacGregor, Laura. (2003). The language of shop signs in Tokyo. *English Today*, 19(01), 18–23.
Madison, Soyini. (2005). *Critical Ethnography: Method, Ethics, and Performance*. Thousand Oaks, Calif.: Sage.
McCarty, Teresa L. (2015). Ethnography in language planning and policy research. In Francis. M. Hult & David Cassels Johnson (Eds), *Research Methods in Language Policy and Planning: A Practical Guide* (pp. 81–93). West Sussex, UK: John Wiley & Sons, Inc.
McGuire, Josephine. (1997). *English as A Foreign Language in China: Past and Present*. Southampton: Centre for Language in Education, University of Southampton.
McKay, Sandra Lee. (2003). Toward an appropriate EIL pedagogy: Re-examining common ELT assumptions. *International Journal of Applied Linguistics*, 13(1), 1–22.

Ministry of Commerce of the PRC. (2019, November 15). China's newly instilled investment to the "Belt and Road" countries amounted to US $ 11.46 billion in the first three quarters of 2019. http://www.mofcom.gov.cn/article/i/jyjl/e/201911/20191102913928.shtml (accessed 3 February 2020)

Ministry of Education of PRC. (2000). *Quanrizhi Putong Gaoji Zhongxue Yingyu Jiaoxue Dagang* [English Language Syllabus for Full-time Ordinary Senior Secondary School]. Beijing: People's Education Press.

Ministry of Education of PRC. (2001a). Jiaoyubu guanyu jiji tuijin xiaoxue kaishe yingyu kecheng de zhidao yijian [The Ministry of Education guidelines for vigorously promoting the teaching of English in primary schools]. http://www.moe.gov.cn/edoas/website18/level3.jsp?tablename=23&infoid=8770 (accessed 3 November 2008)

Ministry of Education of PRC. (2001b). Guanyu Jiaqiang Gaodeng Xuexiao Benke Jiaoxue Gongzuo Tigao Jiaoxue Zhiliang de Ruogan Yijian [Some Recommendations on Strengthening College Undergraduate Programs and Enhancing the Quality of Teaching, Ministry of Education]. http://www.moe.edu.cn/edoas/website18/81/info7281.htm (accessed 22 July 2010)

Ministry of Education of PRC. (2004). Putong Gaodeng Yuanxiao Benke Jiaoxue Pinggu Fangan [University undergraduate education evaluation program]. http://www.moe.edu.cn/edoas/website18/level3.jsp?tablename=1528&infoid=15008 (accessed 20 April 2011)

Ministry of Education of PRC. (2009, December 24). Data on Enrolment, Number of Graduates, Number of New Entrants of Schools of All Types and Level Providing Formal Programs. http://www.moe.gov.cn/edoas/website18/89/info1261469797229789.htm (accessed 22 July 2010)

Ministry of Education of PRC. (2011). *2009 National Education Development Statistical Bulletin*. Beijing: China Education and Research Network.

Ministry of Education of the PRC. (2010, July 29). *Guojia Zhongchangqi Jiaoyu Gaige He Fazhan Guihua Gangyao* 2010–2020 [The outline of China's medium and long term education reform and development plan 2010–2020]. http://old.moe.gov.cn/publicfiles/business/htmlfiles/moe/info_list/201407/xxgk_171904.html (accessed 1 February 2020)

Ministry of Education of the PRC. (2013). Jiaoyubu Guanyu 2013 Nian Shenhua Jiaoyu Lingyu Zonghe Gaige De Yijian [Opinions of the Ministry of education on deepening the comprehensive educational reform in 2013]. http://old.moe.gov.cn/publicfiles/business/htmlfiles/moe/s7229/201303/148072.html (accessed 22 January 2020)

Ministry of Education of the PRC. (2017, May 25). *Action Plan on Language Services for Beijing 2022*. http://www.moe.gov.cn/s78/A19/moe_814/201705/t20170525_305759.html (accessed 16 January 2020)

Ministry of Education of the PRC. (2018). Curriculum plan of senior high school and curriculum standards of Chinese and other subjects (2017 Edition). http://www.moe.gov.cn/srcsite/A26/s8001/201801/t20180115_324647.html. (accessed 22 January 2020)

Ministry of Education of the PRC. (2019a, April 12). Statistics of international students in China in 2018. http://www.moe.gov.cn/jyb_xwfb/gzdt_gzdt/s5987/201904/t20190412_377692.html (accessed 22 January 2020)

Ministry of Education of the PRC. (2019b, January 22). UNESCO officially publishes Yuelu Proclamation on its website. http://en.moe.gov.cn/news/press_releases/201901/t20190124_367985.html (accessed 22 February 2020)

Nan, Zhou. (2007, August 20). Promote Olympic Chinese rather than Olympic English. *Jinri Xinxi Bao*.

National Bureau of Statistics of China. (2010, July 23). Statistics of 2010 Chinese population census. http://www.stats.gov.cn/tjsj/pcsj/rkpc/6rp/indexch.htm (accessed 22 January 2020)

Nelson, Cary, Paula A. Treichler & Lawrence Grossberg. (1992). Cultural Studies: An introduction. In Lawrence Grossberg, Cary Nelson & Paula A. Treichler (Eds.), *Cultural Studies* (pp. 1–16). New York: Routledge.

Ng, Mee Kam, & Peter Hills. (2003). World cities or great cities? A comparative study of five Asian metropolises. *Cities*, 20(3), 151–165.

Nidemike. (2008, July 28). Beijing Olympic volunteers. http://www.taisha.org/test/news/200807/20080728145745.html (accessed 30 March 2009)

Nightingale, David & John Cromby. (1999). *Social Constructionist Psychology: A Critical Analysis of Theory and Practice*. Buckingham England; Philadelphia: Open University Press.

Nishioka, Shunsuke, & Naureen Durrani. (2019). Language and cultural reproduction in Malawi: Unpacking the relationship between linguistic capital and learning outcomes. *International Journal of Educational Research*, 93, 1–12.

Niu, Daosheng. (2008). *English and China* (1st edn.). Beijing: China Social Sciences Press.

Norton, Bonny & Kelleen Toohey. (2002). Identity and language learning. In Robert B. Kaplan (Ed.), *The Oxford Handbook of Applied Linguistics* (pp. 115–123). Oxford: Oxford University Press.

Norton, Bonny & Yihong Gao. (2008). Identity, investment, and Chinese learners of English. *Journal of Asian Pacific Communication*, 18(1), 109–120.

Norton, Bonny. (1995). Social Identity, Investment, and Language Learning. *TESOL Quarterly*, 29(1), 9–31.

Norton, Bonny. (2000). *Identity and Language Learning: Gender, Ethnicity and Educational Change*. Harlow, England; New York: Longman.

Nunan, David. (2003). The impact of English as a global language on educational policies and practices in the Asia-Pacific region. *TESOL Quarterly*, 37(4), 589–613.

Nye, Joseph S. (1990). *Bound to Lead: The Changing Nature of American Power*. New York: Basic Books.

Oda, Masaki. (2007). Globalization or world in English: is Japan ready to face the waves? *International Multilingual Research Journal*, 1(2), 119–126.

Office of the Leading Group on Foreign Affairs of the Beijing Municipal Party Committee of the CPC, Foreign Affairs Office of Beijing Municipal Government, & The Organizing Committee of Beijing Speaks Foreign Languages Program. (2008). A Follow-up Survey and Analytical Report on Foreign Language Environment of Beijing. http://www.beijing.gov.cn/zfxxgk/110042/smjwy52/2008-04/13/content_86553.shtml (accessed 1 October 2010)

Official Website of the Beijing 2008 Olympic Games. (2003). The Olympic Emblem. http://en.beijing2008.cn/spirit/beijing2008/graphic/n214070081.shtml (accessed 17 June 2010)

Official Website of the Beijing 2008 Olympic Games. (2005a, December 9). Gongyingshang jizhun jiawei yu quanyi huibao [Entry prices for service suppliers and their rights and interests]. http://www.beijing2008.cn/94/48/article211994894.shtml (accessed 12 November 2010)

Official Website of the Beijing 2008 Olympic Games. (2005b, June 26). One World One Dream'. http://en.beijing2008.cn/17/74/article212027417.shtml (accessed 25 June 2010)

Official Website of the Beijing 2008 Olympic Games. (2007a, June 20). Aifly becomes Beijing 2008 Olympic Games Language Training Services Supplier. http://en.beijing2008.cn/bocog/sponsors/headlines/n214099347.shtml (accessed 1 May 2009)

Official Website of the Beijing 2008 Olympic Games. (2007b, March 2). English First (EF) selected as official language training supplier of Beijing 2008 Olympic Games. http://en.beijing2008.cn/76/26/article214022676.shtml (accessed 1 May 2009)

Official Website of the Beijing 2008 Olympic Games. (2007c, April 11). Press conference on English signage standardisation campaign in Beijing. http://www.beijing2008.cn/62/23/s214032362.shtml (accessed 13 June 2010)

Official Website of the Beijing 2008 Olympic Games. (2008, April 11). First English-language Paralympic training book distributed. http://en.beijing2008.cn/paralympic/news/news/n214310879.shtml (accessed 7 March 2011)

Official Website of the Beijing 2008 Olympic Games. (2012, November 11). Shi Zhengfu Tuijin Beijing Shimin Jiang Waiyu Huodong [The Beijing Municipal Government pushes forward BSFLP]. http://www.beijing.gov.cn/shipin/fangtan/15074.html (accessed 15 January 2020)

Official Website of the State Council of PRC. (2007, April 11). Beijing Shimin Jiang Waiyu Huodong Guihua Bei Lieru Renwen Aoyun Yichan [BSFLP was listed in the cultural Olympic heritage list]. http://www.gov.cn/govweb/wszb/zhibo37/content_578768.htm (accessed 15 January 2020)

Ogilvy Group, & Millward Brown ACSR. (2008, March 10). The Project 2008 Poll. http://www.ogilvy.com.cn/webapp/cds/news/newsview.jsp?newsid=106 (accessed 5 December 2010)

Organising Committee of the BSFLP. (2003, May 27). The Action Plan for the BSFLP (2003–2008). http://www.bjenglish.net.cn/ministry/ (accessed 30 May 2010)

Overholt, William H. (1993). *The Rise of China: How Economic Reform Is Creating A New Superpower*. New York; London: Norton.

Pallavi, Alyar. (2007, June 27). Crazy about English in China. India's National Newspaper. http://www.thehindu.com/2007/06/27/stories/2007062750611100.htm. (accessed 17 July 2010)

Pan, Lin. (2011). English language ideologies (ELI) in Olympic Beijing. *Applied Linguistics Review*, 1, 75–97.

Park, Joseph Sung-Yul. (2009). *The Local Construction of A Global Language: Ideologies of English in South Korea*. Berlin; New York: Mouton de Gruyter.

Patton, Michael Quinn. (2002). *Qualitative Research and Evaluation Methods* (3rd edn.). Thousand Oaks, Calif.: Sage Publications.

Pavlenko, Aneta. (2001). *Multilingualism, Second Language Learning and Gender*. Berlin; Hawthorne, N.Y.: Mouton de Gruyter.

Pavlenko, Aneta. (2002). Poststructuralist approaches to the study of social factors in second language learning and use. In Vivian Cook (Ed.), *Portraits of the L2 User* (pp. 277–302). Clevedon: Multilingual Matters.

Pennycook, Alastair. (1994). *The Cultural Politics of English as an International Language*. Harlow, Essex, England; New York: Longman.

Pennycook, Alastair. (1998). *English and the Discourses of Colonialism*. London; New York: Routledge.

People's Daily. (2001, July 13, 2001). Xinhua Commentary: A Historical Event for the Chinese Nation. http://en.people.cn/english/200107/13/eng20010713_74935.html. (accessed 20 August 2019)

People's Daily. (2007, March 14). Soft power: A new focus at China's two sessions. http://english.peopledaily.com.cn/200703/14/eng20070314_357578.html (accessed 25April 2011)

Pew Research Center. (2008, August 5). An Enthusiastic China Welcomes the Olympics http://pewresearch.org/pubs/918/china-olympics. (accessed 5 December 2010)

Phillipson, Robert. (1992). *Linguistic imperialism*. Oxford England; New York: Oxford University Press.

Piller, Ingrid & Kimie Takahashi. (2010). At the intersection of gender, language and transnationalism. In Nicholas Coupland (Ed.), *The Handbook of Language and Globalisation* (pp. 540–554). Malden: Blackwell.

Piller, Ingrid, & Jinhyun Cho. (2013). Neoliberalism as language policy. *Language in Society*, 42 (1): 23–44.

Piller, Ingrid, & Kimie Takahashi. (2006). A passion for English: desire and language market. In Aneta Pavlenko (Ed.), *Bilingual Minds: Emotional Experience, Expression and Representation* (pp. 59–83): Multilingual Matters.

Piller, Ingrid, Kimie Takahashi & Yukinori Watanabe. (2010). The dark side of TESOL: The hidden costs of the consumption of English. *Cross-Cultural Studies*, 20, 183–201.

Piller, Ingrid, Zhang, Jie, & Li, Jia. (2020). Linguistic diversity in a time of crisis: Language challenges of the COVID-19 pandemic. *Multilingua*, 39(5), 503–515. doi:https://doi.org/10.1515/multi-2020-0136

Piller, Ingrid. (2001). Who, if anyone, is a native speaker? *Mitteilungen des Verbandes Deutscher Anglisten*, 12, 109–121.

Piller, Ingrid. (2007). English in Swiss tourism marketing. In Cristina Flores & Orlando Grossegesse (Eds.), *Wildern in luso-austro-deutschen Sprach- und Textgefilden: Festschrift zum 60. Geburtstag von Erwin Koller* [Roughing it in the linguistic and textual wilds of Portuguese, Austrian and German: Festschrift for Erwin Koller on the occasion of his 60th birthday] (pp. 57–73). Braga, PT: Cehum – Centro de Estudos Humanîsticos.

Piller, Ingrid. (2012). *Intercultural Communication: A Critical Introduction*. Edinburgh: Edinburgh University Press.

Piller, Ingrid. (2015). Language ideologies, In Karen Tracy, Cornelia Ilie & Todd Sandel (eds.), *The International Encyclopaedia of Language and Social Interaction*, 917–927. West Sussex: Wiley-Blackwell, Wiley.

Piller, Ingrid. (2016a). *Linguistic Diversity and Social Justice: An Introduction to Applied Sociolinguistics* (1st edn.). Oxford; New York: Oxford University Press.

Piller, Ingrid. (2016b). Monolingual ways of seeing multilingualism. Journal of Multicultural Discourse, 11(1). 25–33

Piller, Ingrid. (2019). On the conditions of authority in academic publics. *Journal of Sociolinguistics*. doi:0.1111/josl.12393 (accessed 1 February 2020)

Pound, Richard. (2003). *Report to the 115th IOC Session*. Prague: Olympic Games Study Commission, IOC.

Power, Carla. (2005). Not the Queen's English. *Newsweek International*. http://www.newsweek.eom/id/49022.2005-03-07 (accessed 1 October 2009)

Puzey, Guy. (2007). *Planning the Linguistic Landscape: A Comparative Survey of the Use of Minority Languages in the Road Signage of Norway, Scotland and Italy.* Unpublished M.Sc dissertation, The University of Edinburgh, Edinburgh, UK.

Pym, Anthony. (1996). Translating the Symbolic Olympics in Barcelona. Language and Literature Today. *Proceedings of the XIXth Triennial Congress of the International Federation for Modern Languages and Literatures,* 1, 363–372.

Pym, Anthony. (2003). Olympic Translators, in Barcelona and Elsewhere. In Georges Androulakis (Ed.), *Translating in the 21st Century: Trends and Prospects Proceedings* (pp. 795–799). Thessaloniki: Aristotle University.

Qu, Shaobing. (2007). Yuyan Fuwu Yanjiu Lungang [The outline of language service Research]. *Journal of Jianghan University* (Humanities Sciences) (6), 56–62.

Ramo, Joshua Cooper. (2004). *The Beijing Consensus.* London: Foreign Policy Centre.

Ramo, Joshua Cooper. (2007). *Brand China.* London: Foreign Policy Centre.

Rampton, Ben. (1990). Displacing the 'native speaker': expertise, affiliation, and inheritance. *ELT Journal,* 44(2),97–101.

Rassool, Naz. (2013). The political economy of English language and development: English vs. national and local languages in developing countries. In Elizabeth J. Erling & Philip Seargeant (Eds.), *English and International development: Policy, pedagogy and globalization* (pp. 45–67). Bristol: Multilingual Matters.

Reed, Howard Curtis. (1981). *The Preeminence of International Financial Centers.* New York: Praeger.

Reed, Howard Curtis. (1989). Financial center hegemony, interest rates and global political economy. In Yoon S. Park & Muse Essayard (Eds.), *International Banking and Financial Centers* (pp. 247–268). London: Kluwer Academic Press.

Research in China. (2008). *China's Education and Training Industry Research Report* (2007–2008). Beijing: Research In China.

Rickard, Peter. (1989). A history of the French language (2nd ed), London and New York: Unwin Hyman Ltd.

Rifkin, Benjamin. (1998). Gender representation in foreign language textbooks: A case study of textbooks of Russian. *The Modern Language Journal,* 82(2),217–236.

Ryan, Richard. M., & Edward L. Deci. (2000). Intrinsic and extrinsic motivations: Classic definitions and new directions. *Contemporary Educational Psychology,* 25(1),54–67.

Sassen, Saskia. (1991). *The Global City: New York, London, Tokyo.* Princeton. NJ: Princeton University Press.

Schieffelin, Bambi B., Kathryn Ann Woolard, & Paul V. Kroskrity. (1998). *Language Ideologies: Practice and Theory.* New York; Oxford: Oxford University Press.

Schlick, Maria. (2003). The English of shop signs in Europe. *English Today,* 19(01),3–17.

Shardakova, M., & Pavlenko, A. (2004). Identity options in Russian textbooks. *Journal of Language, Identity & Education,* 3(1), 25–46.

Shen, Qi. (2015). Strategic transformation for the construction of our national foreign language competence under the guidance of the strategy of "One Belt and One Road". *Journal of Yunnan Normal University* (Humanities and Social Sciences Edition), 47(5), 9–13.

Shim, Doobo & Joseph Sung-Yul Park. (2008). The language politics of "English Fever" in South Korea. *Korean Journal,* 48(2),136–159.

Shohamy, Elena. G. (2006). *Language Policy: Hidden Agendas and New Approaches.* London; New York: Routledge.

Sieber, Joan E. & Barbara Stanley. (1988). Ethical and professional dimensions of socially sensitive research. *The American Psychologist*, 43(1),49–55.

Smith, Adrian & Dilwyn Porter. (2004). *Sport and National Identity in the Post-War World*. London; New York: Routledge.

Spolsky, Bernard, & Robert L. Cooper. (1991). *The Languages of Jerusalem*. Oxford: Clarendon Press.

Spolsky, Bernard. (2004). *Language Policy*. Cambridge: Cambridge University Press.

Spolsky, Bernard. (2009). *Language Management*. Cambridge: Cambridge University Press.

Stanway, David. (2008, August 8). Beijing pushes for language victory. http://www.guardian.co.uk/education/2008/aug/08/chinglish.olympics. (accessed 10 August 2008)

Stuker, Sebastian, Chengqing Zong, Jurgen Reichert, Wenjie Cao, Muntsin Kolss, Guodong Xie, Kay Peterson, Peng Ding, Victoria Arranz, Jian Yu, & Alex Waibel. (2006). Speech-to-speech translation services for the Olympic Games 2008. In Steve Renals, Samy Bengio & Jonathan G. Fiscus. (Eds.), *Machine Learning for Multimodal Interaction* (pp. 297–308). Berlin, Heidelberg: Springer.

Su, Yingying. (2017). Thinking and exploration on the talent training mode of less commonly taught languages of the Belt and Road. *Foreign Language Education in China* (Quarterly), 10(2),3–7, 95.

Sunderland, Jane, Maire Cowley, Fauziah Abdul Rahim, Christina Leontzakou & Julie Shattuck. (2000). From Bias "In the Text" to "Teacher Talk around the Text": An Exploration of Teacher Discourse and Gendered Foreign Language Textbook Texts. *Linguistics and Education*, 11(3),251–286.

Takahashi, Kimie. (2006). *Language Desire: A Critical Ethnography of Japanese Women Learning English in Australia*. Unpublished doctoral dissertation, University of Sydney, Sydney.

Takahashi, Kimie. (2011). L*anguage Desire: Gender, Sexuality and Second Language Learning*. Bristol, England: Multilingual Matters.

Talbot, Mary, Karen Atkinson & David Atkinson. (2003). *Language and Power in the Modern World*. Tuscaloosa: University of Alabama Press.

Tang, Xiangyu. (2010). The opium war and the opening of China. http://historyliterature.homestead.com/files/extended.html. (accessed 19 August 2010)

Tange, Hanne. (2009). Language workers and the practice of language management. *Corporate Communications: An International Journal* (2).

Tedlock, Barbara. (2000). Ethnography and ethnographic representation. In Norman K. Denzin & Yvonna S. Lincoln (Eds.), *The Handbook of Qualitative Research* (2nd edn. pp. 455–486). Thousand Oaks, Calif.: Sage Publications.

Thurlow, Crispin & Adam Jaworski. (2010). Trade signs and business cards in Gambia. In Crispin Thurlow & Adam Jaworski (Eds.), *Tourism Discourse: Language and Global Mobility*. Houndmills, Basingstoke, Hampshire; New York: Palgrave Macmillan.

Tollefson, James W. (1991). *Planning Language, Planning Inequality: Language Policy in the Community*. London; New York: Longman.

Tollefson, James W. (2000). Policy and ideology in the spread of English. In Joan Kelly Hall & William Eggington (Eds.), *The Sociopolitics of English Language Teaching* (pp. 1–21). Clevedon, U.K.: Multilingual Matters.

Toohey, Kristine Margaret & A. J. Veal. (2007). *The Olympic Games: A Social Science Perspective* (2nd edn.). Wallingford, Oxfordshire, UK; Cambridge, MA: CABI Pub.

Torkington, Kate. (2009). Exploring the linguistic landscape: the case of the 'Golden Triangle' in the Algarve, Portugal. *Paper presented at the Lancaster University Postgraduate Conference in Linguistics & Language Teaching.*

Translators Association of China. (2019). 2019 China Language Services Industry Development Report Beijing: The Translators Association of China.

Translators Association of China. (2020). Translator Association of China: A brief history. http://tac-online.org.cn/en//tran/2009-10/12/content_3180484.htm (accessed 28 January 2020)

Trochim, William M. (2006, October 20). Nonprobability Sampling. The Research Methods Knowledge Base. http://www.socialresearchmethods.net/kb/sampnon.php. (accessed 30 March 2009)

Tsung, Linda. (2009). *Minority Languages, Education and Communities in China*. Basingstoke, England; New York: Palgrave Macmillan.

Urciuoli, Bonnie, & Chaise LaDousa. (2013). Language management/labour. *Annual Review of Anthropology*, 42, 175–190.

van Dijk, T. A. (1993). Principles of critical discourse analysis. *Discourse and Society*, 4(2), 249–283.

van Dijk, T. A. (1998). *Ideology: A Multidisciplinary Approach*. London; Thousand Oaks, Calif.: Sage Publications.

van Leeuwen, T. (1993). Genre and Field in Critical Discourse Analysis: A Synopsis. *Discourse Society*, 4(2),193–223.

Vertovec, Steven. (2007). *New complexities of cohesion in Britain: Super-diversity, transnationalism and civil-integration*. Report for the Commission on Integration & Cohesion. Wetherby: Communities and Local Government Publications.

Vessey, Rachelle. (2013). Too much French? Not enough French?: The Vancouver Olympics and a very Canadian language ideological debate. *Multilingua-Journal of Cross-Cultural and Interlanguage*, 32(5),659–682.

Vessey, Rachelle. (2018). Language Policy and Planning and the Olympic Games. In Angela Creese & Adrian Blackledge (Eds.), *The Routledge Handbook of Language and Superdiversity* (pp. 227–240). New York: Routledge.

Wamsley, Kevin & Michael K. Heine, (1996). Tradition, modernity, and the construction of civic identity: The Calgary Olympics. OLYMPIKA: *The International Journal of Olympic Studies*, V, 81–90.

Wang, Hui. (2006). Background, problem and thought: Languae planning in China facing the diffusion of English in Globalisation Time. *Journal of Beihua University* (Social Sciences), 7(5),53–58.

Wang, Lidi, & Jie Zhang. (2008). Interpreting for Beijing Olympics. http://www.doc88.com/p-116715930177.html. (accessed 1 February 2020)

Wei, Yehua Dennis, & Danlin Yu. (2006). State policy and the globalization of Beijing: emerging themes. *Habitat International*, 30(3),377–395.

Wen, Bo, Hui Li, Daru Lu, Xiufeng Song, Feng Zhang, Yungang He, Feng Li, Yang Gao, Xianyun Mao, Liang Zhang, Ji Qian, Jingze Tan, Jianzhong Jin, Wei Huang, Ranjan Deka, Bing Su, Ranajit Chakraborty & Li Jin. (2004). Genetic evidence supports demic diffusion of Han culture. *Nature*, 431, 302–305.

Wen, Qiufang, jing Su, & Yanhong Jian. (2011). Guojia Waiyu Nengli De Lilun Goujian Yu Yingyong Changshi [A Model of National Foreign Language Capacity and Its Trial Use]. *Foreign Languages in China*, 8(3),4–10.

Wen, Qiufang. (2019). Reexamining the concept of "national language capacity" – The achievements of and challenges on national language capacity development in China in the past 70 years. *Journal of Xinjiang Normal University* (Philosophy and Social Sciences), 40(5),57–67.

Wikipedia. (2009, October 28). Li Yang. Wikipedia, The Free Encyclopedia http://en.wikipedia.org/w/index.php?title=Li_Yang_(Crazy_English)&oldid=322562229. (accessed 20 February 2010)

Wikipedia. (2010a, May 10). Beijing. Wikipedia, The Free Encyclopedia. http://en.wikipedia.org/w/index.php?title=Beijing&oldid=361279438. (accessed 10 May 2010)

Wikipedia. (2010b, May 16). Beijing West Railway Station. Wikipedia, The Free Encyclopedia. http://en.wikipedia.org/wiki/Beijing_West_Railway_Station. (accessed 13 June 2010)

Wodak, Ruth. (2001a). The discourse-historical approach. In Ruth Wodak & Michael Meyer (Eds.), *Methods of Critical Discourse Analysis* (pp. 63–95). London; Thousand Oaks, Calif.: Sage Publications.

Wodak, Ruth. (2001b). What CDA is about – A summary of its history, important concepts and its developments. In Ruth Wodak & Michael Meyer (Eds.), *Methods of Critical Discourse Analysis* (pp. 1–13). London; Thousand Oaks, Calif.: Sage Publications.

Wodak, Ruth. (2007). Critical discourse analysis. In Clive Seale (Ed.), *Qualitative Research Practice* (pp. 185–201). London; Thousand Oaks, CA: Sage Publications.

Woodward, Amber. R. (2008) *A survey of Li Yang Crazy English. Vol. 180. Sino-Platonic Papers*. Philadelphia: Department of East Asian Languages and Civilizations, University of Pennsylvania.

Wu, Jianse. (2007). Translating China and reconstructing Chinese cultural identit(ies). *Neohelicon*, 34(2),137–148.

Wu, Xiaogang. (2007, May 24–27). Economic transition, school expansion, and educational inequality in China, 1990–2000. *Paper presented at the ISA Research Committee on Social Stratification and Mobility* (RC28) Spring Meeting, Brno, the Czech Republic.

Xia, Liping, & Xiyuan Jiang. (2004). *Zhongguo Heping Jueqi* [China's Peaceful Rising]. Beijing: China Social Sciences Press.

Xinhua. (2005, August 15). English signs in Beijing "lost in translation". http://www.chinadaily.com.cn/english/doc/2005-08/15/content_469176.htm (accessed 10 June 2010)

Xinhua. (2006). Beijing launches exams to improve residents' English proficiency. http://en.people.cn/200603/29/eng20060329_254254.html. (accessed 8 August 2008)

Xinhua. (2007a, February 27). Work begins on removing Chinglish from English signs in Beijing. http://en.beijing2008.cn/48/19/article214021948.shtml. (accessed 10 June 2010)

Xinhua. (2007b, March 14). Soft power, a new focus at China's "two sessions". http://english.mofcom.gov.cn/aarticle/subject/lhsessions/lanmua/200703/20070304459721.html. (accessed 6 December 2010)

Xinhua. (2008a, June 5). Beijing Olympic volunteers corps launched. Olympic Channel http://en.yp.cctv.com/20080605/108230.shtml (accessed 30 March 2009)

Xinhua. (2008b, August 17). Beijing taxi drivers don't think their English good enough. http://news.xinhuanet.com/world/2008-08/17/content_9421180.htm. (accessed 4 February 2011)

Xinhua. (2008c, December 15). China's tremendous changes over the past three decades. http://news.xinhuanet.com/video/2008-12/05/content_10459451.htm. (accessed 14 December 2010)

Xinhua. (2008d, August 23). Commentary: Beijing Olympic Games to shine in history. http://en.people.cn/90001/90780/91345/6484027.html. (accessed 11 February 2020)

Xinhua. (2008e, August 24). Rogge: Beijing Olympics 'truly exceptional Games'. http://www.chinadaily.com.cn/olympics/2008-08/24/content_6966766.htm. (accessed 15 January 2020)

Xinhua. (2008f, August 28). Chinese economy where to go post-Olympics. http://news.xinhua net.com/english/2008-08/28/content_9728929.htm. (accessed 30 May 2010)

Xinhua. (2018, December 22). Yearender: Beijing 2022 embraces Olympic Agenda 2020 through innovation. http://www.xinhuanet.com/english/2018-12/22/c_137691954.htm?from=timeline. (accessed 1 February 2020)

Xinhua. (2019, May 10). BOCWOG launches action plan on volunteer services for Beijing 2022. http://www.xinhuanet.com/english/2019-05/10/c_138049161.htm. (accessed 16 January 2020)

Xinhua. (2020, January 9). Recruitment of volunteers for 2022 Winter Olympic Games, with the number exceeding 630000 in one month. https://baijiahao.baidu.com/s?id=1655238935721019670&wfr=spider&for=pc. (accessed 1 February 2020)

Xu, Fan. (2009, November 24). Beijing Changzhu waiji renkou bili wei 0.6% [Foreigners represent 0.6 percent of Beijing's total population]. http://www.chinadaily.com.cn/zgzx/2009-11/24/content_9025848.htm. (accessed 28 May 2010)

Xu, Xin. (2006). Modernizing China in the Olympic spotlight: China's national identity and the 2008 Beijing Olympiad. *Sociological Review*, 54(s2), 90–107.

Xu, Ying. (2011). Beijing jianshe shijie chengshi zhanlue dingwei yu fazhan moshi [Research on strategic goals and development model of Beijing as world city]. *Urban Studies*, 18(3), 72–77.

Xu, Zhichang. (2002). From TEFL to TEIL: Changes in perceptions and practices–Teaching English as an international language in Chinese universities in P. R. China. In Andy Kirkpatrick (Ed.), *Englishes in Asia: Communication, Identity, Power and Education* (pp. 225–244). Melbourne: Language Australia.

Xue, Yan. (2003). Yujian cheng shijie chengshi: Shanghai yu guoji de chaju zai nali? [Desire to build a world city: What is the difference between Shanghai and internationals?]. *International Market*, 1, 18–19.

Yamane, Yusaku. "Chinese Patriots burn with English fever." *The Asahi Shimbun*. 2 July 2005. Accessed Oct. 2005 http://www.asahi.com/english/Heraldasahi/TKY200507020151.html

Yang, Aixiang. (2003, October 28). Criticising China's college English testing system: English test brings disaster to the country and the people. 21st Century Talent Report. http://www.people.com.cn/GB/jiaoyu/1055/2156626.html. (accessed 20 August 2010)

Yang, Yiming. (2015, November 24). It's urgent to improve national language capacity. *People's Daily*.

Yang, Zhenwei. (2007). "Lvse Aoyun" – Lvse Beijing Jianshe De Cuihuaji ["Green Olympics" – the catalyst of Beijing's ecological construction]. *Journal of Forestry Research*(7), 5–6.

Zhang, Jie. (2011). *Language Policy and Planning for The 2008 Beijing Olympic Games: An Investigation of An Olympic City and A Global Population* (PhD), Macquarie University, Sydney, Australia.

Zhang, Lianqing. (2009, December). Emphasizing global vision and international perspective. *Beijing This Month* (Beijing Speaks Foreign Language Program Special Issue), 14–23.

Zhang, Luxiong. (2005, July 19). Tongyi de yingyu jiaoyu ying cong heshi kaishi [When shall unified English education begin?] *Issues of the Reform of China Educational System*. http://www.dajunzk.com/yingyujxue.htm (accessed 16 November 2008)

Zhang, Qihua. (2005, August 9). English dominance in China: Put the cart before the horse. *Chongqing Daily Newspaper*.

Zhang, Tuo & Zhang, Chongfang. (2008, August 4). Beijing municipal tourism bureau: Beijing Olympics is to welcome 450,000 foreign tourists. http://news.sina.com.cn/c/2008-08-04/151116058772.shtml. (accessed 28 March 2009)

Zhang, Weiwei. (2016). Zhongguo Zhenhan: *Yige Wenmingxing Guojia De Jueqi* [China shakes the world: The rise of a "civilised country"]. Beijing: China Citic Press.

Zhang, Wen, & Qi Shen. (2016). Studies of language services in China in the past decade. *Journal of Yunnan Normal University* (Teaching and Research on Chinese As A Foreign Language), 14(3),60–69.

Zhang, Yue. (2014). Free phone translation service helps foreigners as they navigate Beijing. http://www.chinadaily.com.cn/kindle/2014-07/28/content_17941809.htm (accessed 5 February 2020)

Zhang Zhiguo. (2019). Guoji Zuzhi Yuyan Zhengce Tedian Diaocha Yanjiu [An investigation into the features of language policies in international organisations]. Yuyan Wenzi Yingyong [Applied Linguistics] (2),51–60.

Zhao, Shiju. (2012). Cong Yuyan Fuwu Neirong Kan Yuyan Fuwu De Jieding He Leixing [Definition and types of language service from the angle of its contents]. *Journal of Beihua University* (Social Sciences) (3), 4–6.

Zhao, Shiju. (2015). Quanqiu Jinzheng Zhong De Guojia Yuyan Nengli [National language capacity in global competition]. *Social Sciences in China* (3), 105–118.

Zhao, Shiju. (2016). National language capacity in global competition. *Social Sciences in China*, 37(3),93–110.

Zhao, Yong & Keith P. Campbell. (1995). English in China. *World Englishes*, 14(3),377–390.

Zheng, Yongnian. (1999). *Discovering Chinese Nationalism in China: Modernization, Identity, and International Relations*. Cambridge; New York: Cambridge University Press.

Zhong, Weihe. (2019). China's T&I education after 40 years of reform and opening up: achievements, challenges and development. *Chinese Translators*, 40(1),68–75

Zhou, Licheng. (2008). Zhongguo aolin pike xianqu Zhang Bolin [Zhang Bolin, the forerunner in China's engagement with the Olympic movement]. *Chinese Archives*(4), 52–55.

Appendix 1: List of interview participants

NO.	Date	Pseudonym	Ethnicity	Title & Position
1	July 10, 2008	Xie Changbing	Han	Dean of Volunteer Action Center, xxx Provincial Committee of the Youth League
2	July 11, 2008	Du Jie	Han	English teacher at xxx New Oriental School
3	July 15, 2008	Qi Hong	Han	Manager of Medical Service at International Youth Camp
4	Sept 10, 2008	Guo Mao	Han	English teacher at xxx New Oriental School
5	Sept 19, 2008	Sun Lin	Han	Manager of Language Service for Marathon contest
6	Sept 26, 2008	Hu Junfang	Han	English teacher of Senior Grade 2 in Beijing NO. xx Secondary School
7	Aug 8, 2008	He Yonghui	Han	Taxi driver in Beijing
8	July 13, 2008	Zhao Chan	Han	Olympic volunteer of media operation at Main Press Centre (MPC) (recruited from University A)
	Sept 22, 2008	–	–	Follow-up interview with Zhao Chan
9	Aug 3, 2008	Ji Haiqiang	Yao	Olympic volunteer of hotel service for Nikko Hotels International (recruited from University B)
10	Aug 3, 2008	Sun Hui	Han	Olympic volunteer of spectacular service at the National Stadium (Bird's Nest) (recruited from University B)
	Sept 23, 2008	–	–	Follow-up interview to Sun Hui
11	Aug 3, 2008	Li Jie	Han	Olympic volunteer of transportation service at shuttle bus station for athletes in the Olympic village (recruited from University C)
12		Zhou Shen	Han	Olympic volunteer of spectacular service at the Laoshan Velodrome (recruited from University C)
13		Wu Linna	Han	Olympic volunteer of spectacular service at Workers' Indoor Arena (recruited from University D)
	Sept 20, 2008	–	–	Follow-up interview to Wu Linna
14	Aug 7, 2008	Zheng Suduan	She	Olympic urban volunteer at Purple Bamboo Garden (recruited from University B)
15		Wang Xia	Han	Olympic urban volunteer at Purple Bamboo Garden (recruited from University B)

(continued)

NO.	Date	Pseudonym	Ethnicity	Title & Position
16	Sept 20, 2008	Feng Sanghui	Han	Olympic volunteer of spectacular service at Beijing National Aquatics Center (Water Cube) (recruited from University E)
17	Sept 21, 2008	Chen Zheng	Manchu	Coordinating assistant of outdoor cultural and artistic activities in the big event group of the International Youth Camp (recruited from University B)
18		Wei Ru	Hezhe	Coordinating assistant of outdoor cultural and artistic activities in the big event group of the International Youth Camp (recruited from University B)
19		Zhu Ning	Han	Olympic volunteer of spectacular service at the National Stadium (recruited from University B)
20	Sept 22, 2008	Jiang Fangqi	Han	Olympic volunteer of media operation at Olympic News Center (ONC) (recruited from University F)
21	Sept 22, 2008	Shen Manli	Han	Olympic volunteer of doping testing service (recruited from University F)
22	Sept 22, 2008	Han Yun	Han	Olympic volunteer of media operation at Shun Yi rowing site (recruited from University F)
23	Sept 22, 2008	Yang Yijing	Han	Olympic volunteer of language service for Olympic venues (recruited from University F)
24	Sept 22, 2008	Qin Si	Han	Olympic volunteer of VIP accompanying and (Spanish) language service (recruited from University F)
25	Sept 22, 2008	You Qingchuan	Han	Group leader of the urban volunteer booth at the gate of BFSU (recruited from University F)
26	Sept 22, 2008	Xu Jian	Han	Olympic volunteer of VIP accompanying and (English) language service (recruited from University F)
27	Sept 23, 2008	He Ying	Han	Olympic volunteer of spectacular service at Capital Indoor Stadium (recruited from University G)
28	Sept 23, 2008	Lu Xin	Han	Manager assistant of the International Youth Camp (recruited from University B)

(continued)

NO.	Date	Pseudonym	Ethnicity	Title & Position
29	Sept 24, 2008	Shi Na	Han	Examiner of the English proficiency test for Olympic drivers and Olympic volunteer of VIP accompanying and (English) language service (recruited from University F)
30	Sept 27, 2008	Zhang Qing	Han	Olympic volunteer driver at Wukesong Culture and Sports Center (recruited from University H)
31		Kong Pei	Han	Olympic volunteer driver at Table Tennis Stadium of Peking University (recruited from University H)
32		Chao Feixiang	Han	Olympic volunteer driver at Main Press Center (recruited from University H)
33	Sept 27, 2008	Hua Shuo	Han	Olympic volunteer driver at Beijing National Aquatics Center (Water Cube) (recruited from University H)
34		Jin Yuan	Han	Olympic volunteer driver at the Olympic Inner area (recruited from University H)
35		Tao Bin	Han	Olympic volunteer driver at International Broadcasting Center (IBC) (recruited from University H)

Note:
1. Pseudonyms are used for all participating individuals and institutions throughout this dissertation.
2. Transcripts are labelled by dates following the order of *date-month-year*. I transcribed in the interview language. For the full list of transcription conventions, see Appendix 2. English translations in this book are mine.

Appendix 2: Key to transcription conventions

Symbol	Function
. . .	pause
–	truncation
[ ]	translator's supplement to incomplete utterance
(. . .)	a section cut from the transcript
CAPS	emphatic stress
≫ . . . ≫	spoken rapidly
≪ . . . ≪	spoken slowly
@spoken laughingly@	the utterance between the two @s is spoken laughingly
erm	hesitation marker

Index

accurate English 168
Action Plan on Language Services for Beijing 2022 216–219
Action Plan on Olympic Volunteer Services for Beijing 2022 219
agency 38, 128, 130, 228
Aifly 51, 78, 80–81, 85–87, 97, 114–115, 131
Albanian 209
alchemy 83, 87, 102
American English 159–161, 196, 198
Anglo-American culture 130, 204
Arabic 8–9, 45, 68, 78–79, 88–92, 194, 201, 209, 212, 221
artificial intelligence 199, 220, 224, 226
automated translation software 220
autonomous learning 220
Azerbaijani 9, 209

barbarian tongue 29
Beijing citizen 34, 37, 66–68, 70, 73–77, 102–104, 107, 110–118, 121, 147–148, 157, 163, 228
Beijing English Testing System 64, 66, 76–77
Beijing Olympic Action Plan 33, 62–64, 157, 167, 181, 186
Beijing Olympic Multilingual Service Centre 78, 201–202, 220–221
Beijing Speaks Foreign Languages Programme 51, 64–75, 104, 202
Belarusian 209
Belt and Road initiative 21, 208, 212–214
birthright mentality 192
Bosnian 9, 209
Braille 41, 64
brand effect 79, 84
British English 160, 170, 196–197
Bulgarian 209

capital 25–27, 30, 87, 94, 98–102, 117, 125, 128, 132–139, 194
– cultural 25–26, 145
– economic 25–26, 94
– linguistic 25–26, 100–101, 125

– social 25
– symbolic 87, 94, 99–100, 194
capitalism 26, 132
Catalan 12
Chinese-English bilingual education 74
Chinglish 69, 75, 167, 168, 170, 198
civil servant 68, 75, 124, 147
closed-door policy 29
collectivism 30, 121
College English Test 94, 114, 148
colonialism 29, 110
complex linguistic event (*see also* linguistically complex event) 4
constructive approach 19
Conversational English Reader 52, 146–150
Coubertin, Baron Pierre de 1, 34
Crazy English 81, 85, 86, 94–97, 100, 114
critical approach 57, 60
critical pedagogy 144–145
cross-cultural communication 8, 12, 25, 144, 162, 227
Cultural Revolution 30, 116

data analysis method 56–60
– critical discourse analysis 56–57, 144
– content analysis 58–59, 150
– multimodal discourse analysis 52
– triangulation 17, 58–59
data collection method 50–55
– interview 54–55
– participant observation 55
– recruitment 53–54
– research site 52–53
degradation 144
dilemma 59, 125–131
discursive construction 144, 150
distortion 144
domestically-focused country 142
dominant language 25, 110, 120, 142, 168, 200, 228

educational equity 125
EF English First/Education First 51, 78, 80–85, 136, 138, 189–190

empowerment 52, 97
English desire 95, 131
English dominance 203, 207
English fever 51, 93–94, 97, 100–101, 119–121, 143, 163, 203–204
English hegemony 142, 204
English language learning and teaching celebrity 64, 93–101
English language teaching 45, 61, 69, 86, 95, 116–117, 141–142, 163–164, 166, 177, 181
English learning trajectory 126–127, 131
English Proficiency Index 136–137
English proficiency 44, 73–77, 84, 95, 98, 102, 114–116, 120–139, 143, 164
English Town system 82–83
English varieties 146, 160, 198, 200
English-centric education policy 125, 131
English-only 142, 203
Estonian 209
ethnic minority 54, 128, 184, 196–197
exclusion 25, 144, 153
expanding circle 84, 101, 110

fading glory 28–29
fallacy 163
feminism 144–145
Filipino 209
foreign language media 78, 116–118
foreign language popularisation 49, 58, 64–65, 67–68, 70, 72, 100, 102, 110–118, 132, 143
foreign language speaking population 65–67, 72, 104–110, 143
foreign resident 108, 197
formal education 79, 86, 161, 207
French 7–12, 15, 41, 44–45, 52, 79, 88–92, 99, 107–112, 165–166, 173, 181, 192–194, 197, 201, 205, 207, 209, 212, 221–224

Gaokao 125–129, 204–205
gender bias 144, 164
gender role 155
German 9, 12, 45, 78, 88–90, 99, 107, 109, 194, 201, 205, 209, 212–214, 221–222
global citizenship 142

global competitiveness 142
global governance 11, 214, 215, 226, 227
global lingua franca 84
global mindset 121, 142
global power 96, 213–215
global/world city 132–142, 162, 186, 188, 191, 194, 197
– Global City Assessment Index 141–142
– Global City Index 134–135, 137–138
– Global Power City Index 133–134
– Quality of Living Index 133
globalisation 6, 8, 26, 28, 57, 71, 85, 108, 110, 120, 133–134, 168, 188, 203, 205, 208
globalised new economy 25–26
globalness 138

Han people 184–185
hard power 33, 142, 205
harmonious society 155, 157, 162, 165, 185, 194, 197
harmony 1, 163, 184–185, 195
Hezhe nationality 128
homogeneity 155, 226
human-computer dialogue 218
human right 8, 32, 36

identity (see also identity construction)
– citizenship 142, 150, 158–159, 164
– civic 13
– cultural 102, 128, 172
– gender 144–145, 150–155
– individual 49, 120
– national 1–3, 13, 28–33, 49, 120, 184–185, 195
– occupational 151–153, 155, 158
– racial 158
– regional 13, 49, 120
– social 56, 59, 145, 150
identity conflict 57, 128
identity construction 13–15, 49, 60, 119–120, 128, 143, 144, 146, 171 (see also identity)
identity crisis 30–31
identity marker 184, 191
identity option 144–166
iFLYTEK 220
image crisis 32–33

imagined community 102, 144, 150, 158, 162
imagined interlocutor 144–145
imagined learner 145
immersion programme 82
Indo-European language 3, 41
inferiority complex 29, 32, 95
information technology 71, 207–209, 211–212, 217, 225
informative function 187
inner circle 109, 139
instrumentalist view 102, 121–122
intercultural business communication 26
intercultural communicative competence 73, 114
intercultural competence 142–143, 146, 159, 162
interdisciplinary talent 67
international city 39, 44, 62–63, 65
international language environment 62–74, 104, 108–110, 116–118, 132, 143, 202
International Olympic Committee 2–3, 6–13, 36–39, 40–41, 51, 64, 88–89, 91, 182, 192, 199, 203, 215
– language management of 6–13
– official language 6–10
– unofficial language 9
– working language 6, 9, 11, 91
international organisation 6–8, 12, 214, 227–228
international stance 35
international student 59, 88, 108, 214
internationalisation 14, 18–19, 62, 69–70, 85, 102, 118, 120, 138, 141–142
internationalism 3, 82, 85
internationally-oriented country 142
interpreter 12, 59, 78–80, 82, 88–91, 93, 201, 208, 212
investment 108, 120, 125, 127–128, 130, 142, 145, 182, 203, 211, 214
Italian 12, 45, 78, 88–89, 209, 224

Japanese 42, 44–45, 68, 78, 88–90, 92, 107, 194, 197, 201, 205, 209, 212, 221–223

Knowledge Map Based Intelligent Q-A System for the Beijing Winter Olympics project 222–223

Korean 41–45, 78, 88–90, 92, 107, 109, 194, 197, 201, 212, 221–224

language
– as human capital commodity 27
– as labour 26
– as problem 226
– as resource 206, 224, 226
– as right 6–9
language access for emergency response 80
language and script 19, 24
language barrier 37, 41, 45, 64–65, 87
language challenge 40–41, 227
language code 172, 189
language commodification 25–26
language consumer 22–23
language consumption 22
language expert 22–23, 42, 69, 72, 77, 218, 223
language family 128, 185
language ideology 17, 76, 132, 168, 203, 215, 224
language learning 17, 27, 37, 51, 55, 59, 63–63, 66, 68, 70, 72–74, 87, 93–116, 119, 125–131, 143–145, 157, 168, 191, 206
language management 6–12, 21, 104, 227–228
language need 13, 21, 90, 142, 201
language norm 22, 24
language object 166, 170
language policy and planning
– acquisition planning 5
– actor 19, 22, 31, 192, 227–228
– corpus planning 5, 168
– language-in-education planning 5, 142
– prestige planning 4–5
– status planning 4–5, 12
language policy
– bottom-up 15, 192
– de facto 12, 16–17, 27, 77, 170
– expanded view of 16–18, 57, 143
– mechanism 16–18, 58, 64, 73, 77, 146, 170–172, 197
– overt/covert 7, 16–17, 27, 58, 143, 146, 166, 170–172

– policy device 16–17, 77, 146
– top-down 27, 49, 101, 168, 228
language practice 10, 13–17, 21, 25, 27,
    49–50, 52, 55, 73, 121–122, 143, 147,
    150, 171–172, 192, 194, 198, 227–228
language professional 21–22, 80, 209,
    212–213
language proficiency 5, 24, 63, 66, 68,
    72–73, 105–106, 112, 114, 132, 134, 143
language service
– auxiliary 24
– basic 24
– content of 23, 207
– definition of 21
– development of 18–22, 29, 225
– language education service 24
– language knowledge service 24
– language rehabilitation service 24
– language tool service 24
– language use-related service 24
– language-related technology service 24
– provider of 21–22
– recipient of 22–23
– technology-supported language service 41,
    44–48, 65, 70, 92, 101, 221–223
language service market 22, 65, 71, 209
language service provider 71, 78,
    199–200, 209
language services industry 20, 22, 71, 80,
    92, 199, 207–212
language skill 5, 9, 12, 14, 27, 72, 224
language test 17, 27, 64, 72, 77, 89
language training 5, 10–11, 17, 24, 27,
    67–68, 70–71, 74, 78, 80–89, 101,
    114–116, 127, 136, 138, 147, 161, 163,
    199–202, 218, 220
language welfare 23
language work 25–27
language worker 25–27
language-related disability 23
languages other than English 21, 80, 91, 110,
    124, 126, 143, 181–182, 197
legacy 6, 39, 88, 199–203, 216,
    219–220, 224
less commonly taught language 5, 68, 107,
    205, 207, 213
Li Yang 81, 85–87, 94–100

linguistic diversity 110, 198, 226
linguistic labour 25
linguistic landscape 17, 27, 51–52, 57–59,
    75, 101, 166–167, 169–171, 173,
    182–183
linguistic market 25, 59, 102, 111
linguistic need 4, 49
linguistic sign
– bilingual sign 51–52, 63, 65–66, 69–70,
    119, 167, 173, 175, 178, 181, 183, 194
– directional sign 64, 167, 192
– guiding sign 51, 63–64, 186, 192
– metro sign 43–44
– monolingual sign 52, 173–175, 182–183
– multilingual sign 52, 63, 181–182, 192
– official/top-down sign 171, 173–182,
    192, 197
– public sign 5, 41–44, 69, 75, 166–169,
    171–172, 186–187, 198, 222–224
– road sign 42, 69, 171–172
– unofficial/bottom-up sign 192
linguistically complex event 3–6, 14, 27,
    199, 227
Liu Wenli 87, 94, 97–101
lost generation 30, 116
low practicability 122–125

machine translation 5, 24, 41, 91, 203,
    210–211, 218, 220, 222, 224, 226
Machine Translation for the Beijing Winter
    Olympics" project 222
Mad about English 119–120
mandatory learning 125
mass media 70, 93, 117
Masters in Translation and Interpretation
    80, 212
meaning-making resource 144, 149, 156
minor language 91, 107
misrecognition 18
modernisation 18, 28, 30–31, 34, 62, 102,
    120, 138
monolingualism 7–8, 138, 195, 198, 201,
    205, 215
motivation in language learning
– intrinsic 111
– extrinsic 111
multilingual service hotline 70

multilingual service 12, 20, 24, 41, 45, 70–71, 78, 87–88, 91–92, 198, 201, 218, 220–221
multilingual talent 20, 79–80
multilingualism 7–8, 12, 15, 19, 26, 198, 201, 205, 207, 215, 226
multimodal text 156, 158

Nanai 128
national cohesion 31
national image 2, 32–34
national language capacity 21, 142, 198, 205–207, 215, 221, 224, 226
National Olympic Committee 8–9
national pride 29, 31, 104, 155
nationalism 29, 96, 139
native speaker standard 82, 160, 168
native speaker superiority 81–85, 191
native speaker 42, 83, 102, 150, 160, 165, 168–169, 191–192, 197–198
native teacher 81–82, 190–191
nativeness 191, 195
natural language processing 24, 220
New Oriental 81–82, 113, 160
non-Anglophone country 5, 60, 125, 199–200, 227
non-native (English) speaker 83, 110, 191–192, 198, 200
non-Western developing country 2

Olympiad (*see also* Olympic Games)
– Abu Dhabi 2019 136
– Athens 1896 1, 3
– Athens 2004 12
– Barcelona 1992 12, 15
– Beijing 2008 37, 40, 51, 66, 74, 78–81, 87, 91, 110, 147, 161, 163, 183, 198, 201–202, 213, 216, 224
– Beijing 2022 198, 213, 216–217, 219–221, 225–227
– London 1908 35
– London 2012 12, 14, 200
– PyeongChang 2018 85, 136
– Rio 2016 40, 136, 200
– Seoul 1988 5, 38, 41, 80, 121, 136, 200
– Sochi 2014 11, 15, 84–85, 136, 200
– Sydney 2000 12–14, 37–38, 40, 88
– Tokyo 1964 38
– Tokyo 2020 85, 136, 200, 227
Olympic Agenda 2020 215–216, 220
Olympic bid 11, 32–33, 35, 37, 91, 98
Olympic brand 2, 191
Olympic Charter 7–9, 11–12, 192, 216
Olympic family members 11
Olympic Games
– Ancient 1, 3
– contradiction of 2–3
– Modern 1–6
– scale of 2, 4
– socio-politics of 86, 97
Olympic host city and country
– Abu Dhabi, the United Arab Emirates 136, 200
– Athens, Greece 1, 3, 12
– Barcelona, Spain 12, 15
– Beijing, China 28–39, 40–41, 213–215
– London, the United Kingdom 12, 14, 35, 108, 132–140, 200
– PyeongChang, South Korea 85, 136, 200
– Rio, Brazil 40, 136, 200
– Seoul, South Korea 5, 38, 41–46, 49, 80, 121, 134–140
– Sochi, Russia 11, 15, 84, 85
– Sydney, Australia 12–14, 36–38, 40, 88, 135, 140
– Tokyo, Japan 38, 85, 132–140, 200, 227
Olympic language services provider 77–93
Olympic Movement 2–5, 7–9, 12–13, 34, 120, 192, 199, 215
Olympic organiser 64, 97, 110, 170, 201
Olympic participant 88, 201
Olympic studies 13
Olympic visitor 53, 63, 108, 110, 171, 197
Olympic volunteer 5, 10–11, 31, 54, 60, 72, 76, 82, 85–87, 89, 97, 114, 119–126, 128, 148–149, 153, 155–156, 175–176, 218–219
"Olympic Winter Games Term Portal" project 221–222
Olympism 7, 216
online translation 24, 41
Open door policy 120
Opium War 29

Organisation Internationale de la Francophonie 10
oversimplification 145
ownership 195, 196, 198

patriotism 30–31, 86–87, 94, 96, 100, 102, 121, 157
Persian 209
policy maker 21, 59, 77, 142, 203, 207
Polish 45, 89, 209
political economy of language 25–27
Portuguese 9, 45, 78, 88, 89, 209
post-Olympic era 50, 204–205, 207
poststructuralism 27, 144–145
power 56–57, 75, 77, 87, 125, 132, 134, 138, 145, 154, 170, 182, 183, 191, 197, 213–214
power distance 9, 138
power relation 6, 25, 56, 57, 145, 150, 172, 197
private English teacher 190
Putonghua 55, 63, 184, 185, 195, 196

race 3, 36, 121, 145, 150, 159, 165
reform and opening up 30, 32, 36, 38, 62, 203, 207
research design 49–61
research question 49–50
resistance 101, 128, 130, 165, 204–205
role model 64, 93–94, 100
Romance language 12
Russian 8–9, 11, 45, 68, 78, 88, 90, 92, 107, 109, 128–130, 145, 194, 201, 205, 209, 212, 221, 223–224

salience 170, 172, 188, 192
Samaranch, Juan Antonio 2, 36, 89
second language acquisition 145
semiotic analysis 56, 144
sexuality 145
sign language 41, 64
signage standardisation 65, 69, 75, 167–170, 180, 186, 197, 223–224
Sino-centric world view 28
social actor 22, 192
social class 164

social education 67, 73
social resource 45, 67, 74, 123
socio-economic transformation 28
sociolinguistic context 170–172
soft power 33–34, 142, 186, 205, 206, 208
Spanish 8–9, 12, 42, 44–45, 78, 88–90, 92, 107, 109, 124, 194, 201, 205, 209, 212, 224
speech recognition 91, 218, 220, 226
sport sciences 13
sport sponsorship 84
sporting event 1, 4, 14, 80, 82, 85, 224, 228
spread of English 7, 10, 50, 57, 59, 85, 93, 100, 110, 120–121, 124, 131, 143, 204
Standard English 160, 167–170, 197–198, 224
stereotype 144–145, 154–155, 165
subordination 29, 144
superdiversity 15
supernational organisation 6, 9
symbolic function 188
symbolic power 18, 25
symbolic value 6, 9, 81, 99–100, 102

taxi driver 54, 60, 68, 75, 112, 115–116, 148, 152–153, 155
telephone translation 41, 63, 70
Tetun 209
Thai 89, 209, 212
ti [internal essence] 97, 203
ti-yong tension 127–131, 203–204
tourist information centre 45–46, 70–71, 171
translation and interpretation service supplier 78–80
translation company 67, 71, 74, 78–79
translation technology 24, 211, 226
translator 10, 22, 24, 44, 71, 78, 80, 82, 89, 203, 208–209, 212, 218, 220
Translators Association of China 20
Turkish 44–45, 209

upward social mobility 59
urban civility 157

Vietnamese 209
visibility 144, 170, 172, 182, 186, 194, 198

volunteer training 73, 113, 218
volunteerism 202–203

Wall Street English School 82
window industry 65–66, 73, 118
world city hierarchy 132
world Englishes 138

yong [external utility] 97, 102, 203
Yuan-pei Translation 78–80

Zhongxue wei ti, xixue wei yong
  [Chinese learning for essence
  – Western learning for utility] 97

www.ingramcontent.com/pod-product-compliance
Lightning Source LLC
Chambersburg PA
CBHW031423150426
43191CB00006B/378